Experiences of War

The American Airman in Europe

ROGER A. FREEMAN

Experiences of War

The American Airman in Europe

ROGER A. FREEMAN

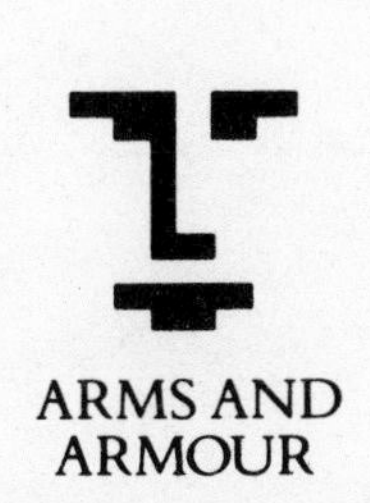

ARMS AND
ARMOUR

Arms and Armour Press
A Cassell Imprint
Villiers House, 41–47 Strand, London WC2N 5JE.

Distributed in the USA by Sterling Publishing Co. Inc.,
387 Park Avenue South, New York, NY 10016-8810.

Distributed in Australia by Capricorn Link (Australia) Pty. Ltd,
P.O. Box 665, Lane Cove, New South Wales 2066.

British Library Cataloguing in Publication Data
Freeman, Roger A. (Roger Anthony) *1928–*
Experiences of war: the American airman in Europe.
1. Europe. World War 2. Air operations. 2. United States. Air Force
I. Title
940.544973
ISBN 0-85368-888-5

Designed and edited by DAG Publications Ltd. Designed by David Gibbons; edited by David Dorrell; typeset by Ronset Typesetters, Darwen, Lancashire; camerawork by M&E Reproductions, North Fambridge, Essex; printed and bound in Great Britain by Butler & Tanner Ltd, Frome, Somerset.

Contents

Acknowledgments

A full list of the contributors whose names appear adjacent to their quotations in the narrative is to be found at the end of the book. To meet the aim of this work, ranks are omitted and it is hoped that this is not seen as disrespect, for some contributors eventually advanced to high command officers. *Experiences of War: The American Airman* exists solely through the interest and willingness of these contributors' co-operation, and to all I offer my sincere thanks.

Acknowledgment and thanks are also due to Patricia Keen, Vic Maslen, Dave Osborne and Geoff Ward; to Ian Mactaggart and George Pennick for photographic work, to Bruce Robertson for editorial guidance and Jean Freeman for preparing the manuscript.

Roger A. Freeman, 1990

Introduction

When the global conflict, that became known as the Second World War, erupted in 1939 there were many military strategists who believed that its outcome could or would be decided by air power. With victory in 1945 there were still those who believed that it had been achieved because of air power, and others equally convinced that it had not. However, there was no disputing that air power in its many forms had played a full part in the conflict and that a considerable portion of war budgets had been directed to air forces. Foremost was the United States of America which harnessed a large part of its great industrial capacity to produce and sustain the largest air force of all the combatants.

The main arm of US air power was the Army Air Forces, a semi-autonomous branch of the US Army. As with most other nations, the aeroplane had originally been brought into use as an aid to army and navy operations. Once the potential of air operations was recognized, some nations moved towards creating independent air forces, the first being the British. There were those senior officers in the US Army Air Service, later US Army Air Corps, who desired to see this happen in the United States, but their inter-war endeavours to create a separate service were suppressed by traditionalists in both the Army and Navy. The air leaders gave prime consideration to the doctrine of strategic bombardment, where aircraft could be used to destroy by bombing an enemy's war productive capacity in his homeland. It was a muted creed as beyond the Air Corps' own command, apart from the objections of Army and Navy hierarchies, the current isolationist governmental policy would be compromised by such assertions. The rise of belligerent regimes in Europe and the troubled international situation during the latter part of the 1930s eventually caused the US to begin rearming. Under President Roosevelt's administration air power plans received favour, eventually with massive investment in aircraft and associated production. While severance from the Army was denied, the creation of the Army Air Forces, a few months before the United States became involved in hostilities, afforded a high degree of independence.

The main facet of USAAF air power advancement was its doctrine of daylight high-altitude precision bombing applied to strategic objectives. At the beginning of the Second World War, bombing operations at heights of over 25,000 feet were considered by most nations to be untenable due to the thin, low-temperature atmosphere and the difficulties of accurate bomb-aiming. The USAAF, however, having developed the necessary equipment to overcome these obstacles, had put into mass production a fleet of four-engined heavy bombers fitted with a reliable crew oxygen system, engine supercharging and an advanced bombsight. With two types of heavy bomber, the Boeing B-17 Fortress and the Consolidated B-24 Liberator, it was planned to equip a vast bomber fleet to assail strategic targets. In development was a larger and even more advanced bomber, the B-29 Superfortress, incorporating a pressurized cabin affording sea-level atmosphere for the crew and so dispensing with the inhibiting oxygen system. This would enable even higher operational altitudes to be attained and sustained.

Although Japan's attack on Pearl Harbor and her conquests in the Far East were of immediate concern to the US, it was agreed with Britain and other allies that Germany and her European partners constituted the greater threat. The policy would be to beat Germany first while fighting a containing war in the Pacific and South-East Asia. Thus the USAAF prepared to test its doctrine and pursue a campaign of strategic bombing against Germany's war industry. Even before America became embroiled in war with Germany, there were plans for such an event with the United Kingdom as a base. Production was arranged for an eventual force of 4,000 bombers deployed in 75 combat groups, the chief operational formation; each bomber group consisted of four squadrons, the basic unit. The majority of these groups would use heavy bombers to fulfil the strategic mission and the remainder would be equipped with medium or light bombers. In a supporting and defensive role would be 25 fighter groups of three squadrons each with a total of 1,500 aircraft. The whole force would be three times larger than the indigenous British air strength. Under a system whereby US air forces were given numbered designations at their various global locations, that in the UK became the 8th Air Force which, as originally planned, would command four-fifths of the total US combat air strength overseas.

In the event, while the 8th Air Force was the largest air striking force ever assembled, it did not attain the fulfilment of the original plan. Many of the groups earmarked for it were sent to the Pacific or Middle East to meet pressing commitments. Of the 8th Air Forces's initial group allocation to reach the UK, the greater proportion was used to form the 12th Air Force sent to support the Allied invasion of North Africa in late 1942. The following autumn the 8th's medium bombers and tactical fighter units were transferred to the 9th Air Force, to support the planned cross-Channel invasion of the continent. Around the same date, half the bomber force still to be sent to the 8th was diverted to the Mediterranean Theatre of Operations to form another strategic air force, the 15th. However, the headquarters of the 8th Air Force was renamed the US Strategic Air Forces in Europe (USSTAF) and assumed control of both the 8th and the 15th. While the deployment was not as originally envisaged, at the time of peak inventory (in the summer of 1944) in the European and Mediterranean Theatres of Operations there were 62 heavy bomber groups (B-17 and B-24), 14 medium bomber (B-25 and B-26), four light bomber (A-20), 46 fighter (P-38, P-47 and P-51), 17 troop carrier (C-47) and six reconnaissance (mostly F-5 and F-6), plus six night fighter and several miscellaneous special duty squadrons. This vast force embraced 14,000 aircraft at more than 300 locations in eight different countries, operated and sustained by 630,000 personnel.

In total, during the three years of conflict, those sent to demolish the Axis tyranny amounted to nearly three-quarters of a million men and women, the majority, 525,000, in what was termed the European Theatre of Operations (ETO) which encompassed the countries of north-west Europe. The remainder served in North Africa and later Italy – the Mediterranean Theatre of Operations (MTO). During these years of combat operations, more than 81,000 airmen were missing in action, of whom more than 49,000 were killed and nearly 33,000 made prisoner, while another 13,000 were wounded. These casualties give some indication of the scale on which operations were conducted; for against Germany and her European allies the USAAF launched the largest air fleets of all time.

The 20th century has, through the medium of mass communication, affected change in the populace as never before. National characteristics which were little different from one generation to another in preceding centuries were notably altered in just a decade or two by the 1900s. The electronic and printed media, plus speedy transportation, spread information, opinions and ideas, producing a noticeable change in behaviour and outlook with each succeeding generation. Nowhere is this more marked than in that front-runner of modern mass communication, the United States. Here national loyalties and customs survive, if diluted, but attitudes of the young, as elsewhere in the western world, are in general now well removed from those prevalent in the early part of this century. Even in the military services, steeped in tradition and bound by order, such change is evident. The professional American airman of today may be as patriotic and committed as his grandfather of the Second World War but he is of a very different mould. The rapid pace of social and material advancement is responsible.

Perhaps this evolution is more evident to the United States' closest ally, supporter and critic – Britain – than it is to Americans themselves. For the British have observed the US serviceman in isolation from his homeland for a half century and thus contrast the GI of the early 1940s with the blue-clad airmen currently in their midst. In general, today's young US airmen are good ambassadors for their country and conduct themselves with far more propriety than the wartime generation that descended on Europe. But, overall, the GI (which has become the generic term embracing men of all ranks and branches of the Second World War US Army and Army Air Forces) presented a refreshing and distinctive vitality to the Old World. To those young Americans their nation was the bastion of what was right in a world of wrongs. While this intrinsic air of superiority irritated their battle-weary ally, whom the US had replaced in the international pecking order, it also brought a much-needed and infectious optimism to the war scene. His unflinching allegiance to the Flag gave the GI an unwavering conviction that the cause was just and that the tyranny faced must be overcome. These young men, the majority servicemen only for the war's duration, conveyed a simple honesty of purpose; they were not saints and among them were a goodly number of sinners, yet in their efforts to fulfil the task entrusted they were confident and rarely divided.

This work is not a re-telling of the USAAF's part in that conflict but an endeavour to evoke the character and presence of those young American airmen through the medium of their own words. To show what they suffered, endured and enjoyed both in combat and everyday living in those momentous years.

1
Heading East

The USAAF's expansion in manpower was rapid; an influx of volunteers during 1942 and the gatherings of the draft (conscription) produced disorder. In the urgency to train men for specific tasks, soldiering often went by the board. Henry Heckman, an armourer, put it: 'Some of us had to learn to change step during the spare time from our schooling.' Men who had received little training themselves suddenly found that they had to teach others. In the cause of expediency, problem personnel tended to be transferred from one unit to another and eventually removed from the mainstream. One such collection was encountered by Bill Barnett:

'After getting drafted in February 1943, I proceeded to Basic Training in Virginia and then Anti-Aircraft Fire Control School in North Carolina. From there I was assigned to the cadre at an AA base on the Gulf of Mexico, where my job was to help train an odd gaggle of fresh ex-civilians consisting of French Cajuns, American Indians and Spanish-speaking Texans, most of whom couldn't understand English. We had to have interpreters to give orders!'

From a USAAF personnel strength of around 300,000 at the outbreak of war in December 1941, intakes increased by 100,000 or more per month until at the end of June 1943 it stood at 2,197,114 – which was 31.4 per cent of the total US Army strength. Throughout this period the priority was to form and train combat groups on a tight schedule for deployment overseas. Initially this was achieved by taking personnel from existing groups within the four domestic air forces (1st, 2nd, 3rd and 4th) to form the cadres of new groups, to which graduates from flying and technical schools were assigned as available. The new group was expected to have completed all phases of training and be ready to move overseas as a self-contained formation in 90 days, although for several reasons – chiefly lack of equipment or sufficiently trained personnel – individual groups took longer to form and complete training. This creation of combat groups eventually gave way to replacement training where, without the haste of the early months and with greatly enhanced instruction, the aim was to give, for example, a fighter pilot 120 hours' flight training and a bomber crew 90 days in all phases before despatch overseas.

When brought together, the men of a multi-place aircraft varied considerably in the degree of individual experience and it was the responsibility of the crew captain to assess capabilities and build that interdependence that would be vital in combat operations. The lessons were sometimes learned in unexpected ways as in the incident Bob Boyle, a 489th Bomb Group pilot, relates:

'Co-pilot Corey had never before seen the inside of a B-24. He had just graduated from aviation cadet pilot training. It was up to me to train him to fly the B-24, even as we all trained together to become a team.

'We arrived at Davis-Monthan Field, Arizona, on December 31 1943 to begin this training. One day we had been to a bomb range for practice bombing. On the way back I demonstrated to Corey the stall characteristics and recovery procedure of a B-24. I then let him try. He recovered too abruptly and the plane fell into a secondary stall, shuddering and shaking as is typical of that circumstance. We cut back on the power and recovered with smoother use of the elevator and rudders and continued on our way.

'We learned afterwards that the rest of the crew had been in a state of near panic. When the plane began to fall and vibrate, they wondered what was wrong. When we cut the engine power back, the "wheels up" horn sounded. (It is designed to alert the pilot if his wheels are up when power is cut for a landing.) Those in the fore area ahead of the bomb bay and in the nose could hear it and thought it was the bail-out signal, and a comedy circus ensued. Sgt Kaplan (ball turret) had gone to the nose during the bombing practice – as he was also the enlisted armourer – to assist the bombardier. Sgt Ewoldt (nose turret) had gone to the auxiliary power unit just below the flight deck to review its operation with the flight engineer. Both Kaplan and Ewoldt had left their parachute packs near their assigned stations. Thus, the crawl space beneath the flight deck connecting the nose area aft to the bomb bay had Kaplan heading aft and Ewoldt heading fore, with no room to pass.

'Luckily, co-pilot Corey had laughed aloud. It was the nearest thing to an aerobatic maneuver he had experienced in the normally "straight and level" flying B-24. The two men fighting to pass each other and bail out heard the laughing and by this time the plane had leveled off, so they knew everything was all right.

'We learned a lesson. Communication with each other is a must. I assured them that I'd never again intentionally do any unusual maneuver without telling them first.'

The first unit of the USAAF to arrive in the ETO was a quartermaster company sailing from New York for Liverpool, England, on 22 April 1942. A few days later the personnel of the 15th Bomb Squadron, trained to fly the Douglas A-20, embarked on a similar sea journey. Although the first air unit to leave for Europe, they were not the first USAAF members to serve in Europe as, even before the United States entered hostilities, observers and advisers had been sent to Britain and the Soviet Union. There were also those United States adventurers who, attracted by combat flying, had joined the British or its Commonwealth air forces and who now transferred to the USAAF. Harding Zumwalt was one of these pilots:

'The exhilaration of flying made me want to make it my career. My ideal was the cockpit of a fast fighter plane, while doing what I could for the British war effort. The United Kingdom Refresher Course, a product of the Clayton B. Knight Committee, was established to recruit and train pilots to fight for the British. When I learned of this excellent opportunity, I joined – especially after a couple of good-looking blondes in the recruiting office explained the program to me. I attended flight training at Spartan School of Aeronautics in Tulsa, Oklahoma – then, on to Canada for RAF uniforms. Finally I arrived in England and completed operational training in Spitfires. By this time the United States was in the War and I, along with many of my buddies, transferred to the US forces.

'Prior to signing with the RAF, I had attempted to join the US Army Air

Corps without success because of the glasses (corrective lenses) which I have worn since childhood – so I will always be grateful to God for answering my prayers and leading me to the British who gave me the chance to realize my dream.'

In the summer of 1942 the German Afrika Korps drove the British land forces back through Libya to Egypt, precipitating a crisis. As an aid to checking this drive, a small force of B-24 Liberator heavy bombers en route to China were diverted to the Middle East where they were joined by a group of medium bombers (B-25 Mitchells) and one of fighters (P-40s). The headquarters for these and other units was eventually designated as the 9th Air Force. Thus at an early date the USAAF found itself committed in two areas on operations against the European axis powers. The Allied decision to land forces in Morocco and Algeria brought a large deployment of USAAF units in western North Africa, which were grouped under the 12th Air Force. On the successful outcome of that campaign, the 12th followed the armies to Sicily and then to southern Italy, absorbing the tactical units of the 9th Air Force and transferring its heavy bombers to the 15th Air Force when that organization was established in November 1943 for strategic bombing.

The majority of support personnel and fighter pilots sent to the UK came by sea across the North Atlantic. For the Middle East the sea route was initially round the Cape of Good Hope. Following the North African landings, Casablanca was utilized and later a variety of Mediterranean ports. Apart from the movement of two single-seat P-38 Lightning-equipped groups in July and August 1942, only multi-engined, multi-crewed aircraft crossed or circumnavigated the Atlantic by air. Air bases in Labrador, Greenland and Iceland provided refuelling stops on the route to Prestwick, Scotland, while a better weather route to the south ran from Florida through Puerto Rico, British Guiana, Natal (Brazil), Ascension Island, Liberia, Dakar, French Morocco and then to England or MTO destinations.

The northern route proved costly in men and aircraft for the medium and light bombers that passed that way in the autumn of 1942 and thereafter this traffic was directed to the south except in summer months. The long overwater legs still demanded precise navigation, particularly the location of the mid-Atlantic Ascension Island. Awareness of this lay behind the oft-quoted jingle, 'If you should miss Ascension, your wife will get a pension'. The route was varied depending on weather conditions and aircraft duration. Four-engined bombers making the direct flight from Natal to west Africa would mostly leave Morrison Field, West Palm Beach, Florida, staging through Trinidad and Belém (Brazil), prior to a direct 2,000-mile flight to Dakar and then on to Marrakesh (Morocco). Heavy bombers, taking the North Atlantic route, made direct flights from Gander in Newfoundland to Prestwick.

For most of the men in service movement, it was their first time on an oceangoing vessel and a particularly impressive event if making the crossing in one of the British 'Queens', then the largest and fastest oceangoing passenger liners impressed as troopships. Henry Heckman was one of many thousands who travelled this way:

'The ground crews and administrative personnel of our group waited at Camp Kilmer, New Jersey, for two weeks before we received the orders to move to the port of embarkation – New York. When we were boarded on the mighty *Queen Elizabeth*, I was in a party of 21 men who were assigned to one half of a former stateroom on "B" deck. There were about a dozen men who filed in ahead of me into the area, and who were claiming the nearest of the three-decker bunks to the door. They were thinking about the need to get topside if there was an emergency. However, having done a lot of reading about ships, I recognized two painted-over and dogged-shut portholes, so I made a fast trip and claimed the middle bunk by these portholes. Feeling clever and having stowed my gear, I decided to open one of the portholes to view my line of escape. On looking down I got a shock for the boarding pier was way, way below and my immediate thought was, "What a hell'uva way to jump!"

'After we left New York there was an announcement over the public address system that all portholes on "B" Deck and above ("A", main promenade and boat decks) could be opened during daylight hours. I opened mine and looked down at the sea and was relieved to find that my original judgment of the height to the water was wrong. It didn't look anywhere near as far to jump – if that dread necessity occurred. Not until my return to the States two years later did I realize that the ship took in sea water as ballast for stability once out in the open sea and discharged it to lessen the draft when entering port. There were 18,000 on the "*Queen*" – according to rumour – including the men of four other bomb groups beside my own. We were on the liner six days, including one day in port, as we had been among the first to board, but for this reason we were some of the first off when the ship reached Greenock, Scotland.'

Another sent to Europe on *Queen Elizabeth* was fighter pilot Royal Frey, who noted with amusement the muddled attempts at security:

'To conceal our being Army Air Force personnel from any enemy agents who might see us board at the port, we were ordered to remove our AAF shoulder patches and collar insignia before we left the Miles Standish holding camp. This was ridiculous because they left us with our pilot wings on our shirts!'

Others who voyaged by sea often had a somewhat convoluted journey to reach their designated theatre of operations; even in the later stages of the war the route to one's permanent combat station could be far from direct, as Harland Little experienced:

'As a replacement crew we went to the "Big Adventure" by an Atlantic ocean trip, landing at Marseilles. We waited there at a depot for transportation to Italy which turned out to be a French ship with a British crew and troops from many different countries on board. The ship went first to Algiers where many of these troops disembarked and then after a 36-hour voyage we arrived at Naples. Another replacement depot and then the Air Force furnished "First Class" transportation – Italian freight wagons! Our crew's private Pullman was filled with straw for sleeping and our food was K-Rations. Even so we enjoyed the rail trip as it gave an opportunity to get a good look at Italy and its people. At Bari, on the east coast, the 15th Air Force put us into trucks [lorries] to transport us to our combat base at Castellucio, between Foggia and Cerignola. The accommodation was tents located in an olive grove and this was winter time.'

Those who travelled by sea went in fear of U-boat attack, but very few of the troop-carrying vessels with airmen aboard were ever sunk. The principal enemy of those journeying by air was inclement weather and this did claim many lives. Navigation was largely dependent on the skill and dedication of individual navigators, but however accomplished they were the rage of the elements could mar and deflect. The medium and light bombers with their shorter endurances were more at risk from the vagaries of the weather, particularly along the northern route. A good idea of the hazards faced can be obtained from the following account written by Edward Laube, the bombardier of 'Man-o-War', a 386th Bomb Group Marauder:

'England was our destination, flying what was then known as the northern route. The trip would take us to Langley Field in Virginia, Bangor in Maine and then Goose Bay in Labrador. We picked up our K-Rations, consisting of a round can of cheese, three or four biscuits, bouillon cubes, a bar of chocolate, tea and some cigarettes. The rations were given to us in the event of making an emergency landing somewhere along the way. Fat chance of survival along that route with thousands of miles of untamed and mostly uncharted territory. We joked about the rations and barked like dogs when we were hungry enough to eat the "dog biscuits". Little did we know that these little dog biscuits would be our food for a week or so when we first arrived in England.

'Our airplane joined a flight of three other planes and headed up to Langley Field, where we arrived late at night and dined on scrambled eggs, bread and beer. The following morning we left early in the morning for Bangor, running into foul weather, including snow – and our airplanes without de-icing boots. The concern was that the snow or ice would laden the wings and create problems for flying. All our training was flying in the warmer latitudes of our country, with virtually no experience in flying in this type of weather. This lack of experience would prove to give us some anxious moments.

'We breezed through Bangor and on to Goose Bay. It was still early in the year with snow on the ground piled up pretty high. As a group we were prepared and had the clothes for the weather. This outpost was desolate, with heaters to keep the engines from freezing. We slept in the ever-popular Nissen huts, a round half of a cylinder that had a pot-bellied stove in the center heated by coal. We carried our own sleeping bags and slept in long handles.

'We waited for suitable flying conditions to make the first leg to Greenland to a base named Bluie West 1. The airfield was located at the end of a long fjord; we would be landing on a glacier. We were given pictures of the correct fjord with the knowledge that there were other fjords around. We were also told to rely on the radio beacon at the end of the fjord before heading down to the landing field. The distance from Goose Bay to Greenland was about 800 miles, or four hours' flying time. The distance to Iceland was just about the same.

'We departed at the crack of dawn, bearing in mind we were near the North Pole with daylight coming about 2am and darkness setting in about 11pm. Since we could fly about six hours, we would be stopping at Greenland for gas and food and be on our way.

'The morning we left provided absolutely the most beautiful sight I had ever set my eyes upon. The sun was barely rising on a perfectly clear day where visibility was probably several hundred miles. The islands were spread out below, covered with snow and connected by the bluest of water reflecting the blue sky. There were icebergs or floes everywhere. We were carrying an armament and ordnance officer, who appeared relaxed, although both of them would have been more comfortable crossing the ocean on a troopship. After three hours Greenland was visible, standing like a huge mountain and totally covered with snow. The radio beacon was working great and barring any mishaps we would soon be landing at BW1.

'We found the proper fjord, which was about 20 miles across and rising several thousand feet above the water. It seemed like the wings were almost touching the sides of the mountains, which rose majestically on either side of the water. A beautiful sight indeed! With the magnificent visibility the distances were completely deceiving to the point that the landing area was easily visible from a distance of 30 miles. The landing was to be on a permanent glacier which was moving only a few inches a year. We would be heading directly into the upward-sloping mountain, which would eventually rise to several thousand feet. Nevertheless it was time to become nervous, although being busy helped. In actuality there was plenty of room after the landing for the airplane to take off again.

'The landing was uneventful . . . we gassed up, had something to eat and were back on our way. We were advised that we had two choices on the way to Iceland. The shortest distance was over the highest point in Greenland, rising to 13,000 feet. Since we hadn't flown in cold climates we were not aware of the sharp drop in temperature that would take place as we climbed over the mountain. The cylinder head temperature kept rising while oil pressure kept dropping. Assuming that oil was over-heating, the oil cooler shutters were opened. Actually what happened was the oil was freezing and the shutters should have been closed. Since we couldn't climb over, we turned around and while descending the oil readings returned to normal. The engineer, then realizing what was happening, closed the shutters. Lack of knowledge nearly had us in trouble.

'The balance of the trip to Iceland was uneventful. There we were in the higher latitudes with daylight lasting 24 hours per day. Having to spend the night in Iceland we had an opportunity to visit Reykjavik. The city proved to be relatively modern – most of us were expecting to see Eskimos chewing on whale blubber. Thus far the weather had been ideal, but this was to change.

'Our next stage was Stornoway, in the Hebrides Islands, a distance of about 900 miles. The approach to Scotland would be difficult because of the seemingly ever-present cloud cover plus the mountainous areas. We had heard that one of the groups that preceded us had lost a crew trying to find an open spot to let down, hitting a mountain in the process.

'After the briefing we were advised that there was a front that we possibly could fly over. The alternative was to fly underneath at an altitude of 100 feet . . . a dangerous way to do the job, particularly keeping that low for several hours. Our flight leader attempted to climb above the front but without success. Down we went to the deck. After a couple of hours of skimming the water one of the engines began backfiring, much to our distress. During the flying careers of us all, ears were always attuned to the purring of the engines. The slightest misfire always alerted everyone, even those peaceably sleeping.

'The engines returned to purring and everyone relaxed after a period of smooth running . . . then we got the bang, bang again. The two passengers were visibly shaken, promising cases of whisky if only we would make it to land. Then we had an unexpected surprise! While the front was fog almost to the sea, we ran right over a German U-boat that was on the surface, probably charging batteries. We scared the hell out of ourselves and the Germans, although we were gone before they could react to our sudden appearance and disappearance. During the balance of the time the engine periodically acted up, but managed to take us the rest of the way.

'Our next problem was to make landfall in the proper place. Before we reached the main island we began passing over small islands. The beacon was functioning and we landed in Stornoway without further incident and would soon be going on to our permanent base near Colchester, England. When we landed at Boxted, code-named "Heartache", we happily found, in a few days, that all planes made it safely across the "pond". We never did get the promised cases of liquor from our passengers.'

Several aircraft disappeared without trace, individual fates a matter of speculation with mechanical failure, if not weather, a possibility and often a combination of both as the reason for loss; a reminder that the state of the art at this time often made flying a dangerous enough business without the hostility of the enemy. Those who became lost during these trans-Atlantic crossings could sometimes be rescued, as John Chopelas, a 452nd BG radio-operator, recalls:

'In March 1944 our B-17 crew was on its last leg of the north Atlantic route to the UK. We were headed for Prestwick on Scotland's south-west coast but, soon after leaving Iceland, we flew into some terrible weather. My efforts to make wireless contact with anyone were unsuccessful and both pilot and navigator had no better luck. We were lost. Finally, there was a break in the overcast and we observed that we were over water. Moments later, a Spitfire appeared to our right, easing slowly and cautiously closer until we could see the pilot who, by pointing to himself and then ahead, indicated that we were to follow him. We soon arrived at an airfield where we landed on the grass runway. We were informed that we were at RAF Peterhead on the north-east coast of Scotland. When intercepted, we had over-flown Scotland and unknowingly were heading for Norway!

'Our pilot dutifully reported by phone to 8th Air Force and was instructed to take off next morning. Meanwhile we gunners were invited to dinner at the NCO mess where we met the Sergeant pilot who had "rescued" us. He was a Pole who was flying coastal patrol after a tour of combat. After dinner our pilot gave us permission to go to town. Since we had only US money we enquired about changing it for British coin. An English officer, very proper, with clipped moustache and pipe, consulted the London *Times* financial section, ascertained the current rate of exchange and made the transaction from base funds. We all got some notes and sundry coins. We then walked to the gate and waited for the local bus to Peterhead. We were wearing our heavy fleece-lined winter flying jackets and when we boarded the bus we must have presented an outlandish alien sight. It was apparent that we were the only Americans within miles.

'Poor conductor! As he approached each of us to collect the fare, we handed him pound notes, not realizing that this was the equivalent of offering a five-dollar bill for a five-cent fare. The other passengers stared at us, waiting for the exasperated conductor's next move. The Scottish dialect vying against American slang only confused the situation. Finally, one of us had the presence of mind to dig into his pocket and bring out a handful of coins, from which the suddenly relieved conductor extracted the correct amount for the fare. The silence of the staring passengers had become almost embarrassing, until a couple of kids began to giggle and soon everyone was smiling and laughing.

'That night in Peterhead was something to remember. We couldn't buy a drink at any pub. The Scots wouldn't allow it. As soon as we entered, we were immediately recognized as Americans and greeted with open arms. And it seemed every Scot in every pub had either lived in New York or Chicago or had relatives there.'

2

Bases, Barracks and Bother

Initially, one of the most troubling aspects of life in a war zone was the absence of exterior lighting – the blackout. This, at its most severe in the United Kingdom, was utterly bewildering to those who had recently left the bright illumination of US cities. But, as the British said, 'You got used to it.' Or thought you did. Edward Anthis, a bombsight mechanic at the 2nd Strategic Air Depot, would always remember the blackout:

'That blackout! Once I came out of our bomb-sight shop very late at night and before my eyes became accustomed to the dark I walked straight into the side of a machine shop trailer parked nearby. I bounced off, but must have been completely disorientated for after a while I realized I must be walking around on the airfield and not to where I thought I was going. Just couldn't see a thing, black as black; it must have been misty, cloudy and no moon. No horizon, no lighting anywhere. For 20 or 30 minutes I staggered about on the airfield telling myself not to panic. Thought about calling for help but guessed no one would hear me. Eventually the mist must have thinned a little for after making out the silhouette of some trees, groped my way along until I found a hard path. Not a funny experience.'

Negotiating the British blackout on a bicycle required daring and luck, according to a consensus of opinion from those with this experience. Fighter pilot Harding Zumwalt was one of the courageous:

'The screened light on our bicycles only dimly illuminated the road a few feet ahead so we learned to follow the white line that was painted up the center of most English roads. Okay until you ran into one of the fog patches that were common at night; then we were all over the place. I consider I was lucky to have survived bicycle riding in the blackout; a lot of men didn't and ended up in hospital. We did part of our training in Bournemouth and sea fog often came in after dark. When this happened the only way to find your way home late at night, after everything had shut down, was to walk with one foot on the kerb and the other in the gutter. This way you found the street corners. Occasionally Bournemouth was bombed by a hit-and-run enemy aircraft. That brought some illumination that we would have been happy to do without.'

Another aspect of the war zone was secrecy; no place names or road signs, nor must one mention the base name or location in public. 'Careless Talk Costs Lives' was the slogan, suggesting a spy listening round every corner. Secrecy meant security but was often taken to silly extremes, particularly by those seeking a convenient excuse for some action or lack of it. Men who had relations in the same theatre of operations were not supposed to know where they were, but it was usually not difficult to overcome this with a word in the right place. Elinor Fredricks, a member of the Women's Army Corps:

'It was impressed on us that you never mentioned the location of your base when you were in Britain. Soon after our battalion arrived from the States and went to the replacement center at Stone, I was amazed to receive a phone call from my brother, who I knew was stationed in England, but not exactly where. Surprised, I asked him how he knew where I was. He replied that he guessed I was just a stone's throw away. The WACs then moved down to Bushey Hall, VIIIth Fighter Command Headquarters near Watford. The second night I was there, in my brother walks. And our movements were supposed to be secret!'

The living conditions in the United Kingdom were generally the best experienced by USAAF men serving in the ETO and MTO. Half a dozen pre-war RAF establishments with heated brick-built barracks had a standard of accommodation, judged by the lucky few who served there, as far better than many of the training installations in their homeland. The 'tin can' Nissen huts, the most common utility barracks building on most of the early constructed airfields in Britain, may have left much to be desired but they afforded far more comfort than the accommodation available to or fashioned by units operating elsewhere. In fact, they could become quite cosy, as this extract from 381st Bomb Group navigator John Howland's diary, written on the winter night of February 1944, suggests:

'This evening we are just sitting on our cots around the tin stove in the middle of our big room. I spent most of the evening reading a book of short stories and Jim Tyson is doing the same thing. Baker has also been reading and Liddle is writing letters. Ted Homdrom is running a correction curve on a compass he swung today. Frank Palenik is working on his bicycle and Bill Doherty and Pat O'Phelan are giving Georgie (our dog) a bath. That poor little mutt is the most dejected looking creature I have ever seen. They are using Lifebuoy soap and a shaving brush to lather him up and then, while Bill holds him, Pat pours water over him. But I don't think they are getting Georgie very clean. They just dried him off with some turkish towels and Bill has him all wrapped up like a Hindu in a turban. Frank says we are having a stand-down, so we should be able to log a few extra hours in our sacks tonight.'

In the usually cool, often cold, British climate the crucial element of Nissen hut comfort was the form of heating and fuel available. The standard fitment was a small cast-iron solid fuel stove which was assessed by all as being quite inadequate, although it was more likely the poor quality fuel supplied by the British rather than the stove that was at fault. Ignition was a major problem for most fire-minders; it was a standard joke that one became warmer trying to get the thing to light than ever one did from the fire. There were various improvisations when it came to fire stimulants. James Sayre of the 401st Bomb Group:

'We solved the problem of getting the stove fire in our hut going. We saved some of the Very pistol flares used in the planes, cut them open and sprinkled a little of the powder over the fire when we lit it. That really got us a nice blaze.'

Stove frustration drove Al Jones and his hut mates to more desperate measures at Shipdham:

'A room in our barracks accommodated the four officers of our crew with double bunk beds at either end. We had a small stove in the middle of the room but never enough solid fuel. Outside in the squadron compound was a large pile of coal surrounded by a high barbed wire fence. We could never figure out why it was there as we were never allowed to draw from this stock. So we did a bit of improvising. With scrap B-24 parts, mainly oxygen tanks and hydraulic tubing, we rigged up our own oil-burner. A tank was fastened outside the room with tubing running through the wall into our stove. A valve regulated the flow of oil which dripped into a moulded clay pot placed inside the stove. The oil was waste from B-24 engine sumps which had to be regularly changed.

'When lighted the fire gave out good heating and made the room real warm. However, this contraption was reckoned to be dangerous since similar installations had caused serious fires. The British were responsible for fire safety and around every two months their fire inspector would drop by, usually when we were on a mission, and confiscate the rig because it didn't meet safety requirements. The first we'd know is when we found it gone. This meant we had to secretly build another oil-burner and hope we'd have warning of the next visit. To us the risk of a fire was nothing compared with the freezing state of our room if we didn't heat it.'

Out by the aircraft dispersals, in the ground crew shacks constructed out of old packing cases and salvaged materials, sump oil heating was common and not subject to fire regulations. In Italy, where the winter could be as unpleasant as in England, oil and gasoline heating was officially sanctioned even in tented dwellings. The 9th Air Force enjoyed similar facilities to the 8th until it began its trek through southern England to Normandy and then towards Germany. Sometimes French châteaux and farmsteads or blasted barracks on former Luftwaffe airfields provided cover, but for the most part it was as 362nd Fighter Group pilot Don Clark describes:

'For most of the 9th Air Force fighter outfits that followed the armies across France it was a case of tent living. We went from the summer dust of Normandy to the freezing winter mud of the Metz area. There were usually four pilots to one tent, which had a small ditch dug around the outside to take rainwater. Any covering we could find was put on the ground inside. We each had a GI folding canvas cot to sleep on and heating was provided by a GI stove placed in the middle of the tent, for which we were issued one 5-gallon can full of coke a day. We kept pretty warm and hadn't much room to complain when we knew there were infantry guys out there who only had a foxhole.'

In North Africa the GI tent was also the standard shelter for both air and ground crews but sometimes, in the early weeks, even less comfortable alternatives were prescribed, as Ashley Woolridge, a 319th Bomb Group pilot, discovered:

'The next day we flew to Algiers (Maison Blanche). This is the place where we were to start our feudin' career. It was a rough looking set-up. The squareheads had been dropping a few bombs. We found some concrete floor space in some old French barracks and set up housekeeping. I had three GI blankets. I would start the nights with one over and two folded under me. It got so cold at night that by morning I would have one thickness between me and the concrete and the rest on top. That sleeping on concrete made your joints ache until you got used to it. We had lots of problems at Algiers. To start with, our ground personnel were at Tafaroui, so we had to crew our own ships. All gas was in 5-gallon cans so we had to pull 960 gallons worth of cans up on the wing by means of a rope and pour it in. Besides this, we had to load our own bombs . . . '

With more permanency in Italy and Corsica, tent life was supplemented by do-it-yourself building, ranging from packing case shacks to quite elaborate block and tin-roofed bungalows, the latter on adjoining 15th Air Force outposts in the Foggia area of Italy where local building material could be had. On other 15th Air Force fields the tent persisted throughout a year's occupancy of the site, as Stan Staples sampled:

'The squadron area had at one time been the hub of some farmer; his buildings, made of clay brick, had been converted into the mess facilities, squadron stores and equipment building, operations office and medical department. The living quarters were made up primarily of heavy tents erected over wooden bases and 3-4ft high framework sidewalls. The squadron area was all dirt – no grass, and when it rained the dirt/clay combo turned to a sticky mud/clay gumbo that was anything but pleasant. Some efforts were made by all hands to build up pathways of brick, rock and gravel in order to stay out of the mud as much as possible, but having little more to work with than our hands, the results were not first-class.'

The sunny Italy of summer could be pleasant but at some locations the conditions were far from pleasant – like those endured by Jack Collingwood of the 27th Fighter Bomber Group:

'While stationed at Santa Maria, Italy, the landing strip was so thick with dust that our chaplain and several officers ventured into the nearest supply sources and purchased as much chewing tobacco as they could. They returned with it and passed it out to anyone who wanted it. The purpose was to keep one's mouth as moist as possible. However, it either served the purpose or you got sick. I tried hard but finally bit the dust. A pun but true.

'At Castel Volturno landing strip, located in the marshland area near the ocean, the 27th fought off mosquitoes as big as their aircraft – or so it seemed; the place was inundated with them. We were ordered to wear nets over our heads and long-sleeve shirts with gloves. Even then we were frequently attacked. We were given insecticide bombs to fight them back. However, the situation became serious enough for the Army general in charge of the medical staff to oversee spraying of the area. Even then many of our group came down with the dreaded malaria.'

Sanitation was basic at forward airstrips, a hole in the ground, and even at more permanent sites in Italy latrines left much to be desired. Ted Newby, a 460th Bomb Group bombardier:

'Right after arrival and the erection of our tents, our only latrines were a couple of 55-gallon drums welded end-to-end to form one long tank – which was sunk into the ground with the top protruding about 18 inches. Two 2 × 4s were placed across the open top and one did a balancing act to keep from falling in.

'One day I was "on the throne" and two middle-to-old-aged peasant women came along the path and stopped to ask if they could do my laundry. Shamelessly I negotiated a deal with them to handle my laundry needs.

'Later they built deluxe eight-holers with screened vents and a screen door – first-class.

'Out at the hardstands there were several of the primitive one-holers for each squadron. There was something about flying off to war that activated my bowels, so prior to every mission I mounted one of the drums. Often one of my latrine companions was Frank Guida, a pilot on another crew. Frank had a grandmother who lived north of Spinazzola and every so often on his day off he would fly up and buzz her house. Our little duel BMs became sort of a ritual for the two of us.

'I finished up on August 6 and my crew went to Ploesti on August 10 and made it back OK. Guida's plane blew up over the target. There were no chutes.'

3
Discipline and Digressions

The relaxation of military discipline was fairly general in combat areas and it would appear that the more primitive the living conditions, the less evident the acknowledgment of rank. Stan Staples recalls that:

'Then as 2nd Lieutenants, we saluted the squadron CO, but as a rule it did not extend on down to the regular squadron mission pilots. Uniform and dress requirements were minimal, but it was the custom to wear one's blouse, "pinks" or "greens" and tie at Sunday dinner.'

Conduct was much dependent upon the views of commanders. In the dust or mud of a forward airstrip with men tired by effort and lodged with discomfort, parade ground behaviour could not be sustained or expected. But even in the more orderly stations in England, some commanders ran easy regimes where salutes were occasional and dependent upon the situation. In certain instances, where an individual of low rank might have some special skill or reputation which could be cultivated to advantage, he was often treated with the minimum of military commitment. Don Bevan, who served with the 306th Bomb Group at Thurleigh in 1942, was such a case although the arrival of a new Group Commander required a return to traditional conduct:

'When Armstrong arrived to replace Col Overacker as Group CO, Majors Wilson and Wright hustled me over to Headquarters to sketch the new Commander – sort of an artistic bootlicking mission.

'I wasn't yet flying combat; I was an armorer but serving as an artist to decorate the drab combat hut of Major James W. Wilson's 423rd Squadron with likenesses of his fighting airmen. Wilson had relieved me of all duties and details to function freely as a true artist – he formed an innocent opinion of artists from a movie he'd seen.

' "Bevan," he said, "I know what you artists are all about . . . you don't have to *salute* any more."

'But now, standing at the Group Commander's door preparing me for a solo entrance – he turned to me visibly concerned: "Bevan, do me a favour, *salute* one more time." The actor Gene Raymond, an aircraft recognition officer, was sitting through the session with Armstrong; both in their stylish trenchcoats and hats. Pure Hollywood all the way.'

There were, as in any military organizations, those who saw no reason to relax traditional conduct, believing that in so doing discipline and order degenerated. Officers, both commissioned and non-commissioned, pursuing this policy, were often identified as those of a domineering nature. As Stan Smith found, these individuals did not always endear themselves to their superiors:

'Some officers you could never please, they never got off your back. Others were great; never pulled rank unless they had to. We worked three shifts in our bomb-sight shop and I'd say we worked pretty hard. One weekend I got a pass out and made a reservation at a hotel in Cambridge. When I arrived back an MP arrested me for being AWOL. This was on command of a major who didn't think I should have left camp. Well, the charge didn't hold up in court because I had a pass. The major didn't like to be beaten and then hit me with the 104th Article of War and turned me over to our CO for punishment. The CO assessed the papers, turned to me and said that for the next week, every time the Red Cross Clubmobile comes by at 10 o'clock, I was to report to his office for doughnuts and coffee.'

New commanders might consider conduct a little too lax in the command assumed and decide to tighten up. The method of achieving a general understanding that the CO was not to be ignored could rarely be as good-naturedly effective as that devised by Major Simmons of the 544th Bomb Squadron. It certainly impressed Henry Heckman, one of his men at Grafton Underwood:

'Like on most wartime airfields in England, our squadron site was out among the hedgerows and separated from the rest of the camp except for access roads. Our guys soon discovered that they could get off base without having to pass the MP post by lifting their bicycles over a gate, crossing a cow pasture, riding over a plank someone had laid over a deep ditch, into a lane and down to the main highway. We called it the Burma Road. The MPs knew what was going on but there wasn't any real fuss until we got a new squadron CO. One of his first acts was to restrict the whole 544th Squadron to base – "Just to show the boys who's boss." he said. He knew damn well that a lot of guys would go into town anyway by using the Burma Road. After it got dark the major sent MPs into town to arrest everybody they found from the 544th. Of course, as soon as they started going into the pubs and asking to see passes, the word was spread to other pubs that if you were 544th you better run before the MPs arrived. Meanwhile our new CO went down to the ditch by the lane and took up the plank, knowing all those who hadn't been picked up by the MPs would soon be pedalling home in the dark, fast. He trapped a dozen guys in the bottom of that ditch that night, including the Group bombardier, who wasn't even in our squadron.'

Having trained together, relationships between officers and men in an aircrew were usually informal but the requirements of rank still had to be respected; in any disagreement the officer still held precedence. Getting back at an officer in pursuing a disagreement can rarely have been so neatly emphasized as that heard by Bill Sullivan of the 379th Bomb Group:

'At mission interrogation our tail gunner mentioned that he had seen two enemy jets. The navigator questioned this, saying that he had not seen them. The tail gunner, resentful at being doubted but mindful that the navigator was an officer, replied: "You must have had your head up your ass-trodome, sir." '

Equally, the authority of rank was the ruling factor with officers. A shrewd lieutenant did not try to tell his superiors what to do. For junior officers the anonymity of the radio in air-to-air communication allowed an opportunity for comment that would never have been ventured directly on the ground. Bud Koorndyck, a 398th Group pilot, heard this amusing jibe:

'Our CO, Colonel Bob Miller, always wanted to make a good show when we returned from a mission, particularly when we flew over the Division HQ which was not far from our base. When the Colonel led a raid you could be sure that as soon as we crossed back over England he'd be on the radio telling people to close up the formation – "sock it in, sock it in". On one trip the Colonel was doing his thing on the radio and called Major Caldwell who was leading one of the squadrons. Caldwell didn't answer, probably his radio was giving trouble. This occurred to the Colonel because he called over the radio: "Leader, if you receive me wiggle your wings." There was no reply so he repeated the call. Then over the radio came an unidentified voice: "Colonel, if you can hear me, stick your head out of the window and wiggle your ears." Miller never found out who it was.'

Inevitably some individuals did not accept the disciplines of military life easily and appeared to go out of their way to antagonize those in authority. Premeditated defiance was the exception, most trouble arising from an individual who simply acted on impulse and without thought or regard for his military status. Such seems to have been the case with the junior officer who gave Bill Cameron, 67th Bomb Squadron CO, cause for concern:

'As a 23-year-old Squadron CO, I considered myself a good judge of character. And so it was when a lieutenant, whom we will call Charlie, was assigned to my squadron. He arrived, swathed in bandages following an aircraft accident. I was sympathetic. Further, he seemed to be more mature than most of my young officers, exhibited a positive personality and otherwise impressed me very favorably. He would do well, I concluded.

'Then one morning I was called into the Group Commander's office and received a chewing out from one end to the other because of a telephone call my lieutenant had made to the base (monitored of course) attempting to learn if a mission was scheduled for the following day. Charlie was summoned to my office to discuss the matter, a gentleman's discussion in the beginning, a shouting affair (I did the shouting) at the end, because Charlie insisted that the matter was not worth discussing! Of course, it was to happen again.

'In the meantime, and while a feeling of goodwill still existed, I learned that my lieutenant had been picked up in London for beating up a couple of senior officers. It seems that he was having dinner with a well-known movie personality, female of course, when the two officers attempted to move in on him. I was able to convince the Base Provost Marshal to travel from Shipdham to London (in a Jeep) to intercede, which he did successfully. No thanks from Charlie. The lieutenant was beginning to irritate me.

'Shortly after this incident he asked to be allowed to check out an airplane to shoot landings. I had no intention at that time to push him ahead of others, and so refused. The next thing I am told is that Charlie is up with a crew in a B-24 shooting landings! How that could happen I didn't know, but I did know that I had given him a direct order and that he not only ignored it, but had convinced my operations people that he had my permission.

'About this time I discovered that an old friend of mine was a surgeon in the 30th General Hospital at Nottingham. In conversation with him I learned that my lieutenant had had his injuries treated there, and that they were the result of an unauthorized flight in a British Tiger Moth trainer. My friend also told me that the hospital staff were greatly relieved when free-wheeling Charlie was released! You can understand that my patience was nearing an end and my target was Charlie.

'However, fate took a hand when Charlie and the crew he was flying with were interned in Switzerland. I heard later that he was seen in London, wearing Captain's insignia; unauthorized of course. Was I to see him again? Yes, a few months after the war and while dancing in a Fort Worth hotel, there was Charlie.

We looked directly at one another but there was no "Hello" on either side! And so, the episode involving this lieutenant had finally ended. A few years later I was to learn from a good friend that Charlie had achieved the rank of Colonel and was well thought of. Perhaps I was not such a bad judge of character after all?'

A desire to indulge in a little mischief while he served with the 493rd Bomb Group at Debach, England, is admitted by John Hutchinson:

'There must have been a rebellious streak in me; a subconscious desire to kick out against the orders we were subject to around the base or something. This manifested itself in resentment of those officers who had Jeeps assigned for their use, while I had to walk or cycle to and from my squadron barracks to the communal site On occasions when leaving the Officers Club when a party was in progress I'd take one of the Jeeps parked outside and drive it to the squadron area and leave it someplace. The Jeep would be recovered by the MPs but as they didn't know who took it, could do nothing about it.

'One night I took a Jeep and decided I'd drive it way out into the scrub on one side of the field. I took it as far as I could go and then walked back to my barracks, laughing to myself that the MPs would have a long search to find the Jeep. A couple of days later I get called in by my squadron operations officer, Captain Frank Baker, who proceeds to quiz me about a Jeep found in the woods. Of course, I professed ignorance of the matter. He said he knew I was the guy taking the Jeeps. "Not me, Frank," I assured him. "Well," he concluded, "the Jeep in the woods belonged to the Group Operations Officer and if he got to find out the name of the man who took it that guy would be in real trouble. If you're still going joy-riding in Jeeps you better see it's not one of the top people." I told him I'd spread the word around, but he knew it was me.'

Another snub to authority was the purloining of government property. Among the rank and file it was not seen as a crime and if you were apprehended there was no disgrace; it was just hard luck. Because of these activities, particular items or commodities in short supply had to be guarded or put under lock and key. Prominent was fuel for heating and the observations of 379th Bomb Group bombardier Harold Smith are not untypical of the situation prevailing at many bases in England:

'The winter of 1944–45 was exceptionally cold and our barracks had the usual heater. A 50-gallon oil drum customized. There was a shortage of coal and it was rationed. If you happened to be out on a mission the day the coal was delivered you were out of luck. It became fair game to steal coal from barracks that had received the delivery in our absence. At night if you heard a noise outside of your barracks, you would scramble out of bed and end up chasing someone trying to run with a coal scuttle full, only to have to empty it as he ran so he wouldn't be caught. Then we found out about the bomb boxes. They were made out of pine wood which was great when you burned it but it burned fiercely and only for a short time. The front of your body would be so hot you would have to get away from the stove and your back would be freezing. When the Ordnance people found out what was happening to all the boxes they put out a warning, but the stealing continued. Eventually they put up barbed wire around the area.'

It was also fair game to take non-personal effects of men missing in action – those articles supplied by the Air Forces: clothing and equipment. This was illegal and individual base administrations took measures to prevent these unauthorized acquisitions, but the articles were often removed before any protective action could be taken. In fact, in many instances crews who had been forced to put down at another airfield after a combat mission found, on returning to home base, that their lockers had already been plundered. The practice was difficult to stamp out because it had become something of a tradition. However, in some cases an individual's personal belongings were distributed, an action that found any apprehended culprits in deep trouble. Naturally, the 'fair game' attitude relating to Air Force equipment was an excuse by the morally uninhibited thief to steal anything that took his fancy, be it GI or private property. These men were few, but there always seemed to be one ready thief in a unit. When a new B-17 landed at Burtonwood and its crew were incautious enough to leave their belongings on board while they reported to the flight office, they found most gone when they returned. The plunderers were a nearby anti-aircraft crew. No doubt they thought it a great joke. One of the robbed, John Howland, saw this in a different light, as he recorded in his diary after trying to obtain replacements:

'Tried to buy a hack watch to replace the one stolen back at Stone; but there is so damn much red tape to go through I think I will just let it go and use my faithful old Gruen. It is really upsetting not to be able to get needed equipment here in the combat zone, and one of the worst conditions I find we have to put up with is that our private property is not safe. For myself, I can honestly say I would not think of stealing another man's equipment; but after losing a hack watch and my navigator's chronometer,I don't think I would be gentle if I caught someone stealing from me.'

One can imagine the mirth of the perpetrators responsible for the theft described by Dave Davidson of the 7th Photo Group. The victim must have been less amused:

'A C-47 transport from Africa came into our base at Mount Farm one day. Among the stuff it carried was cheeses cured in camel dung. At the time they were unloading all this stuff, an RAF messenger drove up on a motorcycle, parked the machine and went into the control tower. When he came out, the bike had disappeared. It was on its way to Africa – the C-47 crew had put it on the plane, closed up and taken off.'

Finding the thief was often difficult and when one did, justice was not always forthcoming. This was the case for Anthony Hmura, who traced his robber through an unusual incident:

'When we flew from our training session in Northern Ireland to our combat base in England, we were told to leave our baggage behind and that it would be sent along by sea. Everybody in my crew got their bags except me. A friendly sergeant in the Supply Office managed to get me some clothes and helped to put a tracer on my two missing bags. One day I got a call from him that my bags had arrived. The one with my blankets and overcoat was okay but the other, that had all the valuable articles – camera, films and so on – I'd brought from the States had been emptied and filled with old fatigues, towels and other worn stuff just to bulk it out. This burned a hole in me and by the time I reached my barracks I was really mad. In my anger I took a blow at the door to let off steam but only succeeded in bruising my knuckles which made me feel worse not better. Well, I got over it and was able to borrow clothes and other things.

'Then, coming back from London on a crowded train, the pal I was with managed to find seats for us in one of the small compartments. Sitting opposite were two other soldiers and from the cross pistols insignia on their collars I knew that they were Military Police. As I didn't want to talk with any MPs I just ignored them, preferring to talk to my pal or look at the ceiling and the floor. It was when I looked at the floor that I got a shock. One of the MPs was wearing the civilian shoes I'd had stolen in Ireland. At first I was speechless and just wanted to hit the guy but I restrained myself and finally shouted, "Those are my shoes you have on!" He asked me what I meant and when I told him they'd been stolen he said he bought them from his buddy beside him. His friend said that he'd bought them from another guy. At first I thought I was being given the run-around so I decided to act friendly and sure enough they were able to give me the soldier's name and the outfit he was with.

'At first I was going to write him but my crew talked me out of it and suggested I get the proper authorities to deal with it. This I did and finally received an order to attend a Court Martial where this man was to be charged for stealing my property. I was asked to identify my shoes and a shirt but not allowed to listen to the trial. In the end all I received back was the shirt and shoes. None of the other items had been recovered and the thief got away with it because he said the bag had been marked salvage from the belongings of a man who had been shot down. How the court could accept that when no missions were flown from Northern Ireland I don't know. After that I didn't have much faith in Army justice. I felt I was the one who was made to look foolish.'

The authorities were not lenient if a crime was proven, with prolonged confinement for serious wrongdoers. England and Italy had US military prisons. Petty larceny and infringement of military regulations would be dealt with by the unit, the enlisted man offender being reduced in rank or given a week or two KP (kitchen parade), involving washing dishes and peeling potatoes. Officers were usually fined, the fine generally being extracted from pay.

4
Pranks and Pastimes

Regulations were a challenge to many people who appear to have derived great satisfaction from flouting them in some manner or other. With an average age of 21, youthful nature undoubtedly had some bearing on this behaviour. There was rarely any malice in this action, but if something was forbidden there was always a temptation to attempt it. For example, rules were strict about the use of rifles and pistols issued to specified personnel for guard duty and personal protection; but this did not prevent Nissen hut barrack rooms being perforated by bullet holes, nor did it prevent hunting expeditions. If apprehended the punishment could be a period of confinement or substantial fine. Although the tell-tale shot would bring the military police, the temptation to pull a trigger was often too great, as Marvin Speidel tells:

'During the period of the cross-Channel invasion in early June, we were told to wear sidearms around the base as there was a possibility of paratroopers being dropped as a counter move by the Germans. There were warnings about misuse but the novelty was too much for some people to resist. One evening our ball turret gunner exhibited his marksmanship by blasting a rabbit seen near our barracks. Needless to say there wasn't much left of the bunny after it was hit by a .45 bullet. The shot must have been heard by an MP, for we soon got word that the Provost Marshal was heading our way. The remaining evidence was quickly hidden but the ball gunner couldn't locate any gun oil with which he might clean the signs that his weapon had been fired. In desperation he grabbed someone's bottle of Vitalis hair oil and swabbed the barrel with that. When the Provost arrived he demanded to inspect each gun and sniffed the barrels. When he came to the guilty one, he made an exclamation and barked: "What the hell did you clean this piece with soldier?" The ball gunner feigned innocence and said he didn't know. The Provost must have had his suspicions but with no smell of cordite for corroboration he couldn't nail the culprit.'

The constitutional right of the US citizen to carry arms was instrumental in the 'no big deal' attitude prevailing among US servicemen when it came to the use of guns. The weapon issued might be Government property and intended for use against the enemy, but a little illegal hunting or unauthorized target practice was not viewed as the serious offence it would be in the British or other Allied services. The US authorities did crack down on offenders, particularly to placate the civilian population of host countries who tended to be alarmed by the casual use of handguns and rifles. Bullets whistling around the countryside were not appreciated, even in the sandy wastes of North Africa, as Ted Newby discovered:

'While in Tunis, en route, a couple of us went out into the desert with a rifle and some bullets and engaged in some target practice. We found some old AA shells with no projectile in them. There seemed to be a detonation cap at the rear end but we knew if we hit the cap it should blow up or something.

'We got back a "safe" distance and took turns firing at it. Fortunately no one hit the bull's-eye. Who knows what might have happened if we had.

'After we spent quite a bit of time shooting out toward the desert, an A-Rab came running over the hill in front of us yelling and waving his arms. When he got up to us he did a little pantomime indicating bullets hitting around his feet. We got the message and retreated before we started an international incident.'

For pilots, the ultimate snub to regulations was indulging in 'buzz jobs' – very low flying, often dangerously low, just above roof and treetops. An exhilarating experience but a grounding offence if apprehended. Many commanding officers tended to turn a blind eye to this activity, feeling that it built pilot confidence, particularly with fighters that often had to fly at hedge-hopping heights in the course of operations. There was, however, no justifiable reason why a high-altitude B-17 or B-24 should be skipping over the countryside at hedgetop height frightening (or thrilling) the inhabitants and scaring livestock. Thus, apart from the exhilaration of 'fanning the foliage', there was the gamble of being caught in the act and identified. Al Jones, a 44th Bomb Group bombardier, offers the reason and example:

'I think we were typical of most combat crews when we first arrived in England. We knew we were going into a situation from which we might not return but looked at it from the standpoint that it would probably happen to the other guy. We were therefore a little cocky and looked for excitement before combat had sobered us down. A favorite way of letting off steam was buzzing. Popular "targets" were other airfields. On one local flight we decided to give some of our fighter friends a thrill. After all, they were always buzzing the bomber fields. We picked out a field with a mobile runway control vehicle at the end of the runway and turned in toward it as if we were on a landing approach. As Pete let down, we turned to the fighter airfield radio frequency and listened. Almost immediately the tower is screaming at us that we had our wheels up. The screams got louder the closer we came in toward the runway. Then we saw the men in the control vehicle jump out and run. Pete takes the B-24 down to about three feet over the runway, flies the whole length at that height and climbs away. No doubt leaving some pretty mad runway control people.'

Such escapades took place on what were test or cross-country training flights that should properly have been conducted at altitudes of several thousand feet. Buzzing was a practice that practically all junior officers indulged in at some time or other. Bomber pilots in the MTO were no less inhibited, as B-24 nose gunner Harland Little confirms:

'We enjoyed the days we flew "training" missions. One of our favorite tricks was to buzz the tents of a different group down the road to see if we could blow them down with our prop wash. Another favorite was buzzing small sailboats in the Adriatic, which made things a little rough for the fishermen. Sometimes we'd do a little "splash" target practice nearby. I guess we were far from popular with Italian fishermen.'

Although buzzing and aerial extravagance by fighter pilots were indulged, there were limits to official acceptance, as Jack Ilfrey discovered:

'In mid-December 1942 we (the 94th Fighter Squadron) had to leave the mud at Youks-les-Bains and move to hot, dry and very dusty Biskra. It was common practice for pilots who scored a victory to do a roll over the field upon return – provided the plane wasn't damaged – to let the ground men know of the success. Of course, it was in my nature to have to try and do something more spectacular, so I made a habit of diving down, buzzing across the field, pull up, do my roll and then pull up into a half loop, rolling out at the top. The group CO, Lt Col Ralph Garman, didn't like this exhibition too much, even though he knew it was good for the ground crews' morale.

'The day I got a double victory and feeling my P-38 was in good shape, I was going balls-out on the deck, pulled up and did a double roll and on into a half loop when an engine quit. I had the plane on its back and was just starting to roll out; no airspeed to speak of, ground not far below me; and I looked to have lost it. Well, I survived a really close shave. Even though I had just become his first ace, Garman was livid. Restricted me to quarters and cut off my liquor allowance. After a good reprimand and my promise not to do it again I was back hunting Jerries. But, of course, I had to think up some other trick. Returning from a mission soon afterwards, I buzzed the Colonel's headquarters tent which was near some palm trees on the edge of the field. I must have been a little too low for, as I pulled up, I saw Garman run out, shake his fist and jump in his Jeep. As I landed and taxied in to park, the Colonel's Jeep got behind me and collected a lot of the dust my props were throwing up. By the time I'd got out and was about to jump off the wing to meet the stern-faced Garman, I was pretty sure I was going to be grounded or transferred. At that moment a command car drove up and out jumped General Pete Quesada from 12th Air Force HQ. He was laughing a storm! Instead of being chewed out, I was presented with a fifth of scotch by the General (in appreciation of my knocking down five Jerries) while I listened to him reminding my Colonel how he, Garman, had pulled various stunts when as a Lieutenant he flew under Quesada's command back in the 'thirties. Despite my "free spirit", Ralph Garman later gave me the best letter of recommendation I ever received in the service.'

This was just one more example of what one of the regular pranksters termed 'the foolin' around syndrome'; more truly defined as an uninhibited zest for non-conformity. Much was of a fairly harmless nature, or a show of youthful exuberance like that noted by Barky Hovsepian:

'The gunners on my crew were 18 and 19 years old. Craving youthful excitement and a desire to aid in the war effort, they scoured the land for empty bottles – any variety. When they had collected a sufficient number, they put them on board our plane before an operational mission and later dropped them through the camera hatch, commencing at the IP. This produced a screaming whistle when the bottles reached terminal velocity. It was psychological warfare! I doubt if the enemy below heard them over the sound of sirens, anti-aircraft guns or the drone of all the bombers, but it did help our gunners psychologically.

'Another prank they had concocted was to steal the 100-pound dummy bomb that was used to indicate our 787th Bomb Squadron Orderly Room. They smuggled it on board and it too was dropped through the camera hatch at "bombs away". On our return, we heard that inquiries were made as to the whereabouts of the bomb/sign. Of course, the search proved fruitless and a new sign was installed.'

Most pranks were played on fellow soldiers or airmen. Sometimes this horseplay would develop into a rivalry between friends, each intent on outsmarting the other. Whitmal Hill and a fellow mechanic in the 441st Sub Depot had such an ongoing exchange:

'My friend Bobby and I continually played tricks on each other to the point that whatever happened one would blame the other automatically – to the amusement of the other men living in our barracks. The capers included welding knife, fork and spoon together, drilling holes under the handle of a mess cup so that it leaked as soon as it was filled, sewing up pockets and sleeves, and so on. Two other guys did the same sort of thing, but one trick boomeranged on the perpetrator. Gene nailed Gabby's shoes to the wood floor and when Gabby discovered this Gene expected retaliation. When Gabby wasn't around Gene put his own shoes under Gabby's bed and Gabby's under his. Sure enough when Gene wasn't around Gabby nailed down the shoes under Gene's bed. There was a lot of laughter from the other guys when he learned what he had done.'

Retaliation frequently featured in barrack pranks, the usual objective being to cause a high degree of discomfort or inconvenience to the victims. Royal Frey of the 20th Fighter Group:

'One time Altman and Lundin, who shared the first room inside the main entrance of our barracks, came back happy from an evening at the mess bar. The rest of us were already asleep but these two went from room to room waking people, joking, jostling and singing on the bed; good-natured kind of stuff and we all took it with a smile. Next day we got together to think up a trick to pay them back and somebody came up with a good idea. That evening when Altman and Lundin were kept entertained at the bar, the rest of us went back to the barracks and wheeled in the 35 bicycles which were parked outside. We piled these one on the other in Altman and Lundin's room. By the time we finished, the bikes were stacked to the ceiling and when the guy who had been holding the door open let go to close it, the bikes settled down behind. Altman and Lundin came back around 11pm and there was a lot of noise as they tried to get in their door. Eventually they succeeded and for the next three hours we could hear them giggling as they struggled to untangle and remove each bike. Their state of inebriation undoubtedly added to their difficulties.'

Youthful fooling in this man's world was not easily accepted by the more senior and serious. George Meshko encountered this disdain:

'Coming back from the "Fox and Hounds" one evening, we were fooling around playing aeroplanes on our bicycles, just kids' stuff I guess. I was an Me 109 and collided with a guy who was a P-47. Ended up on the road about a half block from the base hospital. I got tangled up pretty badly and couldn't walk. Had to crawl to the hospital where they found I'd made a mess of my ligaments in one leg. They put me in bed, my leg in a cast, and elevated it. There I am for about a week with a dozen guys, most of whom have been shot up in combat. Towards the end of my stay a bunch of dignitaries arrive in the sick bay talking to patients. The guy in the next bed, who has his eyes all bandaged, gets a Purple Heart pinned on him. Then one of the officers turns to me and says: "What happened to you sergeant?"

' "I fell off a bike, sir."

'Boy, they didn't think that funny. Did I get the cold shoulder! Guess my feelings were kinda hurt. After all I'd flown 25 combat missions, which was more than any of the others had.'

Newcomers were inviting targets, as Bob Strobell found when he joined the 353rd Fighter Group at Metfield, England:

'In one Nissen hut, when a replacement pilot arrived he would find he had been assigned the bunk just inside the door. He was told by the other pilots in the hut that if he heard the air raid warning go off he was to scamper out that door as fast as he could and dive for cover into the ditch just outside. It was emphasized that if he didn't do this, he was likely to be trampled by a pack of pilots right on his heels, intent on getting out the same door. Air raid warnings were common, but rarely did any enemy activity develop around our base. The newcomer was not to know this and probably expected bombs to fall as soon as the siren went. Sure enough, it wasn't long before the air raid warning sounded one night and out the new replacement rushes, dives into the ditch and comes up covered in mud. And there, standing at the top of the ditch, was a group of pilots with silly grins advising him to get out of there because that was where they went at night when they didn't want to walk over to the latrines. The replacement pilot learned fast. Next night he moved down a couple of beds and waited for a new replacement.'

The newcomer was most susceptible to being duped when it came to the local scene away from the base. Here the 'old hands' could have great fun in bringing recent arrivals discomfort; and in the anecdote related by Whitmal Hill the discomfort probably included punishment for a late return to camp:

'We were coming back to our base at Bassingbourn from a pass to London. At King's Cross station we encountered several men from the B-17 group recently arrived at Nuthampstead, a new airfield a few miles away from Royston town on the opposite side to our base. These guys had obviously been on their first pass to London, for they were not sure which train they should catch. Anyway, they eventually got aboard and away we went. This was late at night and probably the last train. It stopped at several stations and when it pulled into one called Ashwell and Morden, villages a few miles south of Royston, the guy I was with – Thornton – winks at me and says he's going to have some fun. As soon as the train stopped he stepped out on the platform and yells in a fake English accent: "All change for Royston." We guys from Bassingbourn knew that you didn't change. We could hear the doors slamming as all the Nuthampstead guys jumped off. The guard blew his whistle and the train moved off up the line to Royston. I expect the Nuthampstead guys are still looking for the jokers who gave them a mighty long walk.'

Practical joking among members of the crew was particularly marked, a relief from the rigours of combat flying, but also an unconscious bonding activity, much in the way a litter of cubs play. John Wilson, the navigator of a 96th Bomb Group B-17 crew, relates many amusing escapades such as the following:

'Our co-pilot, Charlie, came back from a bike ride in the country with six beautiful fresh eggs which he'd persuaded some farmer to sell him. Charlie was really excited about these eggs – they were the first we had seen in five months – and kept talking about how he was going to have them cooked; no mention of sharing with the other guys in our hut. A little later Charlie had to go with our pilot out to the field to check the plane. Before he went he thought he had hidden his precious eggs where we wouldn't find them, but he was wrong. Next morning Charlie took the eggs to the mess sergeant and told him just how he wanted them cooked. So the mess sergeant gets a greased pan and carefully taps one of the eggs on the edge to break it. No luck. He taps again and still no yolk appears. He carefully looks at all the eggs and says: "Is this some kind of a joke Lieutenant? These eggs have been hard boiled." Charlie was more than a little mad at us; but, of course, we pleaded innocence.'

5
Pets and Petting

Pets were in some part an outlet for affection that would normally have been bestowed on a wife, girlfriend or family. A desire common to the men of military units but rarely allowed fulfilment; apart from being impractical due to the itinerant nature of most forces. The relaxed order of the USAAF enabled men in those units that had some permanency of station to acquire and maintain pets. There was a North African donkey in England and one bomb squadron managed to fly a North American brown bear cub into its Suffolk county base. This was maintained as a mascot until its adult ramblings brought protests from apprehensive locals and the British police, leading to the creature being put down. Exotic pets such as monkeys, parrots, or snakes were smuggled into some British and Italian bases by air. One 96th Group crew had smuggled an African mule aboard their B-17 during the shuttle raid in August 1943 and brought the animal back to England. This cosseted mascot was used in another caper by John Wilson's crew:

'One of the guys goes to our pilot and tells him the tail gunner, Chuck Haywood, is very sick in bed and he should go to take a look at him. So our pilot, who was always very concerned about his crew, goes to the barracks and up to the bed and there's the mule that the boys got in Africa looking at him from under the sheets. Chuck wasn't very pleased because the mule left fleas in the bed!'

The predominant pet and mascot was, naturally, the dog. Every 8th and 15th Air Force station had a canine population, many being adopted local strays. There were periodic efforts by the authorities to limit numbers, particularly after one incident when a dozen mongrels insisted on intermingling with soldiers assembled for a General's parade inspection. Generally, Command tolerated pets, appreciating that they provided some relief from military life. In combat units the situation would arise where the owner of a dog would be killed or missing, the dog then being taken over by another airman or other occupants of the particular barracks. Connie Anszperger tells the story of one such animal:

'There was a dog called Catfish who followed a certain co-pilot of the 524th Bomb Squadron wherever he went around the field. Anytime he wasn't following the co-pilot he'd be chasing his own tail, round and round so much that the tail was cleaned of hair for about three inches back from the tip. One day Catfish suddenly stopped chasing his tail and we learned that the co-pilot had not come back from a mission. Catfish went to every hardstand, round the mess hall, all over the field but couldn't find his man. For several weeks Catfish was never seen to chase his tail. Then one day he started again. It was the day we learned that the co-pilot was safe, a prisoner of war.'

One of the most enduring and endearing relationships was that established by Walter Konantz, a 55th Fighter Group pilot, with a Scotch terrier:

'I was on a short leave in London and, while window shopping, I happened by a pet store that had a Scottie put in the window. Since I had left an ageing Scottie at home when I joined the AAF, I entered the pet shop only to look at the pup and maybe scratch it behind the ears. The lady removed the pup from the window and set it on the floor, whereupon it started wagging its tail and ran over to me like I was its long-lost master. I had no intention of buying, but after that greeting I walked out of the shop with the puppy under my trench coat and headed for the train back to base.

'We lived in a 12-man Nissen hut and housebreaking the puppy did present problems, but Lassie II, as I named her, eventually learned and became the beloved pet of the whole barracks. One afternoon I was scheduled for a maintenance test hop in a P-51 and decided to take the dog for a ride. The cockpit was too cramped to carry her on my lap or the floor, so I spread my heavy jacket over the radio just behind the armor plate of the seat and placed her there. After take-off I looked back at her several times and she appeared to be enjoying the flight. Even after I temporarily forgot about her during my peel-off to land, which subjected the dog to three or four "Gs" and flattened her out like a bearskin rug, she didn't seem to mind. Subsequently Lassie rode with me on several local flights, mostly in the Group's L-4 Cub liaison plane.

'Once, when I was flying a combat mission, someone accidentally let Lassie out of the barracks and she was hit by a GI ambulance and badly injured. The driver knew the dog and took her to the base hospital where a broken left hind leg was diagnosed. Our Flight Surgeon put the leg in a plaster cast, wrapping it around Lassie's middle to prevent movement. We attached an aileron pulley to the end of the cast so she could roll the leg on smooth surfaces. After four weeks the cast was removed and the leg proved as good as new.

'I could not bear to leave the dog behind when I finished my tour and by knocking her out with sleeping pills successfully got her on the troopship and through US Customs in my laundry bag without being apprehended. She wasn't the only smuggled pet; there were four others on the ship that I knew of.'

Apart from being objects of affection, pets were often taught tricks to perform – or encouraged in dubious practices, as Royal Frey discovered:

'Our enlisted men at Wittering had a dog, an ugly short-legged mongrel, which they must have trained not to like officers. You'd be riding down the street on your bike, meet a bunch of enlisted men, exchange salutes, and then this damn dog would take off after you. We noticed this only seemed to happen when wearing our pink officers' pants, so we concluded they'd trained the dog to go for that colour.'

Unit mascots extended to children, particularly young boys who showed an interest in aircraft. In both England and France the occasional youngster would often be seen around the base, sometimes dressed in specially tailored GI uniform. In Italy, where poverty took a hand, groups of young boys were attracted to 12th and 15th Air Force bases where such goodies as chewing gum and chocolate bars were given out. These youngsters often became Americanized, much to the amusement of their benefactors. Dick Halliday, a 2nd Bomb Group pilot, was surprised by the extent of this influence:

'The first evening on our arrival at Amendola air base in Italy we were walking down the main street of our tent city on the way to dinner when we saw a group of Italian kids coming towards us. I would guess they were aged between 10 and 14 years. We had been told there were a number in the camp who were treated as mascots. None of my crew had ever been out of the United States before and flying a B-17 across the Atlantic, staging through foreign countries, to finally reach our combat unit had all been a great adventure and exciting experience for we young Americans. As the kids approached I turned to the other three officers of our crew who were with me and made some comment that we were about to get our first lesson in speaking Italian. My remark was overheard by one of the youngsters who looked up at us and directly at me and said in heavily accented English: "Hubba, hubba, chicken a shit, second lieutenant." '

The USAAF made provision for off-duty entertainment of personnel but this depended very much on the type of unit. The permanent heavy bomber bases in England had squash courts, sports fields, libraries and movie shows; while a tactical fighter group in France, following hard on the ground forces' heels, had to find its own relaxations. Fortunately, the kit for baseball was little and light and this game was to be seen at nearly every USAAF camp. In some localities High Command was able to organize stadium sports events, occasionally within striking distance of the Luftwaffe. Jack Collingwood:

'While in northern Italy on 1st January, 1945, several members of the surrounding army and air force units were invited to attend a most unusual New Year's Day event. Those of us who were lucky enough to be selected knew only that we were going to a football game. We did not know the time or where, being instructed to wait at a given spot to be picked up by an Army truck. We were then taken to a large stadium in Florence. There we learned that there was going to be an American football game between the Army and Air Force personnel, most of whom had played on various college football teams. It was announced as "The First and Last Spaghetti Bowl Game". During the entire time, before the game, during and after, the air force flew fighter coverage. It would have been an exceptional time for the Luftwaffe to have made some attacks as there must have been some 40,000 personnel in the stadium.'

The natural inclination of young men to seek out young women was not muted by overseas service in Europe. The primary recreation for the majority of USAAF personnel was the local womenfolk. A high proportion of such successful associations were of a permanent nature, with several thousand marriages to British, French and Italian girls. The base Post Exchange sold toiletries and other desirable items that were in short supply in Europe and this source was exploited by some men, particularly the promiscuous, to attract girls. The availability of prophylactic kits to any man going off base resulted from a policy whereby the US authorities expected a proportion of men to indulge in sexual adventures, with or without cautioning, and therefore provided for the prevention of infection and impregnation. However, while undoubtedly a progressive attitude, in practice it did encourage many amorous adventurers to see their activities as being condoned. In Britain popular rumour maintained that Yanks were over-sexed, a fantasy also conveyed through 'dirty' stories that were a common, if dubious, feature of personal entertainment, prevalent in many quarters at that time. The subjects of this supposed prowess were amused, if not flattered, and readily repeated these tales among themselves. A 381st Bomb Group navigator recorded this example in his diary:

'Mar 2, 1944 – A Yank story making the rounds deals with one English woman talking to another. In a strong cockney accent one asks: "Do you know Yanks, dearie?"

' "Do I know Yanks? Why just the other evening I was walking home from the pub with a bucket of beer for me old man when I met a Yank. Well Luv, he ups me, downs me, ins me, outs me, wipes his tallywacker on me petticoat, drinks me old man's beer, pisses in the bucket, walks off whistling "God Save the King". And you ask me if I know Yanks!" '

The higher pay of US servicemen, as much as three times that of the equivalent ranks of British and other Allied airmen, undoubtedly played a part in attracting the good-time girls and those engaged in prostitution. In Britain prostitutes quickly saw a means of enhanced income and offered their services at a higher price to GIs. The reputation of the 'Piccadilly Commando' was well known at most USAAF stations in England and from all accounts these girls were well supported by a proportion of young men 'on pass'. When the USAAF moved to the Continent during the liberation of France and the Low Countries, the attentions of prostitutes were more blatant, as Frank Gaccione of the 27th Photo Squadron recalls:

'Directly outside the base was a cafe and a bombed-out building. There always seemed to be girls hanging around outside these places and I soon found out that they were prostitutes. They had a regular business going every night! The ordinary street-walker would be out front and took her clients into the bombed-out building – usually two girls with a line of GIs queueing up! The higher priced girls operated inside the cafe and seemed to have some arrangement with the owner. These girls didn't really want French money, only US dollars or goods – soap, cigarettes, coffee, etc. They were pretty brazen and when the trucks drew up at the camp gate to take the boys into Brussels or Lille on a liberty run they'd try and jump on. They knew the boys would have money to spend. In one section of Brussels there seemed to be prostitutes in most small cafes. They'd call after you when you walked by. Sometimes you found a mother and daughter teamed up. Most guys were too scared of VD to have anything to do with them. VD was very common. We were given sulfa tablets to test against colds and some men accumulated these to use as a "cure" for VD!'

In Italy the poverty induced by war brought many women into this age-old trade, sometimes with the connivance of their families. Harland Little was aware of the situation that existed at his base near Foggia:

'We were not restricted in any way within our relationships with Italian girls and many men from our base had casual or serious affairs with them, most with the knowledge of their families. Often little brothers solicited American airmen for their sisters, wanting money or food. A can of corned beef, items wrangled from the mess hall cooks, cigarettes and candy, were all good for trade. In the valley below the base there was a special place in a wooded area where several local girls were usually available for a few lire of occupational money. The evidence of their popularity was seen by the volume of discarded protective devices. This area was near a field where shepherds grazed their sheep and watched airmen come and go, often receiving cigarettes and other gifts. Most of the girls in Foggia, where we spent our spare time, were attractive and, I believe, from nice families. They did what they did to get food and money for their families – and some because they were attracted to the Americans.'

The presence of American service women in the ETO and MTO was small and chiefly confined to WACs in higher headquarters. This limited deployment suggests that the military authorities in Washington had a narrow view of female presence in the Army. Either they feared for the chastity of the WACs or, conversely, thought the WACs would be more interested in liaisons with the troops than their duties. Many WACs sensed this discrimination, one being Hathy Veynar, who served at 2nd Bomb Division headquarters:

'Initially there was a lot of prejudice against women in US military service. Quite extraordinary and difficult to understand. As an early volunteer for the WAC I was subject to a thorough investigation of my background. They wanted to know everything and I'm sure this deterred a lot of girls from joining. At the time my company was sent overseas one of the tabloid New York papers ran a piece that said WACs had been issued with contraceptives. This was completely false and although it was refuted the damage was done. As a result, we always had to be very careful how we conducted ourselves as some prejudiced male would be eager to give us a bad name. With time the situation eased. Overall I think WACs were excellent representatives of American womanhood of the time.'

USAAF personnel were aware of and accepted the British WAAFs serving the RAF in a wide variety of duties, some involving strenuous manual effort. The apparent cosseting or restriction of American womanhood produced an attitude of curiosity towards the few WACs that appeared overseas. Elinor Fredricks recalls her arrival:

'The boys at VIIIth Fighter Command had been overseas around a year before we arrived. The WAC wasn't even in existence when some of them had left the States. We were something of a curiosity when we arrived. The first morning there were tables set for the WACs at one end of the mess hall. While we ate it seemed like every man was staring at us; it felt like we were something that had dropped in on them from Mars. As the days went by they got used to us, although we always got plenty of male attention. When I got to know the Sergeant I worked with, I asked him why we were such curiosities. He said it was because they didn't know what to expect. Were we broads or were we society women; they didn't know. What they didn't expect was what they discovered: that we were no different from their sisters back home.'

Despite the reputation assumed by their allies, the US airman was no more or no less a sexual adventurer than the men of other nations. The majority conducted themselves well with the girls of Europe and gifts were given out of genuine friendship and knowledge of local shortages rather than with a view to gaining favour. Men stationed in England were soon aware that food rationing was severe and that if visiting in the local community one should remember this. Gifts of foodstuffs were thus the favourite visiting present, although not easily acquired on bases other than those limited items obtainable at the PX. There were ways of overcoming this particular problem if one had rank, as John Parsons observed:

'Our gunnery school at Snettisham was commanded by Major "Fletch" Fletcher. He and I met two English girls in King's Lynn and started to go see them regularly where they lived at Hunstanton. We never went empty-handed, knowing that rations were pretty tight for the British. Major Fletcher would go to the back of the mess hall and tell the mess sergeant: "Lieutenant Parsons and I are going out on the economy tonight. Now we'd like you, Mess Sergeant, to give us the rations we would have eaten tonight. We're not asking for anything extra." The sergeant quickly got the picture; he was talking to his commanding officer. He would bring out steaks, canned fruits and things the British couldn't get. We'd load up the Jeep and go up to Valerie's house and the girls would really set up a dinner. Valerie was married to an RAF officer. They eventually got divorced and she married "Fletch". I went with Joan Henderson, the widow of a Canadian flying officer, but we didn't carry it on after the war.'

Shortages were even more acute on the continent and many US servicemen became benefactors of friends made in the nearby towns and villages. Charles Salter of the 9th Air Division was one who tried to help:

'While stationed with the 394th Bomb Group at Cambrai, I got acquainted with a French family who ran a bar in the town. They had a rough time, with a son crippled in the war. We got to be quite friendly, though I had a little trouble with the language. I would take them things as they didn't have a lot, and they'd invite me to dinner on Sundays. Food wasn't that plentiful so I didn't like to make it more difficult for them. First time I went I asked the daughter of the house what meat we were going to eat. She said: "Lapin, we have plenty of lapin." I didn't know what lapin was. So she wriggled her nose and made ears with her hands. I got it right away – rabbit! Eventually I was moved up to Namur, Belgium. My work there was to go out to the various bases and sort out any administrative troubles.

'On one trip I had to go back to Cambrai and took the opportunity to call in on the French family I knew. I found them distressed. They were in big trouble with our local MPs who had accused them of having stolen US property. This was a couple of pairs of paratroopers boots which I'd bought at the Army Sales Store when I'd been stationed at Cambrai. They'd been seen and reported to the commander of the local MPs, a major, who just wouldn't believe the boots had been come by legitimately and was going to get the town's mayor to bring the family to trial. It was fortunate for them that I chanced by and, being a lieutenant colonel, was able to pull rank on the major and set the record straight.'

In the aftermath of the German retreat public order in the liberated territory often left much to be desired. The purloining of materials and equipment from Allied air bases appeared to be fair game and required some energetic policing activities to recover. The supposed affluence of the US forces found the more assertive native endeavouring to establish a friendship with a GI, as Frank Gaccione discovered:

'We had no shower facilities in our base at Denain/Prouvy and had to go into town to use the public baths. We could catch a trolley [tram] that ran by the base gate and, although we were told to pay the fare, the French wouldn't take it, saying the Germans never paid so why should we. One time I was waiting for the trolley when a Frenchman standing there asks if anybody speaks Italian. I said that I did. He brightened up and said he was in the Italian Army in World War I and stayed behind and married a French woman. A couple of days later this same man comes looking for me and says that he wants me to come to his home and that his wife will cook a spaghetti dinner.

'At this time the Battle of the Bulge was going on and we had been warned that German troops may be in hiding in our area and we should be very careful where we go. Had to wear our helmets and carry carbines if we went off base. So I thanked the man and made some excuse. Well, the man keeps turning up and putting the same invitation and I keep making excuses that I've got to work. I found out he was in charge of civilian labourers on our base. Eventually I gave in and found a buddy who, after all others refused, would come with me next night. So we take a trip into town and the man meets us. As we are walking along I'm thinking about why is this guy so eager for me to go to dinner at his house. When we get to what looks like a bombed building (there were no street lights), he makes for us to go up some stairs, but I told him, "No way, you go first". By the time we got to the top of the stairs to a door, I was expecting Germans to come bursting out with guns blazing. I was really scared and wishing I'd never accepted the invitation. Well, the door is opened and there is an enormous table with men and women of all ages sitting round it. Reminded me of a picture of the Last Supper. We were sat down and were given a good dinner – I don't know what we ate, but it was good. And this man had liquor you couldn't believe – calvados, cognac and everything. I asked him how he came to have so much and he said it had all been buried in the garden back yard.

'I still couldn't figure out why he was so keen to get us to go to his house. When asked, he said his daughter was studying English and that he wanted for her to talk to people who spoke it. Me? With a Brooklyn accent! Somehow this still didn't figure. The following day he was at the base gate asking for me. Could I get him some Gillette razor blades? Next time it was soap, then cigarettes. I then began to catch on why he had wanted to dine me: I would be less likely to refuse his requests. This was the British zone but this man knew that Americans could get things the British couldn't and had set out to use me.'

6
Chow and Booze

Foodstuffs were often far from plentiful for the GI and were actually in short supply when units moved to the continent. Sometimes men were reduced to the packaged K-ration. Frank Gaccione's squadron encountered some shortages and turned to barter with the natives:

'We had a rough time for food when we first got to France as the weather was fogged in and planes could not fly in supplies. No coffee, no salt for a while. Drank concentrated lemonade. We bartered soap for food with the civilians. I was a Lifebuoy man, the bar with a medicinal scent. Soon discovered the French weren't interested in Lifebuoy, they wanted Lux and sweet smelling soaps. So I couldn't deal. Quickly wrote my mother and got her to send Ivory tablets. These I'd split in half and could get five eggs for a half bar.'

Similarly, during the North African invasion of late 1942 men of the 12th Air Force experienced problems obtaining good food. Jack Ilfrey:

'When we first got to Oran and Algiers food was in short supply and what there was was mostly horrible. Some of our finicky big eaters actually got rather hungry. We did manage to get eggs and sometimes the Arabs' chickens and goats just happened to get in the way of our Jeeps. Fruit was plentiful so we ate too many dates and figs to sate our hunger. The result was that most of us got diarrhoea – some cases were severe. When I opened my mother's Christmas gift it was a pack of Dromedary dates. Just to look at the camel's picture on the pack made me feel ill. I didn't want to eat any and there were no takers when I tried to give them away.'

When the Allies moved into Sicily during the summer heat of 1943, water became a problem for the first airmen to arrive. Jack Collingwood of the 27th Fighter Bomber Group:

'The Germans had contaminated all watering locations. Each man was rationed one canteen per day for *all* purposes. This went on for three or more weeks. No baths, short of food, short of water and still trying to operate. Water was then brought in on LSTs and transported to the units in 5-gallon cans. After no bathing for so many weeks, the Army finally brought in some field showers and disinfectants. All men were ordered to shower and while doing so their clothing was sprayed with, we think, DDT.'

Food at established air bases was good. Those who found it wanting quickly revised their opinions if they had the misfortune to eat at a British forces mess. Kitchen staff were forced to make use of vegetables and fruits acquired in the locality if they wanted to use fresh produce. American palates were unaccustomed to some vegetables and in England one gained almost legendary status – the Brussels sprout. A form of cabbage, the edible parts consisted of small tight-leaf clusters taken from the stem and served after boiling. The frequency with which this vegetable was served in dinner meals brought many complaints and the Brussels sprout was soon established as the pet aversion of the US serviceman in England. Edward Anthis, a bomb-sight repairman at the 2nd Strategic Air Depot, was well aware of this infamous reputation:

'In our bomb-sight shop the late shift worked until midnight, by which time the mess hall was closed. So we didn't go hungry, around ten in the evening two of us would take turns in driving a Jeep down to the mess hall and collecting all the left-overs. Once a friend suggested we pull a joke by filling all the pans we took to the mess hall with nothing but Brussels sprouts. This English vegetable didn't suit most American palates and was often on the menu. When we arrived back at our shop and told the others there was nothing left but Brussels sprouts there was a great uproar. To take the joke further I kept eating the sprouts and making as if they were delicious while everyone else was bitching. Funny thing is that I really began to like them and have done ever since.'

That popular speciality of American gastronomy, ice-cream, was not on the military menu. Undaunted, several enterprising units in the UK and Italy managed to locate ice-cream making apparatus locally and improvised ingredients. The results varied but that sampled by Barky Hovsepian was most welcome:

'Our Wing had acquired an ice-cream making machine and once a week this would visit each of the three bases. A plate of ice-cream cost 2/6d [12½p] but it was good. We had to pay cash at the mess, otherwise no ice-cream. Always the same flavor, pale chocolate made by grating the hard tropical chocolate that was available. Although it was never firmly frozen, nevertheless it was enjoyed.'

Generally RAF and USAAF men did not approve of the others' mess hall fare – although RAF men stationed at US bases very quickly appreciated that the standard and variety of food was infinitely better than their own. Americans who fed at some British airfields confessed that they did not know what they were eating and only ate through hunger. Additionally there was the hazard of terminology – two nations separated by a common language – as 91st Bomb Group's Robert Cayer discovered:

'After the flight from Newfoundland to Scotland we landed at Bassingbourn on a late October evening in 1942. It was after dark and the mess hall was closed. An RAF sergeant showed us to a barracks. He asked me if I wanted some biscuits and, being very hungry, I said yes. Imagine my surprise when he carried in three small bed mattresses and put them on my bare bed frame.'

The chief agent in escape from the stress of combat or the boredom of military duties was alcohol. As is their wont, young men often imbibed too liberally in the quest for the blurred euphoria of intoxication. Many men did not drink, many others only in moderation, but there were always those who, usually in the company of their buddies, drank heavily. Beer and liquor were obtainable at the clubs for officers and NCOs that were established on most bases but supplies were restricted and drunkenness avoided. Officer parties were sometimes the exception, but even there the man who could not 'hold his liquor' was not tolerated. Supplies of hard liquor came mostly from the British, which they called 'spirits', notably Scotch whisky, for which many American servicemen developed a preference. The supply was, like most things in wartime Britain, rationed. But there were always those who found ways to obtain scarce requisites, as happened at the Snettisham gunnery school where John Parsons was stationed:

'The mess officer at our little outfit was an enterprising man. The British provided the liquor ration that had to be collected from headquarters at Brampton once a month. The ration included rum, which didn't rate much favor with Americans but was very popular with British sailors. Our mess officer went down to King's Lynn and talked to an English liquor distributor. A secret deal was set up whereby our man collected the full rum ration for our outfit from Brampton and exchanged it, bottle for bottle, for Scotch with the guy in King's Lynn, who had an outlet for rum with the Navy. That way we never ran short of Scotch and, as we were seldom without visitors from other US bases, the word must have gotten around.'

The value of alcohol in relieving combat tensions was accepted by high command and at debriefing on return from a mission crews would be offered a small measure of whisky. This gesture was appreciated more by some individuals than others as Herbert Lancaster, a 493rd Bomb Group B-17 pilot, admits:

'Every mission was a good one when the wheels touched down at the home base and no wounded aboard. Park the plane and on to debriefing; shed all the flying gear and get comfortable. At debriefing Uncle Sam had a "welcome home bar": good old American booze. Just sign your name but only one drink per person. One of my buddies, Pete Peterson, 19 years old, did not drink but he always signed, so I had one more. There were also other non-drinkers who would also sign and let me enjoy. Now it's time to go to the mess – wherever it is! But Pete would always lead the way.'

Another official source of liquor was the sick quarters where it was dispensed for special reasons that proved an attraction to some. George Meshko:

'When there were wounded who needed a transfusion, our medical officer would come through the barracks looking at dog tags for men who had the correct blood group. After he had taken the blood at the dispensary, the donor was always given a shot of whisky. Our tail gunner, Bill Adams, liked a drink and when the Doc approached him for blood Bill said: "Okay Doc, I'll play you shot for a shot." '

Men who wanted to drink had to do it off base in an English pub or French bar as opportunity allowed. A night out on the town might be fun but was not conducive to the best state of health if one had to fly a mission next day. The exuberance of youth forgot such caution and many were those who used the pure oxygen of their aircraft's system to help clear a thick head. There were other dangers from excess as the experience of 55th Fighter Group P-51 pilot Carroll Henry illustrates:

'Coming back from a mission the weather started to close in so I diverted with my flight to a field just outside Paris. That night, with a bunch of other fighter pilots, I went into the city and had a ball and between us we consumed eleven bottles of champagne. Next day the weather was fine and we set off back to our base in England. When I made my landing approach the flying control van fired a red flare at me. I'd forgotten to lower my landing gear! Hadn't appreciated the power of champagne. I'd drunk a lot of water and thought I was okay, but evidently the alcohol was still fogging my brain.'

Wine was plentiful in France and the principal source of alcohol in Italy. In the UK wine was almost unobtainable and, as already stated, hard liquor was restricted and rarely available unless one had the right contacts. The attraction of alcohol was very strong for some individuals, as Art Swanson witnessed:

'There were some guys who got their kicks from seeking out new kinds of liquor to try. We had a man in our section like that. One evening he went down to the sick quarters to see the medics about some minor problem he had, but no one was there. While he waited for the orderly to return he started looking the dispensary over and his eyes alighted on a jug of clear liquid. The label on the side said something about alcohol. So he smelt and tasted it and decided he had made a valuable find that was too good to pass up. Didn't wait for the medics to show up; grabs the jug and comes back to our hut proclaiming, "Hey, fellas, Look what I got!" Well, I like a drink but I wasn't going to touch it. A lot of fools did and got bombed on the stuff. Guess it didn't do 'em much good.'

Those who patronized the English pubs drank various types of beer that appeared weak but had, in fact, a fair alcohol content, usually not discovered until a considerable quantity had been consumed. Many caught in this deception became ill rather than intoxicated. Norbert Jost, the flight engineer of a 379th Bomb Group B-17 crew, overdid the celebrations on completion of his combat tour:

'I finished up my missions on November 5th 1943 after a pretty rough tour. Next day, with some of my crew, I got a pass and went to London to celebrate. We knew a place called the American Bar and here I bought a whole bottle of Canadian Club – which was pretty hard to get. I had to pay £25 – about $100 I guess – but I didn't care because I was so happy that I was alive and going home I wanted to get drunk. Well, I sure did. I was silly enough to drink the whole darn bottle and nearly pass out. You could book rooms at this place but I'd forgotten to get one so my navigator took me up to his and put me on the bed. Soon after he'd gone I began to feel pretty ill. My stomach had been with me 22 years and didn't like what I'd just done to it. I threw up all over my uniform and the bed and was so darn ill I just lay in it. When the navigator with his girlfriend came back he was disgusted. Hauled me onto the floor and pulled the bedclothes off onto me. Boy was he cross and I don't think he ever forgave me as his date walked out.'

On another occasion Norbert Jost aided a friend who had taken too liberally to the English beer:

'My buddy and I were out drinking in a pub and he got ill. I took him to the bathroom and held his head over the toilet just as he threw up. He was so ill he could hardly speak for a while but kept trying to get me to look in the toilet. I told him not to worry about it and pulled the flush. Then I realized that what he'd been trying to say was that he'd lost his false teeth down there!'

Over-indulgence in alcohol was a frequent trap for young men trying to forget the war in their celebrations. Rare were the wayward among the small WAC contingents where a much tighter rein was held by unit commanders. Elinor Fredricks knew one WAC given to this weakness:

'We had a replacement WAC who drank too much and the other girls were always trying to get her into the shower to sober her up. One night she went out dancing and was so drunk the MPs had to bring her home. She made it into bed all right and, as the CQ (Charge of Quarters) for the barrack, I decided to put nothing in my report as the MPs said they weren't going to report it either. Next morning I was called to the WAC Commander's office and asked why I hadn't put this girl's behavior in my report. Evidently the Provost Marshal had seen the MPs half carrying this girl back to camp. Needless to say I got punished and the MPs got punished too. So much for charity.'

As is well known, the demon drink can also unleash aggressive tendencies, as in this amusing anecdote related by Carroll Henry that can have done little to promote a favourable opinion from British onlookers:

'Fighter pilots did have a reputation for going wild when they were on pass. Took a trip to London after a mission when we had lost a buddy. Three of us went to a pub where the bar was upstairs and had a few drinks. I proposed drinking a proper toast to our buddy who didn't come back that day and smash the glass against the wall. Macdonald asked if that was an English custom; I said I didn't know whose custom it was but that was what we should do. So we raised our glasses to the missing guy and then smashed the glasses against the wall. Well, the lady behind the bar thought she had real trouble on her hands, but I explained things and paid for the broken glasses and she settled down.

'Sitting at a nearby table was an Air Force major, a master sergeant and a WAC private who – by the looks they were giving us – didn't go along with our behavior. After a few more drinks Macdonald got to feeling sick and we thought we'd better get him to the men's room quick. Now this room was downstairs, but at the top of the stairs was a little old cubbyhole for women. When we got Macdonald to the top of the stairs I didn't think we had time to get him down them, so I opened the door of the ladies room and pushed him in. He hadn't been there 15 seconds when along comes the little WAC and wants to go in. I told her she'd have to wait as there was a man in there. She didn't like that one bit. Next thing I know, her friend the Major is trying to push me outa the way and I'm not letting him do it. There's a struggle and then we're rolling down the stairs. As luck has it, I'm on top when we get to the bottom. Before I can take advantage of the situation my upper arms are grabbed from behind and I'm lifted up in the air as if I were a sack of feathers. Couldn't move, I'm being held so tight. It's this great big master sergeant. By now the WAC has gone for the MPs and this all-American brawl is getting plenty of attention. We sober down and find that the sergeant is the WAC's brother, that the major is up for promotion to Lt Colonel, just as one of my drinking buddies and myself are hoping to make captain any day. This exchange of information sobers us all up even more and by the time the MPs arrive the scene is all peace and quiet and we're acting the best of friends.'

7
Contact with Allies

It was in public houses (pubs) or bars that most acquaintances were made with servicemen of Allied nations. The uniforms were mostly British but they could contain men from a score of different nations, from every occupied land in Europe and almost every corner of the British Empire and Commonwealth. The encounters could be surprising. Philip Kanarkowski of the 95th Bomb Group:

'While on leave in London in 1944, "pub-crawling" was a favorite pastime for war-weary airmen. At one of these pubs I noticed an airman wearing British blues with a POLAND patch on his shoulder. Being of Polish heritage, but knowing very little of the language, I nevertheless decided to try and give a friendly greeting that I knew – "Yaksha mush", which means "How do you do."

'When he heard this, the exuberant Pole threw his arms around me, kissed me on both cheeks, then hugged me enthusiastically as he proceeded to sing the Polish National Anthem at the top of his voice. This demonstration of patriotic fever got the attention of everyone present who must have thought we were long-lost brothers instead of up till now complete strangers.'

The reception was not always friendly as there seemed to be a generally held view among other Allied servicemen that 'the Yanks' were too highly paid and boastful. In part this was envy and in part resentment but was quickly evaporated by personal contact. The RAF were, understandably, a trifle peeved that the USAAF was taking over centre stage and an undertone of sarcasm was sometimes evident as a result. Tyler Winton, a 385th Bomb Group navigator:

'On 26th July 1943, we suffered grievous flak damage over Kiel and left the target area with one prop' feathered and another windmilling. By stripping everything loosely attached to the aircraft, we managed to stabilize at 1,000 feet and 120 indicated air speed for the long flight home. We eventually arrived over the Wash at dusk and, groping south in the haze, encountered an RAF Lancaster station where we plopped down. Though they were themselves launching a mission within minutes of our arrival, the hospitable RAF fliers not on the schedule insisted on hauling our limp, cold, dirty selves to their mess for a little cheer. The first toast, offered by a merry flight lieutenant, left me pondering whether there might have been some implied censure therein:

' "Here's to America, the land of the push,
Where a bird in the hand is worth two in the bush.
But if, in the bush, a maiden should stand
A push in the bush is worth two in the hand." '

While acknowledging that American airmen were involved in a pretty bloody war, one point of irritation with the RAF men was the seemingly apparent eagerness of the USAAF to adorn their personnel with medals on the slightest pretext. Philip Kanarkowski again:

'Our CO made it mandatory that we wore our combat ribbons while on leave. Some Australian aircrew members I met in a London pub questioned me about my Air Medal ribbon and Oak Leaf clusters. I was oh so proud of these which signified the completion of the 15 missions I had flown up to that time. The Aussies started to laugh and I, not seeing anything to joke about, was ready to cause an international incident until learning the reason for their mirth. They each had around 90 missions under their belts! I was so humiliated and embarrassed I ripped the ribbons off my tunic and threw them across the room. One of the Aussies went over, picked them up and fastened them back on my uniform, assuring me they meant well and had not intended to disparage my combat experience. Another round was bought and the evening in the company of these friendly, boisterous blokes turned out to be one of the best spent in old London. But it taught me a lesson in humility.'

Co-operation between the RAF and USAAF was excellent and allowed the latter considerably more flexibility in logistics and operations than would otherwise have been the case. In particular, it gave the British an opportunity for some counter Lend-Lease, although Stanley Sajdak thought them sometimes a little too accountable:

'In the early days we had difficulty in getting radio parts and equipment. I discovered a large dump of salvaged aircraft near Oxford and told my commanding officer. He told me to get a truck and we drove over to the place and he talked to the RAF people in charge. They told us to go ahead and we filled the truck with gauges, tubes and other equipment we could use. The actual load of parts consisted of covering half the truck bed to a height of five feet. A few weeks later the major received a bill for $3,680 – charged to Lend-Lease!'

At times there was a good deal of friendly taunting, particularly in the air. Henry DeKeyser, a 392nd Bomb Group gunner, observed the following escapade from the waist of a Liberator:

'We were sent up on what was called a swing-the-compass mission. This called for a lot of gentle banking turns to the left and then to the right and the whole thing repeated again with the pilot, radio-operator and navigator involved. The rest of the crew were along for the sights.

'On one of our left turns a British Mosquito flew in alongside of us on the right. This pilot was a whizz because he flew such a tight formation with us that his wingtip was just out of reach. He kept in formation as we went through our banks to the left and right and grinned from ear to ear all the while.

'I was finally able to get the pilot of my ship on the intercom and tell him of this. His reaction was for me to tell the RAF pilot to get the hell away. I signalled the Mosquito pilot and gave him the wave-off. He grinned and gave me thumbs down. All the time I think he was getting closer and closer.

'My pilot asked if he was gone. I told him no. My pilot said we are going in for a landing and to tell the Mosquito pilot to scram. I did and he grinned back and indicated he was going to follow us in. By this time my pilot was angry and said get rid of him. I answered that I know how.

'Reaching over, I unlocked the flexible .50 cal machine-gun from its position and swung it out the waist window. The Mosquito pilot looked at the gun, gave me the biggest grin I have ever seen and a bye-bye wave of the hand, did a wing-over dive to our right and in a flash was gone.'

The tease was just as likely to be played from the American side. Edward Holmes, a flight engineer in the same group:

'Flying over northern England in our B-24H "Alfred IV", we sighted an RAF Stirling four-engined bomber ahead of us. Our pilot, Don Monroe, being a frustrated fighter pilot, caught up with it and proceeded to fly formation, putting our port wing above and a little to the rear of their starboard wing, about 50 feet away. The RAF pilot didn't like it, no doubt thinking we were far too close for safety, so he opened up and tried to pull away but we stayed with them. Next they put a man in the upper turret and turned the guns on us. As Monroe still hung on there, the RAF pilot decided to pull out all the stops and gradually began to pull ahead. Our cylinder temperatures rose towards the danger point so Monroe finally had to turn away.

'The RAF got the laugh on us on another occasion. We were cruising along over England when somebody called out "Fw 190!" I thought it was a joke until, sure enough, an Fw 190 appeared off our starboard wing. Happily it had RAF markings. Its pilot flew along with us for a few minutes and then with a wave, pulled off and left. It was quite an experience to see a 190 so close and not firing at us.'

8
The Army's Way

Personnel in the ETO and MTO soon adapted to the environments of their base and locality but the Army was still the Army whether in the Zone of the Interior or overseas; everyday service life was ruled by the conflicting interests of expediency and bureaucracy. There was a general attitude in command that if a task was ordered it should be performed in a hurry, regardless of importance. Expedition may be crucial in a war situation but it could sometimes endanger lives. Tom Parry relates such an occurrence with humour:

'After completing 33 missions with the 93rd Bomb Group I was assigned to the Base Air Depot at Warton, joining the multi-engine flight ferrying to various bases.

'One morning the multi-engine pilots were summoned to the flight line and informed that we had the honour of flying P-51 Mustangs that day. The single-engine pilots were weathered in at another base and the P-51s were urgently needed at an RAF base on the south-east coast. The P-51 was the hottest operational fighter plane in the world and I had not been in a single-engined plane since basic flying school. While everyone was mulling over the possibility of hiding under the rug or jumping out the window, the Commander informed me that I had the honor of first take-off. But, first, I was to receive training, consisting of a five-minute cockpit check to locate the necessary controls. I had the distinct impression that they wanted to see if I could make it off without killing myself, before sacrificing anyone else.

'A short, cigar-chomping captain went out with me, explaining en route that I needed five degree right rudder trim to offset torque on take-off. I vaguely recalled that torque had something to do with the twisting force of the prop on a single-engine plane. The captain also warned me that the plane fell off to the left in a stall.

'After strapping me into the cockpit and having me turn, push and crank a few things, the engine started and the captain departed. I never felt so alone in my life. After taxying erratically to the runway, I received a green light for take-off, whereupon I seriously considered shutting down and resigning my commission.

'In multi-engine aircraft, you put on full power quickly for take-off, but in fighters you add power gradually for directional control. I applied full power, bounced about twice and was airborne. Before I got the wings level, I was in the 4,000-foot overcast on instruments. After getting things under reasonable control, I reduced power and dropped below the clouds.

'Looking at the field below, I observed P-51s coming off the runway like grasshoppers so, in the interest of safety, I cleared the area immediately and headed south at about 100mph faster than usual. As a result, I found myself over the Channel heading for France while still trying to locate my position on the map. After turning back and finding the airfield, I noted with satisfaction that it was all grass with no runways. At that point I didn't feel capable of hitting a runway but an entire field was in the realm of possibility.

'With the checklist in my hands and the control stick between my knees, I discovered that I had to lower the airspeed before dropping the landing gear. But every time I lowered the flaps to slow down, the additional lift put me up into the overcast. After various experiments, I finally got the gear down, made a wide bomber pattern and landed in what might best be described as a controlled crash.

'After shutdown and giving thanks to any power that might have had a hand in my destiny, I rushed to the Control Tower to watch the show. The radio transmissions from the other 51s, picked up in the Control Tower, went something like this:

' "Hey Jack, where is the flap handle on this bird?"

' "Look down on the left-hand side of your seat."

' "I thought that was the gear handle."

' "Does anyone know the final approach speed?"

' "I think it's around 120, what's the stall speed?"

'The British tower operator looked at me and asked, "How much time do these chaps have in the P-51?" When I replied, "About 30 minutes," he moaned, "Oh my god."

'About every other one would touch down, bounce too high, throw on power and go around. I thought we might have to shoot down the last one after he went around several times but he finally got it on the ground for good.

'This could only happen in wartime and, ever since, I have a hard time believing that we did it. I flew the P-51 on many occasions after that and, remembering the captain's warning about falling off to the left in a stall, always kept my right foot cocked, before I discovered it fell off to the right!'

As for bureaucracy, examples are not difficult to find but Bob Boyle's anecdote is a prize example of cent wise, dollar foolish administration:

'During my cadet pre-flight days another cadet, Fred Borman, was assigned to the same barracks. We hit it off well together. We stayed together through primary, basic and advanced flight schools, then went to B-24 transition school together. Eventually I was assigned to the 489th Bomb Group at Wendover Field, Utah, and Fred to the 490th Bomb Group at Mountain Home, Idaho. In England we ended up at bases a few miles apart.

'Sometime in September or October 1944 I decided to pay a visit to Fred. About four of us in the 489th Training Office shared a Jeep. I thought I might be able to use it for the short ride to Eye, maybe 20 miles, allowing for possible twisting road routes. But no, that Jeep was restricted to the base and could not leave. I then tried the motor pool to get transportation and was practically laughed out of the office for asking to use transportation for a personal visit.

'Then I learned that if I could get a crew together I could take a B-24. The crew minimum consisted of pilot, co-pilot, flight engineer and radio-operator. I did just that. I phoned Fred Borman at Eye and we made some plans. On the appointed day my mini-crew took off from Halesworth, flew 10 or 15 miles (as the B-24 flies) and landed at Eye. We visited for a while and then flew back to Halesworth.

'It was impossible to get ground transportation but a four-engined bomber was available. As we used to say, "There is a right way, a wrong way and the Army way." '

Within the bureaucratic framework 'passing the buck' was an essential element of survival by keeping one's own patch clean. Allow for all contingencies, even if wasteful, to keep the command above happy and avoid reprimand. It was only the government's money you were spending, so better safe than sorry. One noticeable incidence of this philosophy is described by Tom Morrow, ordnance officer for the 1st Bomb Division:

'In early '43, 150 kits of a missile termed Glide Bomb arrived at the Melchbourne storage depot. These were a wing, tail assembly, and servo-guidance mechanism powered by a 12-volt battery; all to be attached to a 2,000lb bomb and designed to be carried one under each wing of a B-17. The 8th Air Force test group at Bovingdon carried out tests on the missile, dropping some on the Grassholm Island Irish Sea test target. Accuracy and reliability left something to be desired, so the units were relegated to inactive storage.

'Around six months later, Hap Arnold journeyed to England and, in review of many items, demanded to know what had happened to the Glide Bomb kits he had sent to the UK. When told that brief tests were inconclusive, he ordered that they be used on missions.

'So the 1st Division was ordered to train a Wing in use and to damn well use them.

'The designated Wing took the project quite seriously. The 50 kits were delivered to each Group and numerous test flights carrying the units in formation to determine proper take-off, assembly and group procedures were performed. After about 30 to 45 days of testing, involving quite a number of hours with the control systems engaged, I had a call from the 379th Group Ordnance officer inquiring how he could requisition replacement special 12-volt batteries essential to the guidance system. Original equipment batteries would no longer hold a charge. Ordnance officers at the other two involved groups on contact confirmed they were starting to experience similar difficulties.

'So, conforming to approved supply practices, with 150 kits on hand it was reasoned that 100 per cent replacement reserve of 300 batteries was in order. The 8th AF Ordnance was requested to procure and deliver, at the earliest, 300 batteries. There, an adequate reserve was considered sound so 600 batteries were requisitioned on USSTAF. That office rounded it up to a nice respectable number of 1,000 and so sent the order to the US. Shortly thereafter, USSTAF was informed that these were of special Delco Remy manufacture, that the assembly line was discontinued, and that a minimum order of 5,000 was required for re-supply. Determination was made that replacements were urgently required so US Procurement were instructed to supply the batteries – ASAP!

'While this was transpiring, one group of the Glide Bomb Wing, with some 12 aircraft carrying 24 Glide Bombs, ran a mission on Cologne. As the bombs had a 1-in-5 gliding angle and could be servo-guided in direction but not altitude, the winged 2,000lb bombs were launched some 20 miles from the target. Reconnaissance photos showed some six, or possibly more, landed within the greater Cologne area, about eight or ten were observed to spin in after release, and the balance were unaccounted for. Upon various HQ evaluations, the project was determined to hold very limited prospects and the remaining kits were returned to depot storage. Mission Scrubbed!

'About a month and a half later, the 8th Air Force supply officer inquired where he should send 5,000 12-volt batteries for Glide Bombs. Told him he knew the project was scrubbed out. He agreed but said, you needed and ordered the damn batteries so where should they be delivered?

'After some phone calls and arguments with my base Ordnance officers, the 5,000 were delivered to two bases. Informally, I was advised that several living huts on those bases had, for some months, the best improvised 12-volt DC lighting in the UK.'

9
Facing the Enemy

The strategy behind the USAAF's deployment against Germany and her Allies had strategic bombardment as the major intent. The heavy bombers, four-engined B-17 Fortresses and B-24 Liberators, were to be used in high-altitude attacks on the enemy's war industry, the destruction of which would render him unable to pursue a modern war, or at least make it very difficult. There were several other missions apart from this major force. The employment of the twin-engined light and medium bombers – A-20 Havocs, B-25 Mitchells and B-26 Marauders – against short-range targets was less well defined, but predominantly they were to support the tactical requirements of the ground forces. Originally trained for low-level operations, the twin-engined bombers were soon driven by enemy defences to work at so-called medium altitudes.

The role of fighters was first seen as defence against enemy bomber operations and then as support and escort for the bombers. P-47 Thunderbolts and P-38 Lightnings were later joined by longer-ranged P-51 Mustangs. Eventually over half the fighter force was developed for tactical employment, in ground-attack ahead of the armies. Ground-attack with fixed gun armament – strafing – also became a successful offensive role for the long-range escort fighters. Small numbers of night fighters, British Beaufighters and Mosquitoes, later replaced by P-61 Black Widows, served with the tactical forces and afforded after dark defence against enemy air activity over the battle area. Aerial reconnaissance over enemy-controlled territory was flown mostly with the camera-equipped version of the Lightning, the F-5. The substantial number of C-47 Skytrains available served both to convey paratroopers to combat drops and act as glider tugs and general theatre air transport.

The daylight heavy bomber war changed little from its opening operations in the summer of 1942 until the campaign terminated in April 1945. Large, close formations would be assembled over friendly territory while gaining altitude. The force would fly to its target and bomb on the aim of the leaders from an optimum altitude of 25,000 feet. Missions could last for anything from four to ten hours, and during half to two-thirds of this noise-ridden flight the crew would breathe oxygen in sub-zero temperatures.

A crew member was expected to fly a 25-mission tour before being taken off operations and returned to the US or given ground duties. During the first year of operations only some 35 per cent of crewmen had a chance of completing their tours. In early 1944, when the odds had improved, the tour was raised to 30 missions and a little later to a required 35 for the 8th Air Force. But during the final years of operations nearly 80 per cent of aircrew stood a chance of surviving. In the MTO, because of the large number of short penetration tactical missions the heavy bombers flew, a tour was set at 50, but distant dangerous strategic targets counted as double missions towards completion of a tour. Medium and light bomber crews in both theatres were expected to complete a 40-mission tour, but later in the war many men flew 60 or more combat trips before being rested.

For fighter pilots a combat tour was assessed by combat hours flown, with 300 the usual requirement in both the ETO and MTO. Thereafter the pilot would be rested or given 30 days' leave in the States, when he was eligible for another tour or a different assignment. Hours flown were also the yardstick of assessment for the period of assignment to other types of combat flying.

For the first American airmen to arrive in the ETO the enemy was rather obscure. Until battle was joined they could but conjecture as to the calibre of what their British allies called 'The Wily Hun'. A mixture of caution and bravado pervaded the early US establishments, as the following observation of Tom Morrow indicates:

'About 6.00pm one cloudy afternoon, a number of us had gathered at the newly opened bar in the officers mess when the air raid sirens sounded. Looking out the window to the area where our men were in a chow line, we saw some of them break for the slit trenches but, apparently taunted as chicken by their fellows, rejoin the line. Then, hearing machine-gun fire to the east of our building, we rushed to the front door just in time to see a Do 217 at tree-top level fly in front of our HQ half-a-mile to the north. With all guns blazing away, he disappeared to the west, hotly pursued by two RAF "Spits". A glance at the chow line area showed not a soldier to be seen! About one minute later there was a clatter on the stairs behind us and a newly assigned "Gung Ho" major burst on the scene, carrying a tommy gun, wearing gas mask, helmet, cartridge belt and .45 pistol, exclaiming: "Where is he? Where is he?"

'Our Wing Executive Officer, Colonel Beaman, had been talking to his assistant, Lt Col Fred. Beaman was leaning against the wash-stand in his HQ office on the 2nd floor (1st floor in England) when the Do 217 flew down the street by the HQ immediately in front of Beaman's window and only a little higher. It shot up several vehicles parked on the street just below. There was a momentary silence whereon Beaman turned to Fred and said, "Kheeeist – I could have spit in his eye!!"

'The next day we learned the 217 was shot down by the Spits some 10 miles to the west of us, near Bedford.'

Even when battle was joined the enemy became someone unseen in the cockpit of a Messerschmitt or Focke-Wulf or behind a flak gun far below. In air warfare the enemy airman was usually remote, the conflict impersonal. Thus, to come face to face with your enemy could be surprising, as Al Zimmerman discovered:

'Shortly after D-Day we were on our first leave and two of my crewmates and myself were getting ready to get in a cab at Liverpool Street station. Across the way was a truck with a British military guard and some other men. When I took a second glance I realized I was looking at the faces of German prisoners. It was a shock as I'd been conditioned by Hollywood movies that all Germans were mature, had thick necks, burr hair cuts and a sabre scar on their faces. In contrast, these youngsters all looked like the kid next door back in the States; blond, soft, delicate boyish features. They were obviously aware I was looking at them and returned my stare with expressions of such clinical detachment that I felt compelled to walk over to the guard and ask, "Are these German prisoners?" "Yes," he confirmed, "a bad lot. They shot some of our lads." He didn't enlarge on what atrocities they had committed but I then realized that these were indoctrinated Hitler Youth, fanatics. It was the first time I'd come face to face with my enemy.'

10
Taking the Strain

'Most of the time things went as scheduled; we flew, got shot at, dropped our bombs, flew out and came home. I don't mean to indicate that it was a routine thing and that we were blasé about it. Far from the truth, but there is no way the written word can convey the tension, apprehension and, yes, the ever-present fear that was the companion to a combat crew. There is no way I can make another understand what it was "really like". If I speak with another who has flown under similar circumstances no words are necessary – he knows; a thousand words, even carefully chosen, will never be enough to indoctrinate the non-combat flyer.'

Few, if any, who flew and fought in the Second World War would disagree with these sentiments of Stan Staples, a Liberator pilot of the 461st Bomb Group, 15th Air Force. Words can never truly evoke 'what it was like' but they can give an insight into the emotions and experience of those who were there. The following extracts from a diary kept by John Butler, a young gunner of the 93rd Bomb Group, touches on much that was familiar to all combatants of the high-altitude air war; the exhaustion, fears, frustrations, discomforts and losses:

'Combat is pretty good. Especially the money. But the raids are very tiresome as the oxygen and excitement really tire you out. A lot of my good friends have gone down. And it seems strange to see them go. At first it bothered me. But now I don't mind it so much. As you don't want to think of that stuff. And to think I used to be afraid of the dark and wouldn't even ride the roller-coaster. But I can say with truth that I'd rather face fighter than flak. A fighter you can do something about, but flak you can't. I really would like to go after those flak gunners some day and blast the hell out them.

'One thing I sweat out and that is my heated clothing. As I am afraid of frostbite. And I am taking every precaution to prevent getting it. This damn war is getting tough. If I don't come back I want the kids to divide my stuff up to suit themselves. But the way I feel about it is that they will never get it as I am coming back from all the raids. We get a bar of candy and package of gum before each mission and it sure tastes good.

'I am now in a different squadron and they give two Mars bars and a package of gum. So it's worth your time to go on a mission. When I get back to the States I am going to buy a whole carton of Mars bars and eat them to my heart's content.'

As an eloquent assessment of a participant's feelings on completion of a combat tour, 305th Bomb Group pilot Saul Levine's words are true to the event:

'As you progressed through your missions your attitude changed with time and experience. First there was the apprehension of the early missions during which you tucked the big bird in there and hoped you would be lucky. Then came the mid-missions and the realization that somehow your luck was holding and you had gotten through the screw-ups and now your chances were improving. After that came the grinding attrition of the later missions in which the experience and hope was there, so you just kept plugging.

'Suddenly the big one arrived; number 35. A milk run you hoped. Wesendorf – where the hell was that; what would the weather be; the bomb load; the fighter cover? God, that red string seemed endless. Number three slot, that felt comfortable after 25 trips as "tail-end Charlie" because you were considered the steadiest man for the spot and wouldn't give the SOB of an Operations Officer the satisfaction of requesting out. Ten-tenths coverage over the target would also help – not the bombing of course!

'The ground and flight checks were completed as usual, perhaps with a little extra care. Crossed fingers from the ground crew on taxying out. More rubbernecking on the assembly, then on course, knowing it would be over for me at the end of this day, one way or the other. The droning hours, the throttle changes, the oxygen checks, more rubbernecking and tucking it in extra close. Nice being up front, instead of Purple Heart Corner worrying about who was crawling up below the contrails. Then, up through the overcast, the ominous black puffs. On goes the flak suit with an extra tug and pat here and there. Then the helmet; looking like turtles now.

'Over the target, very little flak thank God, and bombs away. Then the diving turn to the left and home James, hoping yet not wanting to test the evil eye. England's socked in so a let-down through it with a squadron break-up is next. Not me, I'm hanging on to the lead ship to make sure we can find the field. Damn it, in close. We're through and there, happy day, the runway lights and beacon. Suddenly I felt bigger than life itself; I was on the final approach and no longer in the aircraft, on the controls but outside above the Fortress and it was responding to my thoughts; we were one. What a mystical feeling of power, peace and control all in one. It was over, the wheels touched and I was back inside, taxying to the parking area and engine shut-off. I was bushed; bone dry. Out went my bag and I went slogging to the Ready Room, to the handshakes, the back-slaps and the whisky. Then the barrack and the letter to my wife that I had dreamed of. I had deliberately omitted one mission from the count to be able to surprise her.

'I've never forgotten that out-of-body experience on the final approach, nor have I ever felt that same feeling of elation and control since. I still wonder why I finished that tour and so many did not.'

Added to the strain of combat missions were those many occasions when a scheduled mission at a point in preparation or despatch was suddenly scrubbed for some reason or another. Louis Wust, 453rd Bomb Group pilot:

'In combat, things usually happen so fast that there is little time for much thought or elaborate preparation. The time for my first mission arrived with exactly this suddenness. My only advance notice was my name appearing on the alert list, along with many others, very late on the night of September 24, 1944. Being on the alert list was by no means a definite indication of going out next day, it meant that we had to be prepared to go. So, on some one hundred occasions I prepared for the next day's flight although I actually flew 35 missions. Very early in the morning of September 25th I was awakened by the beam of a flashlight shining in my face. I realized at once I was about to make my debut and, like any first performer, experienced a feeling of great anxiety and fear.'

The first mission, facing the unknown, was a worrier for most and this and the following early sorties while 'learning the trade' were, statistically, the most likely to lead to the loss of a new crew. Stan Staples:

'Not having flown since September 13th 1944 at OTU at Davis-Monthan in Arizona, we were re-introduced to the B-24 on December 3rd 1944, when I was given a check flight. This was followed by four more "training" flights in the area to sharpen our flying procedures and to acquaint us with the way things were done in the squadron. On December 15th I flew, as co-pilot, with an experienced crew to Linz, Austria. What a place to break in a new man. There was no fighter opposition toward our units, but the flak was something else again. As we neared the target the pilot, 1st Lt Bud Summers, instructed us to don our flak helmets and other protective armor vests that had been issued. With the objective coming up, the black puffs of flak were apparent in the distance. Ol' Staples, wet behind the ears, was all eyeballs, sitting up as far as he could to take in this new experience. As I glanced across the cockpit, pilot Summers was crouched down in his seat as far as he could commensurate with his abilities to maintain formation. It didn't take long for the realization to hit me that the bastards were actually shooting at us, and in short order I also slouched down in my seat.

'On the second mission, a seasoned co-pilot flew with our crew, and on the third trip out, a seven-hour hop to Wels, Austria, we flew as our own complete crew. As a replacement crew we were assigned to fly the oldest, war-weariest ships in the squadron and were placed at the tail-end of the squadron formation – the old hands weren't taking any chances with the new kids on the block. As we gained experience, and as new crews came in after us, we were moved up in the squadron formation. With perhaps four crews for each airplane, we were never assigned a permanent, personal ship to fly. As a result we flew almost every plane in the squadron. Perhaps this tended to keep one a bit sharper because although the ships were of the same design, they each had their own characteristics and personalities and to some degree handled a bit differently.'

The 'old hands' were inclined to indulge in a little torment of newcomers and, unkindly, to capitalize on their fears. Bud Chamberlain of the 489th Bomb Group was one victim:

'It was SOP for the pilots of a replacement crew to fly their first combat mission as individual fill-ins with an experienced crew. I went as co-pilot with a Lt Rudy Hoerr who had flown much of his tour. Of course, as it was to be my first taste of combat I was apprehensive. Rudy was certainly going to make me sweat. As we were headed out over the coast at about 10,000 feet he leaned over and offered a cigarette. As we were about to go on oxygen I said I could do without. He insisted: "You better take it. It might be the last one you ever smoke." That placed a new dimension of reality on what we were about to do.'

And, of course, those in command would often feign a blasé touch to quell concern. George Meshko, a 96th Bomb Group gunner:

'My first mission was Wilhelmshaven. I looked out and saw all these bursts of flak around us and excitedly shouted over the intercom: "They're shooting at us!" Back comes the calm voice of our co-pilot: "That's all right, George; they're allowed to." '

For the fighter pilot, operational initiation was devoid of communication with squadron brethren, radio silence being mandatory. Thus attention tended to be concentrated on the aircraft. Robert Strobell:

'When you first start flying fighters on combat you have a tendency to listen to the engine. You watch all the engine gauges – temperature, oil pressure, manifold pressure, rpms – rather intently. And you listen. It probably comes from the revolting thought that it might quit over enemy territory. After a few missions you suddenly get the message. And that is that there is nothing the watching and listening will do to prevent this if it is going to happen, and just as suddenly you are free of this self-imposed tension. But there was one pilot who had a different solution. He carried a pair of pliers in the cockpit. He was an oil gauge freak. If the oil pressure wasn't where he wanted it he took the pliers, broke the glass and crimped the hand to the position he wanted it!'

No one offered the newcomer the cautioning statistics that accrued with operational flying over Europe and the Mediterranean. Nearly one-fifth of the total aircraft losses were to causes other than enemy action. In short, flying for Uncle Sam was dangerous without the participation of the Luftwaffe. Similar non-combat statistics prevailed for the RAF and probably for all committed air forces of the Second World War. Self-assured young men were seduced by the thrill of flying. As a result there were many 'near thing' incidents, like that which befell John O'Grady, a 93rd Bomb Group pilot:

'The purpose of the cockpit check list was to ensure no operation at the controls was overlooked before take-off. We'd been through this so many times we could easily remember it, or so we thought. Got kind of lazy about it. We were shaken out of our nonchalance one morning in the fall of 1943 when setting out on a mission with a full load of bombs and fuel. We pulled onto the runway, got the green light and pushed the throttles full open. As the B-24 picked up speed it started lurching to the left. I immediately tried putting in right rudder but it wouldn't move. Instantly I realized the trouble; we had forgotten to release the rudder lock. The strap holding the lever up was still hanging from the ceiling. I shouted to the engineer standing behind me and while he released the lock I applied full power to the left engines and pulled back on the right to counteract the propeller torque that had pulled us off the runway. As soon as the rudders were free I gave the engines everything. We were now heading for a group of trees on the field boundary and we literally drug the landing gear through the tops. That was some hairy take-off.'

No one appreciated that it was 'some hairy take-off' more than the men in the nose of that particular B-24. One was bombardier Hal Moore:

'Bud our navigator and myself were, as usual, riding in the nose. We didn't know what was happening and thought we were going to crash into the trees. As it was, we only just scraped through the tops. After that trip we never sat in the nose for take-off again. Safer up on the flight deck. This wasn't our regular ship. It was one of the war-weary original B-24Ds the Group brought over. Man, they were dangerous to look at, let alone fly!'

Many who neglected the check list never had a second chance. The wise ones did not leave it to chance, as John Howland learned:

'We were taking a shower in the "ablution room" at Ridgewell. Our co-pilot, Bill Doherty, had a tremendous bruise on his left arm and shoulder. When asked where he had gotten such a bruise, Bill replied: "I tried to recite the check list from memory, and Jim reached over and hit me. At the same time he told me to READ THAT CHECK LIST EVERY TIME WE USE IT.'

But there would always be those fliers who ignored or forgot the laid-down procedures, yet who luck still smiled on. Robert Strobell:

'I returned from a deep penetration with my wingman, both very low on fuel. When we crossed the coast of England I recognized Woodbridge, the emergency landing field with its runway three times as wide and as long as on a standard airfield. If one had to use this emergency field the rule was to come straight in from the coast and land, regardless of wind direction. I did this; went straight in and landed. Soon after I touched down and the tail wheel hit the runway the engine quit – out of gasoline. Just as I came to the end of my landing roll I got the shock of my life as my wingman's P-47 went barrelling by me, going in the opposite direction! He obviously didn't know the rules and as a result we had narrowly escaped a head-on collision on the runway. I had not seen him nor he me until we passed, as when the P-47 is in three-point position you cannot see straight ahead.'

11
Operational Hazards

Leave nothing to chance; checking everything was a definite aid to bettering one's chances of completing a tour. You could not always rely on others as Ralph Patton of the 94th Bomb Group discovered:

'On my first mission, November 26, 1943, I was flying co-pilot on a mission to bomb the Renault factory in a suburb of Paris. When we got into some pretty heavy flak the pilot told me to clip on my chest pack parachute, just in case. I reached under the seat where it was stowed and went to clip it on. To my horror I found that I had rings on my parachute harness and rings on my 'chute pack. No one had told me that there were different packs, ones with rings and ones with clips. On this day my regular 'chute had been taken by the rigger for a repack and a substitute placed in my locker. It was a hard way to find out that the substitute pack had rings on it instead of clips. The trip home was especially long knowing that if we had to jump I couldn't use my 'chute.'

The parachute was a life-saver, but on more than one occasion took life, or threatened to do so, as in 386th Bomb Group's Everett Shue's case:

'One day Operations asked me if I would take a K20 camera and get some pictures of the bomb strike. On an A-26, I was to fly beside the pilot on the jump seat and take pictures out of the bomb bay after the drop. I told the pilot to leave the doors open until I was through taking pictures. On the bomb run when the doors opened and I looked down, I decided to put on my parachute pack in case I fell out. It was the dumbest decision ever made, because when leaning forward to take the first picture the rip cord handle caught on something, spilling out the parachute into the bomb bay. I was trying to gather it in, at the same time yelling to the pilot to shut the doors. I also discovered to my horror that the plane in formation behind and below us was directly in my way if I was pulled out. About that time the pilot behind us broke radio silence and told my pilot to close the doors before that darn fool fell out. The actual time was probably only a few seconds but to me it seemed like hours. I never dropped the camera, but I sure never got any pictures.'

Another personal life-saver was the Mae West flotation jacket which could also threaten one's mobility and safety if inflated in the aircraft; as 384th Bomb Group bombardier Frank Furiga found out:

'We had a couple of bombs stick in the bay – wouldn't release. When we let down over the Channel the pilot suggested I go back and force them off the shackles to let them fall in the sea. I opened the bomb doors, took a screwdriver and went back to the bay. Standing on the catwalk, working on the shackles the bombs were finally liberated. As I turned to go back to the flight deck the lanyard of my Mae West caught on something causing it to inflate. Before I knew what was happening I was wedged tight between two stanchions either side of the narrow catwalk. Having no connection to the interphone, there I stayed. After a while the pilot, concerned that I hadn't showed up, sent the engineer to see what was wrong. When he saw what had happened he laughed so much he darn near fell out the open bomb doors.'

There were similar embarrassing situations – like that witnessed by Dan Turner of the 44th Bomb Group:

'We were under attack by fighters and as I was firing at one I caught sight of the other waist gunner striking his chest with his hand as hard as he could. I realized he had been hit and went over to help. I asked where he'd been hit. He said, "I haven't. When I was tracking a Focke-Wulf with my gun the tabs of my Mae West somehow caught and the darn thing inflated under my 'chute harness. It restricted my movements and I couldn't see down. So I punctured it with a .50 calibre round." '

Mae Wests inadvertently inflating in fighter cockpits were particularly threatening and for this reason many pilots carried a knife for quick puncturing.

Of malfunctions within an aircraft, probably the most hazardous were connected with gun turrets in which some men were crushed. James McMahon was lucky indeed not to have suffered that fate in a 93rd Bomb Group B-24:

'They removed the ball turrets early in '44. I was sent to nose turret school. I said I would never fly in one of those things and did not pay attention during the training. We were warned that there was a "special" way to activate the turret and not to ever turn on a certain red valve before we did other things. All of the turret valves were down where you could not see them. My next mission was in the nose turret. Being 5ft 11in, my feet had to be jammed into a cramped position one on each side of the gun control column.

'I got into the turret as we approached the French coast, reached down and turned on one of the valves. The turret doors were open at the time. The navigator had not closed them yet. Immediately after turning on the valve the turret swung violently to the right. The doors were ripped off and I was thrown half-way out. I found myself looking straight at the No 2 propeller, about six feet from my face, and the ground 20,000ft below. Managing to pull my body out of the slipstream and back inside the turret, I turned off what I thought was the valve that I had turned on. Nothing happened. The turret was still turned as far to the right as it could go. I called to the pilot and told him about my predicament. The pilot told me that if I couldn't get back inside the turret he would feather the No 2 engine and I could bail out if I wanted to. One problem was that nose gunners couldn't wear a chute and I was so large that I couldn't wear a chute harness. There was no way they could get a harness and chute to me. Even if they did manage to get a harness I didn't have room to put it on.

'I received advice from everyone on the ship as to how to get the damned turret to return to a forward position. Nothing worked. Finally someone said they would take the waist gun barrel and use it to pry the turret around so that I could get back into the ship. I was now being repeatedly sucked into the slipstream. Slowly I was losing the strength to pull myself back inside. The only thing that kept me from being sucked completely out and into that propeller was my big feet. They were inside my winter flying boots which were jammed into the small space on each side of the gun control column.

'I became aware that people were working on the turret when I saw the gun barrel being used to try to force the turret back against the hydraulic pressure into a position where I could get back inside the ship. But it couldn't be done. We were now over Germany and as we were the lead crew we couldn't abort! A final attempt was made to help me by using the two waist gun barrels for leverage and slowly the turret was forced to a point where a small space was made so that I could squeeze back inside the ship. It was a very narrow space and I was warned to get out fast as they couldn't hold it much longer. If the turret slipped away from the gun barrels and I was partly in and out I would be cut in two. There was no choice. I pulled my feet out of my boots and pushed myself quickly out of the turret into the ship. I was so exhausted they had to drag me to the flight deck where I sat for the rest of the mission wrapped in flak suits. I volunteered to take the nose turret schooling again and after a short while I wouldn't fly any other gun position. When they made all the bombardiers navigators I became a togglier.'

The worst place to be trapped was the ball turret under the fuselage. The occupant could only escape if the hatch door at his back was clear to open into the fuselage; besides which a parachute could not normally be worn in the turret. Navigator Irwin Pochter tells of the occasion when the ball turret on his B-17 jammed:

'Our mission for the day was Berlin. As we approached the battle lines, all crew members were in combat position and Sgt Donald "Oakie" Forsman, our 18-year-old ball gunner, descended into his turret. Soon after entry Oakie called our pilot, Lt Harry O'Grady, and informed him that, while he could rotate his turret around, the guns would not elevate. They were jammed pointing almost straight down, but not enough to clear the door and allow egress. Several of the crew proceeded to try and free-up the turret, but to no avail. The next voice on the intercom was Harry O'Grady's: "Oakie, do you want us to abort the mission?" The response from the ball turret was, "What's the weather going to be like over the target?" He was informed that we had been told to expect the use of radar with a solid cloud layer below. After a few moments of silence, Sgt Forsman said quietly, "I think we should continue the mission." Again, he was reminded that if we had a problem he would be a prisoner in his ball turret. Firmly he said, "Let's go on."

'As we approached the target, the clouds disappeared and heavy anti-aircraft fire began. We were all so busy the next 15 minutes we didn't have much time to think about Oakie. When at last we left Berlin and headed back to England, both Harry and I called him to check on his condition. To our relief he responded that he was OK but still a prisoner. We realized that with the ball turret guns pointing down we could not land without crushing them and almostly certainly causing death or severe injury to Oakie. He was assured we would not attempt a landing before freeing him. Once our B-17 had descended to a lower altitude over the Channel, several of us got to work on the turret gearing. Efforts at manual cranking were to no avail; it was stuck fast. Finally, in desperation, I took the crash axe from its container and proceeded to hammer at the gear train. When I was exhausted with the effort another crewman took over. We were rewarded when several teeth broke off the gear ring and we were able, at last, to move the turret so its doors could be opened up and the gunner helped out.

'Oakie had spent over four hours in his "prison" and had to sit there watching the flak bursts, knowing if our plane was hit and had to be abandoned he would face certain death. The mental strain of those four hours can be imagined, yet Oakie remained calm and confident throughout.'

A constant worry at high altitude was the oxygen supply, without which anoxia could occur. Failures claimed many lives through the undetected nature of anoxia which first fogged the brain, so the victim was usually unaware what was happening. For this reason frequent oxygen checks were made over the intercom by deputed members to others on the crew. An illustration of how quickly oxygen starvation can dull the senses is told by John Howland in his diary:

'Mar 2, 1944. Although flying at high altitude is routine, we sometimes get a little careless. On this occasion we were flying at 22,000 feet and as we neared the French coast I decided I had better put on my flak suit; so I took off my oxygen mask and reached around to get the 16lb suit of manganese steel armor plate. I must have fumbled around quite a bit and in doing so used up most of the oxygen in my lungs. I worked with the damned suit for a minute or two and finally got my head through a hole in it. I had enough sense to realize I needed oxygen. I put my mask on and turned the auto-mix off so I would get pure oxygen. In a few seconds my head cleared. I discovered that instead of putting my head through the shoulder straps, I had pushed it through the small opening where the apron joined the rest of the outfit and yet, while doing it, it seemed like the only logical place to put my head.'

There was no one to help or check the occupant of a single-seat fighter for oxygen supply. As a result it was estimated that anoxia periodically claimed victims in every fighter squadron. Additionally, the fighter pilot was from time to time hazarded by engine or glycol fumes in his cockpit. Robert Strobell when flying with the 353rd Fighter Group:

'On a mission headed for Germany I had to abort over Holland because the cockpit was filling with gasoline fumes. I turned back and headed home but became light-headed from the foul air. I slid the cockpit canopy back a few inches to get some fresh air, but this only seemed to make matters worse. As soon as I hit the Channel I dove down under 10,000ft and removed my oxygen mask but that didn't help. But the little one-foot-long rubber stretchable hose of the mask gave me an idea. I slid the canopy back a few inches, leaned forward and stuck the hose out into the slipstream. Immediately my mouth was filled with air pressure and the mask flapped violently on my cheeks, so I quickly pulled the hose back in. How about facing the hose backwards instead of forwards? I stuck it out again and promptly lost all my breath to an overwhelming vacuum. Finally I figured out that if I put my thumb over the end of the hose I could admit the right amount of air when it was held forward. It worked, but had me in an awkward position with my head on top of the control column and my face a few inches from the instrument panel. I couldn't see out! However, I could see the compass and set a heading and finally arrived at my base. Landing was tricky but I got down safely. The cause of the fumes was found to be a broken flange round the filler cap of the fuselage located fuel tank.'

1. Lt Ed Laube (on left) and the rest of the James T. Wilson crew listen while Sgt James Dugan describes how he gunned down an enemy fighter. They are standing in front of the Marauder in which the trans-Atlantic flight described in Chapter 1 was made.

2. Sgt Harland Little (standing in the middle of the doorway) and Lt William Hipple's crew about to leave Naples in a railroad boxcar (Chapter 1).

3. Some of the first contingent of WACS, 650 strong, to arrive in the UK claiming their personal equipment bags at the Stone depot (Chapter 2).

4. A sunny spring day at Shipdham, 1943. Typical barracks area at one of the new airfields in the UK. The curved 'tin can' Nissen huts predominated, but these were supplemented by various conventionally configured prefabricated structures, using wood and precast panels with asbestos roofing. [*W. R. Cameron*]

5. Despite the relatively high standard of barracks accommodation in the UK, there was some tent life. The severe winter of 1944–45 was pretty to behold but a chill experience for the ground crew men who used this cover 'on the line', at Nuthampstead. [*398 BG Association*]

6. Commandeered farm and village buildings often served as quarters in Italy. This is the communal area of the 765th Bomb Squadron at Torretto. Officers' Mess and Club far centre. Enlisted Men's Mess and Club on right and Squadron Supply on left. [*S. Staples*]

7. Making 'side walks' among living area tents at Torretto using local brick and rubble. When it rained the mud of sunny Italy was equal to the best in England. [*S. Staples*]

8. Most MTO airfields had canvas cover – fine in summer but rough in winter. These large tents at the 310th Bomb Group's airfield at Ghisonaccia, Corsica, protected parachutes and aircrew equipment.

9. A tedious task in the hot sun at Tafaroui, Algeria. At North African airfields where enemy air raids were to be expected, slit trenches were strongly recommended.

10. William R. Cameron (Chapter 3), a distinguished veteran of early B-24 operations in both the ETO and MTO. By May 1943 only Bill Cameron and another pilot remained 'operational' of his squadron's original 80 aircrew personnel that arrived in the ETO the previous October. A few had been re-assigned or wounded but most were Missing in Action. [*W. R. Cameron*]

11. Staff Sergeant Anthony Hmura of the 445th Bomb Group (Chapter 3).

12. 'Lady Moe', the 96th Bomb Group's North African acquisition, inspecting British artist Frank Beresford's work at Snetterton Heath (Chapter 5). The paint was tasty!

13. 'Lassie II', complete with plaster cast support wheel, receiving encouragement from her master. Walt Konantz had a flying career after the war and often took Lassie with him. The scottie logged over 300 hours' flying time, in twelve different types. When she died in 1953 her body, in a sealed box, was sent 500 miles by air to the family home and buried beside the grave of Konantz's original Lassie who died in 1943. [*W. Konantz*]

14. Walter Konantz and his pet pose on the pilot's personal Mustang (Chapters 5 and 17).

13

14
Saturday Night

15. Harland Little (Chapters 5 and 13).

16. 'That damn dog' (see Chapter 5) was known as 'Sack Time'. The name arose from the animal's predilection for minimum effort – except when trying to bite officers – which enabled his owners to dress him for the part. [*Royal Frey*]

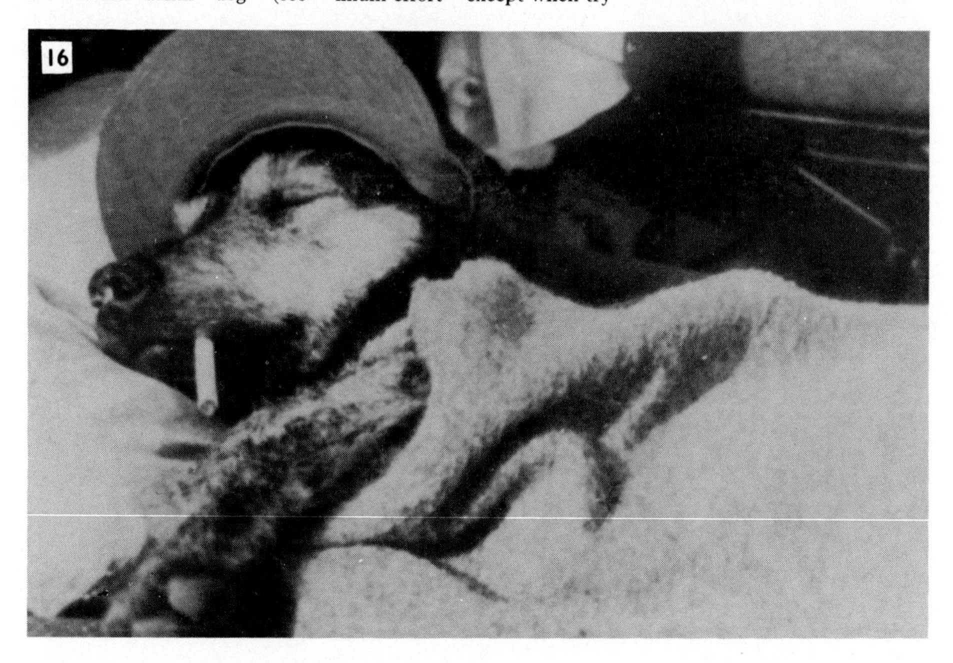

17. George Meshko (Chapter 4) and his pet jackdaw.

18. At the 379th Bomb Group in England the Mess Officer inspects plates of those who have dined. This clean plate parade was principally for the camera of a British newsman in an attempt to counter the widely held view among the severely rationed British that the US serviceman wasted food.

19. The effervescent Carroll Henry (third from left) and some of his fellow pilots in the 338th Fighter Squadron. McDonald is second from right (Chapter 6).

20. Colonel (later Brig General) Barlett Beaman (Chapter 9).

21. Artist Mel Stephens featured several sky warriors in his drawings and this is a reproduction of that done for John Butler (Chapter 10).

22. A photograph taken on 24 February 1944 after the Jim Tyson crew returned from a raid on Schweinfurt (Chapters 10, 11 and 18). Front row, left to right: Frank Palenik (bombardier); John Howland (navigator); Bill Doherty (co-pilot); and James Tyson (pilot). At back, left to right: Charles Churchill (waist gunner); Robert Smith (replacement waist gunner); Arnold Farmer (tail gunner); Sgt Schilling (replacement ball gunner); Richard Jensen (Flight Engineer); and Henry White (radio-operator).

23. Lt Robert Strobell (Chapters 4, 12 and 15).

24. Lt John Greenwood wrapped against the English cold at Polebrook.

25. Lt Don Kammer (Chapter 12) in the cockpit of a P-51 at Raydon, England. His personal flying equipment (G-suit, Mae West, etc.) adorns the US fighter pilot model in the Imperial War Museum's Duxford display in the UK.

26. The wreck of 'Blue Dreams', the B-17 that crash-landed at Steeple Morden and in which Earl Williamson was flying (Chapter 13).

25
Pilot LT. KAMMER
CREW CHIEF S/SGT Lee
ASST CREW CHIEF SGT Croshav
ARMORER CPL Hohl

26

27. 'Buying the farm'. Fire takes hold of a B-24 that crashed off the end of the runway at Halesworth, England, while another Liberator takes off for the mission through the growing column of smoke.

28. Lt Stan Staples, (Chapters 10 and 14).

29. The crew and ground crew of the lead Fortress are presented to the press as the first to fly into and release bombs over Germany (Chapter 15). Brig General Frank Armstrong stands at left end of row. He was the model for the fictional Frank Savage in the brilliant post-war movie 'Twelve O'Clock High'.

30. Against a patchwork of strip-cultivated fields in Yugoslavia and the Nis marshalling yard, a B-17 of the 483rd Bomb Group is consumed in flame. A direct hit by an 88mm shell in the right wing brought disintegration of the bomber in a few seconds.

29

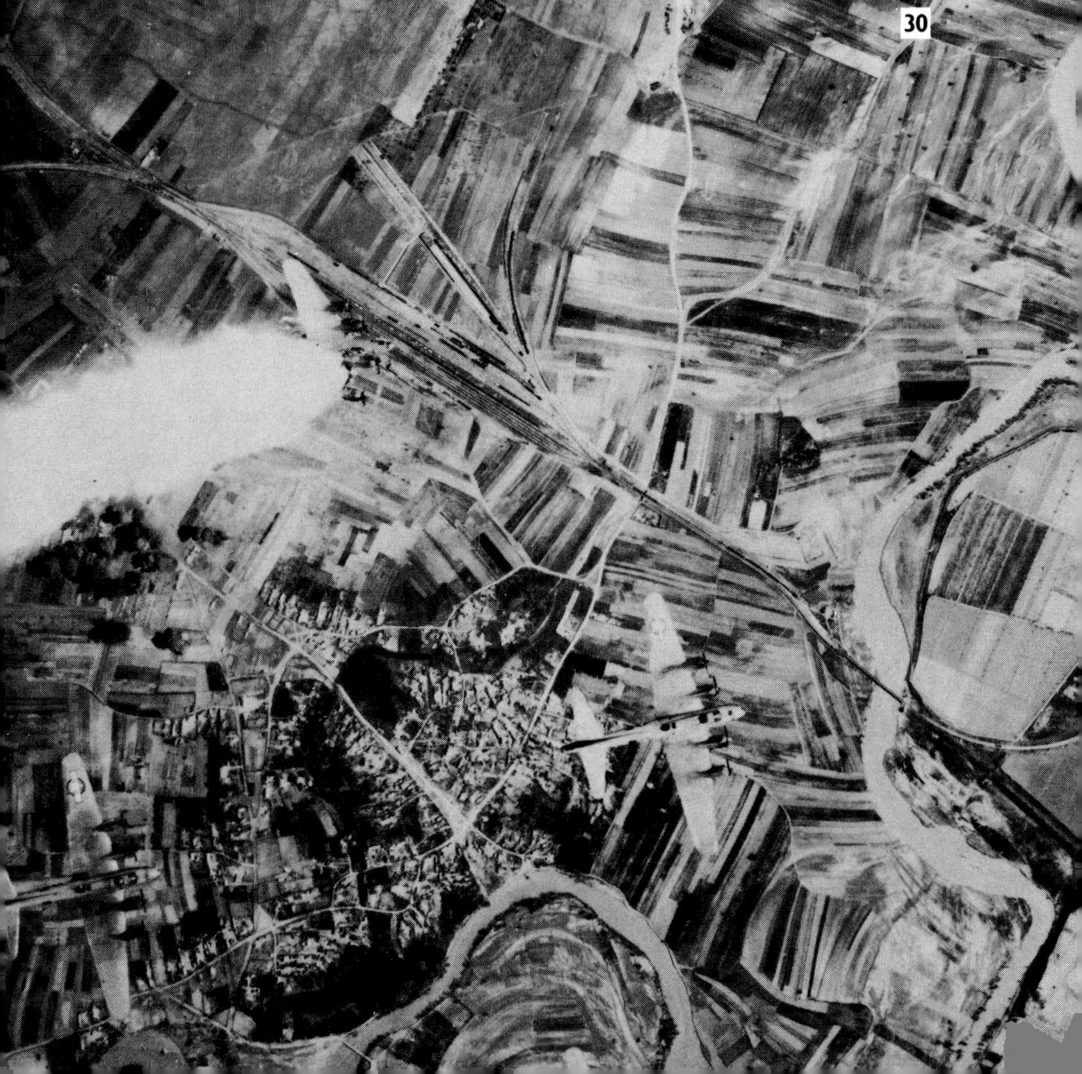
30

31. 'Flak so thick you could get out and walk on it' was the humorous quip. But sights like this were fearful. How could any bomber fly through such a barrage concentration and the many thousands of steel shell splinters slicing around in all directions and survive? Yet most did.

32. The 454th Bomb Group B-24 in which Edwin Range 'sweated out' the deluge of gasoline (Chapter 16).

12
Fatigue and Frustrations

For all high-altitude combat fliers, despite their youth, fatigue was a regular result of missions. The high fliers had an added problem, as 486th Bomb Group's Robert Bee explains:

'To my mind the most significant effect of the high-altitude missions we flew was the state of exhaustion one was reduced to. There was the apprehension suffered during preparation and the early stages of the flight, plus noise and vibration. In the nose of a B-24 there wasn't a lot of vibration if the props were in good synchronization. The props were also responsible for the greatest volume of noise when riding in the nose and bombardier and navigator had to shout close into each other's ears to be heard. You didn't always want the other crew members to hear what was being said so the interphone was not always used. However, the major cause of fatigue on long missions that could be anything up to ten hours – of which seven might be at high altitude – was the effect of atmospheric pressure. At 25,000 feet it is about a third less than at ground level but your inside body pressure remains at ground level. The result is a bodily expansion, enough to worry your digestive system but more evident in that, although you were not really expending much energy as you sat there, you'd come back feeling as tired as a rag. Breathing oxygen kept you from feeling drowsy but once you were back on the ground and relaxed, the exhaustion really hit you. I've known the time I'd just flop on my bed and immediately fall asleep, not even taking my clothes off.'

The behaviour of their bowels was a regular embarrassment to many fliers, particularly as 'going' in the sub-stratosphere was a most difficult procedure. Bob Hanson of the 91st Bomb Group had the solution – or so he at first thought:

'You kinda forgot about the effect of high-altitude flying on your digestion when you were eating and drinking. Mutton stew, Brussels sprouts and beer weren't a good mix if you wanted to fly easy. I learned the hard way. After I'd had my fill of beer the day before, I began to feel that I needed to go someplace fast when we were at 25,000ft. Only problem there was nowhere to go in a B-17. My quick solution was to empty the shells from an ammunition can onto the floor of my radio room. The can wasn't really wide enough and a bucking bomber is no substitute for a latrine – and at well below freezing no place to have your pants down for long. The result was a mess everywhere. Fortunately it soon froze hard and I was able to pitch all into the bomb bay ready to fall when the doors were opened. Only thing, they didn't give you a medal for crapping on Germany.'

Indigestion was another penalty of unmindful eating, but it was the bladder that troubled most. Robert Strobell again:

'The most outstanding feature of the mess hall was the hot cross type buns baked fresh for pilots who rose early for briefing. They were excellent. Two or three of those big buns and two cups of coffee woke you for briefing. Along about the third or fourth mission, flying above 25,000ft, you were hit with heartburn. The oxygen mask prevented a soothing solution, even if you had one. So you soon learned that it was best to have your buns when you got back and lay off the coffee too. It took the same number of missions to learn that you couldn't do much about a full bladder except suffer. On one flight of about four and a half hours, I returned in so much pain that as soon as the airplane stopped in the revetment, I jumped out and let it go back of the tail. Then I looked up to see a farmer, his wife and two kids only 30 yards away at the fence watching the act. All I could do was smile and wave at them.'

High-altitude bomber men made individual arrangements. A few had highly original methods of solving the problem, but none quite as original as that of Coleman Sanders' pilot:

'My regular pilot, Ken "Buzz" Edwards, was a big, handsome guy and of a generally reserved nature. Like all high-altitude aviators there were times when you had to urinate fast because you simply couldn't hold it. Getting out of the seat and going back to the relief tube in the bomb bay was a chore, so most pilots made other arrangements using a convenient receptacle. While we were on long-range training flights in the States, Buzz noticed that if the B-17's pilot's side window was open a few inches anything light placed on top of the instrument panel was whipped straight to and through this opening, all to do with the creation of a negative gravity area. Buzz had the idea that if he stood up and urinated at the instrument panel, the liquid would go right out the window. Sure enough it worked, and from then on whenever he got the urgent call of nature at high altitude that was his unusual manner of relief.

'An occasion arose when Buzz was assigned to fly the lead ship on a mission with a General from Combat Wing in the co-pilot seat. During the flight Buzz, deciding to take his usual relief measures, opened his side window, stood up and aimed at the instrument panel. He'd neglected to tell the General what was going to happen. As you can guess, the General was astonished by what he observed, and even more astonished when he suddenly got a shower. The General had earlier opened the co-pilot window with the result that the area of negative gravity no longer existed. It took a lot of explaining; Generals aren't accustomed to being peed on.'

The very low temperatures at high altitude, sometimes 50 degrees below freezing, made frostbite yet another hazard, particularly so for gunners in the rear of B-17s and B-24s where waist window positions exposed them to an icy blast. An extract from John Butler's diary gives an insight into this problem:

'Took off this morning at 8.30am to bomb the city of Emden, which is a pretty important shipping centre. It was 39 degrees below zero. My heated suit worked very good back in the tail. Being a tail gunner is nice as you have armor around you and all the bad stuff has gone by. We ran into a lot of flak at the target and it was pretty accurate. I heard a loud noise in the tail and got out of the turret to see where we were hit. The flak had put a large hole in the vertical stabilizer. Then some came in at six o'clock and in my hurry to get back in the turret I pulled my heated connection off on my right boot, so my gloves and boots were not working. I checked all my circuits and my fuses. I was beginning to become real cold, then I happened to check my right boot. Put the plug back in. The heat came back to my feet and hands again. A Ju 88 came in on the tail, but he was gone before I could get a shot in. I fired around 30 rounds at some Me 109, but no results. Flak also hit us in the waist. The tunnel gunner had just passed out from lack of oxygen. He fell forward on top of the camera hatch, flak came through the side of the plane and past the spot he was in. The lucky stiff. The Red Cross had hot cocoa waiting for us. It sure tasted good. Harry Fargo flying tail gunner on "N for Nan" froze his hands and feet and had to land at another field so they could get him to a hospital. "Q for Queenee" made a crash landing on our home base but no one was hurt. My guns worked okay.'

Apart from all the other fatiguing factors, there were often periods when men were committed to combat missions in rapid succession, demands that even those in their early twenties found difficult to endure. Pathfinder crews were the most put upon during the spring and summer of 1944, simply because of the shortage of trained men with their skills in radar leadership. Robert Jacobs was one who found it difficult to keep his eyes open:

'At 0230 on 5 June 1944, Lt Litwiller's crew of the PFF aircraft "Liberty Run" was awakened to fly their 24th mission. The target was in the Pas de Calais area, a blissfully short haul, uneventful with no enemy fighters and very light flak observed.

'When the crew returned to Hethel early in the afternoon, the word was out that hot water was available at the "Ablutions". This being an infrequent occurrence, all personnel attempted to take advantage of the opportunity. While in the shower, Litwiller's crew was paged on the Tannoy, told to report to the briefing room immediately ready to fly – which they did – to Bungay, home of the 446th Bomb Group. Upon landing they were surprised to be met by armed MPs and taken to a secured building. There they were informed that "D" Day was 6th June 1944.

'To say that we were excited would have been a gross understatement. This was what all of us had been waiting for and the adrenalin was flowing. Our mission was to lead the 446th Bomb Group to attack the invasion beaches of Normandy immediately prior to the ground assault. In the course of the briefing, we learned that the 446th was to lead the 8th Air Force on the first "D" Day strike.

'We took off at 0220, climbed to 10,000 feet and circled in our prescribed forming area while our engineer fired the specific coloured signal flares as Colonel Brogger, the formation commander, and the 446th aircraft assembled in formation behind us. The mission went precisely as planned with the briefed undercast necessitating bombing by H2X radar. As we approached the French coast the radar navigator called me over to look at his PFF scope. It indicated the vast armada of the invasion fleet standing just off the coast of Normandy – a thrilling sight even on radar. Bombs were away at 0600! We led our formation back to Bungay via Portland Bill and returned to Hethel.

'As we started to undress for a well-deserved rest, we were again paged and subsequently told to get over to Bungay for another mission. We had been up since 0230, 5 June and it was now the afternoon of 6 June, some 36 hours later. During the briefing the flight surgeon gave each of us a pill with the instruction to take it only "when you feel you can no longer keep awake".

'Shortly after take-off my eyelids began to get very heavy. Since we were again leading aircraft of the 446th Bomb Group, I needed to have all faculties clear so I took my pill. It worked marvelously well in that all signs of weariness disappeared and I was again able to perform my required navigation tasks. We flew to Coutances, dropped our bombs and returned to the English coast without incident above a solid undercast. At landfall I gave the pilot a heading for Bungay and relaxed. The next thing that I recall was being shaken rather violently by the engineer. He finally managed to get across that the pilot was calling me over the intercom. The pill had worn off and I had fallen sound asleep! Les (my pilot) informed me that he had been directed by the British Ground Controllers to circle and let down below the overcast so that our formation could be identified visually. There was fear of German intruder aircraft. The formation was now at 1,000 feet and Les wanted a new heading for Bungay. There I was, the lead navigator, feeling half drugged, without the foggiest notion of our position. What to do? I told him to contact the deputy lead and obtain a heading from his navigator while I attempted to sort out where we were.

'By this time it was dark so that the pilotage navigator could not help. We were apparently too low to use Gee because I could not pick up any station clearly. The heading obtained from the deputy lead put us on a track due east. My first step was to find out exactly when the formation let-down had started; thus, I was able to compute a very rough DR position. Around this I drew a circle whose radius was the maximum distance we could have travelled from the let-down area. We were somewhere in the circle, about 50 to 80 miles due west of London and heading straight for Piccadilly according to my best estimate. I called the pilot and told him to monitor channel frequency 6440 for balloon barrage squeakers.

'In the meantime I continued to work with the Gee set and was finally able to pick up one station. Just about then the pilot called on the intercom to tell me he had picked up the balloon barrage squeakers. I immediately gave him a new heading for Bungay away from London. Then for the first and only time during my tour in the UK I used the Gee single station homing procedure that we had been taught at Cheddington when our crew first arrived in England to join the 93rd Group. It worked beautifully and we came across the blue perimeter lights of Bungay just as the second blip aligned with the first. The second station had come in about ten minutes out of Bungay.

'A quick peel off and we were back on the ground at Hethel – time 2345. It had been a very long day indeed!'

Fatigue could lead to disorientation, another dangerous situation. John Greenwood, a 351st Bomb Group navigator, tells of his experience:

'While flying the high squadron position in very high cloud over Germany, I happened to look out of the nose of our B-17 and noticed the other planes in the formation were in a steep climb in contrast to our level flight. There was that strange feeling that strikes when you know something is wrong but can't immediately identify what it is. For a few moments my alarm increased, then I realized ours was the plane that was going places. We were diving down through the low squadron. In the thin cirrus clouds our pilot had gotten vertigo. It took him about 3,000 feet to grasp the situation and level out. We had been flying as an element leader and the No 2 man had followed us down. No 3 stayed up there, having enough sense to realize what was happening. We were never able to regain the formation so jettisoned our bombs and went home. Wasted effort.'

Vertigo was insidious and could take the most unlikely candidates. In fact, few pilots were immune from its effects if they forsook their instruments in clouds. Don Kammer, 353rd Fighter Group:

'We pilots were in our beds, late on a cold evening in February 1945, when another pilot who had been to the Officers Club and was feeling no pain came in.

When he got into bed he did not turn out the light and someone yelled for him to do so. The next thing we knew he had pulled his forty-five and was shooting at the single bare bulb that hung from the ceiling. He shot five times and missed. Everyone started laughing. "You don't think I can hit it do you?" he asked, and promptly shot once more. The light bulb smashed and darkness descended. Next morning the "hot shot" was one of our squadron pilots sent on a combat mission. The weather was bad, poor visibility and a complete low overcast. After take-off he must have disregarded his instruments, become disorientated in the cloud, augered in and was killed. A guy who was steady enough to shoot out a light bulb while the worse for alcohol just didn't seem the kind to fall victim to vertigo.'

13
Buying the Farm

'One of the most apprehensive times for a pilot on any mission was take-off. Always a gut wrench because you knew that if an engine failed or faltered as you broke ground, then the chances were you'd buy the farm. This apprehension was worse after you had witnessed some other crew go in, as I had. To take off over a crashed and burning wreck that a few minutes before had been a perfectly good B-24 with a good friend and his crew aboard in the line-up ahead waiting to turn onto the runway, was definitely not a morale lifter. Once in formation I always felt I gained an inner strength just through seeing all those other planes going the same way. Besides, when you were flying formation you were kept busy and this diverted attention from thoughts of personal safety.'

These sentiments of Robert Vickers are widely endorsed by those 'bits of boys' who had the responsibility of transferring 35 tons of warplane overloaded with fuel and ordnance from earth to sky. The silent prayer was that all engines continued to produce the necessary power. Some multi-engined aircraft did survive an engine failure at take-off but many more 'bought the farm'. Take-off was always critical and especially so for bombers; an apprehensive time for aircrew. Air gunner Harland Little found it so, even when watching his Group's B-24s go to war from a ground vantage point:

'The airstrip at Castellucio was located on a plateau with the runway heading out over towards a deep valley After take-off pilots would gain airspeed by dropping down into the valley. When watching fully loaded B-24s take off you held your breath every time one dipped out of view beyond the runway. You hoped to see the plane rise above the horizon instead of a ball of smoke.'

No combat group escaped take-off crashes; many resulted in fatalities; in other cases the crews escaped with no more than a shaking. Harold Rutka was one of the lucky:

'The crew of the B-24 "Belchin Bessie" had been briefed for a mission to Toussus airfield, south of Paris. Our plane was number three in line for take-off, and was loaded with 52 hundred-pounders and 2,700 gallons of fuel. We started down the runway and all seemed to be normal. I was standing at the waist window and had just said "Wheels up" when we suddenly crashed down on the runway. I was thrown forward and ended up at the bulkhead. The air was filled with white smoke as we slid along the runway. As we came to a grinding halt our first thoughts were to get out before it blew. Our waist gunner had always said that if we had to get out we had better not get in his way; we always thought he had been joking. He tried to pull open the floor hatch but it had jammed. As I cleared the waist window, darned if he didn't go over me and through the window. We had green flight suits and they were white from the smoke. When we took off the parachute harness we had white suits with green stripes.

'The crews that were to follow us had to take off on another runway and thought we had all been killed. A heck of a way for them to start out on a mission. We all survived, and with the help of the medics' whisky – furnished to settle us down – we returned to our huts. As a flier from another crew later observed: "When they came back to the barracks they were dead alright – dead drunk." '

After take-offs, landings stood next in the accident ratings, although most aircraft wrecked on landing from combat missions had suffered some disabling battle damage. Landing gear problems predominated and wheels-up touch-downs were not an uncommon experience. Ed Laube describes an episode in a Marauder that had to be 'bellied in' at Stansted:

'One other time when we returned the nose wheel would not lock in a down position. The main gear would go down and lock but not the nose wheel. The engineer put on a parachute to assess the problem, which was a piece of flak that had sheared off the locking pin. A lucky shot for the Germans and just as unlucky for us!

'We were advised to go to the main depot where airplanes severely damaged would land and be repaired, if possible. We had to land with the wheels up. We were the first airplane to attempt this type of wheels-up landing at this place. The airplane was landed in the dirt alongside the runway per instructions. When the belly of the airplane went across the other direction runway, the bottom was ripped off, beginning at the bomb bay doors. Then the airplane became a giant scoop, piling up tons of dirt and mud into the cockpit. The airplane finally stopped with all accounted for except the aerial engineer, Holstrom. He was buried deep in the mud and dirt. We all immediately began frantically digging with our hands to find Holstrom, listening to his muffled pleas for help. Fortunately he was not at the bottom of the mess but all of us had some anxious moments until we removed him. The airplane was junked! We were all a muddy mess but unhurt.

'After this fiasco of landing in the mud, the runways were sprayed with foam, with the airplanes landing on the foamed runways. Most airplanes could be returned to service after a few days using the newer technique.'

Human error in maintenance activities or through a piloting lapse were the major causes of landing and take-off accidents. In the incident which 91st Bomb Group gunner Earl Williamson recorded in his diary, when the 91st Bomb Group set out for the first major US attack on Berlin, one error led to another:

'Monday, March 6th, 1944 . . . We took off and hadn't been in the air five minutes when gasoline began to pour out of the wing close to our No 3 engine. Someone must have left the gas cap off or at least didn't fix it very tight. Our pilot, Lt Wilkinson, and co-pilot, Lt Maghee, have always been extremely afraid of any gas because one spark and you've had it – as the British say. Our pilot radioed for an emergency landing at our field but they told him he couldn't land for 15 minutes because other "Forts" were taking off. So we flew over an adjacent fighter field only three miles away and radioed for an emergency landing.

'All communications between ground and air do not come over the interphone and, like the rest of the crew, I was ignorant of the fact that we were going to land so soon. The pilot should have let us know on the interphone. The bombardier, ball turret operator, radio man and right waist gunner were all in the radio room. The navigator had just crawled out of the nose. The tail gunner was near the tail wheel adjusting and checking his equipment and I was near him doing the same thing but still on interphone. Suddenly we felt the flaps on the wings come down and the plane start to slow; we realized then we were going in to land. The tail gunner looked back and noticed the tail wheel was still up, which meant that the main gear was still up too. I went to push my interphone button to warn the pilot but at that moment we hit and all hell broke out.

'We were bouncing and hitting along with ten 500-pound bombs and a full gas load. None of us in the rear was braced, as far as I knew. I was going from side to side like a ping-pong ball and landed up near the tail wheel when the plane eventually came to a stop. First thing I heard was gas sizzling, just like those sizzling steaks back in good old America. A spark would fix things: in my daze I knew I had to get out of the plane in a hurry but for some reason I was frozen until the fellows coming from the radio room told me to get out. I stepped out and ran. I thought of the others and looked back to see the co-pilot coming out of the cockpit window. We all got to a safe distance and watched the airfield crash crews swarm around playing extinguishers on the badly battered and smoking plane. About everyone in our crew was shaking and moving around and because of it having difficulty in trying to light a cigarette. A doctor came and looked us over and told us we were all right. How we could all walk away from such a wreck is beyond me. Our pilot said: "I'm sorry boys. I just forgot to put the wheels down." '

A crashed aircraft might end up in a fairly intact state, yet the occupants might be fatally or badly injured by being crushed or thrown against internal equipment. For the fighter pilot, perhaps the greatest hazard in a crash was the gunsight situated directly in front of his face. Alvin Baker, assistant crew chief in the 364th Fighter Group:

'Our P-38s were returning from a mission. One pilot landed too long and seeing he was going to overrun the runway he firewalled both engines in an attempt to lift off again. He was still on the ground when he reached the perimeter track, hit a pothole (actually a filled-in bomb crater) which took off his landing gear, and bellied-in across a farmer's dirt field. With my crew chief, T/Sgt Louis Crane, I started to run towards the plane. Some British soldiers from an AA battery got there first but didn't know how to open the canopy. I got up on the wing, released the canopy, reached down and unbuckled the pilot's harness. The impact of the crash had caused him to strike his forehead on the gunsight and it looked to me as if his brains were hanging out. We carefully lifted him up and onto a stretcher because the ambulance couldn't get across the soft dirt. We guessed he wouldn't make the hospital alive.

'About a month later an officer comes along in a Jeep to where we are working on Major E. E. Bankey's plane. Wants to shake our hands and thank us. Yes, it's the P-38 pilot we thought was dying. The medics had put a silver plate in his head, sewn it up and he was fine.'

14
Alien Weather

While take-offs and landings were critical, weather conditions were a major contributor to flying accidents. Pilots who had trained in a more equable climate in the USA found it difficult to adapt to the European weather and its preponderance of cloud. Moreover, operations were often scheduled and despatched in heavy cloud conditions because the forecast promised good weather in target areas. The launch of missions in bad flying conditions often precipitated several crashes. Tom Morrow, Ordnance Officer at the 1st Bomb Division:

'A mission in early '44 took off as scheduled under deplorable weather conditions. A thick, wet, heavy overcast prevailed with ceilings frequently below 100ft at the bases with resulting poor visiblity. About an hour after scheduled take-off my phone rang. It was Brig Gen Beaman calling. I answered, "Major Morrow, Ordnance." Per his usual summons, the question was "Beaman – can you come up?" Reply, "Yes, Sir!" A short time later, General Beaman, the Divisional Chemical Warfare Officer and I drove to an area north-west of Kimbolton. Here a B-17 had crashed, full power dive at about 70 degrees into soft ground at the bottom of a swale [small dip or valley]. Only about 15 or 20ft of the tail structure and a little of the wings were above ground level. The area was cordoned off with MPs posted to prevent access. At the wreck were several officers and men with a Chemical Warfare decontamination truck spraying a rather small stream of water into the wing wreckage where flame from ruptured oxygen bottles flickered. Bomb loads that morning were either 500-pounders or incendiary bomb clusters.

'The Chemical Warfare Officer and I looked at each other and, almost simultaneously, shouted: "LET'S GET THE HELL OUT OF HERE!!!"

'That we did, expeditiously, clearing the area with guards posted at least 1,200yds from the site. We then left the area to look at another crash in a living area of Chelveston. There we learned that the wreck had blown up just 27 minutes after we vacated the site. On our way back to Brampton we returned to the crash site. The explosion of ten 500lb bombs dug a crater about 30ft deep and 75 to 80ft in diameter.

'That morning our Bomb Division had five crashes owing to the really bad take-off conditions.'

The dangers were intensified by launching missions before dawn when climbing through cloud in darkness presented a high risk of a collision with other aircraft. Near-misses were common. William E. Smith, a 392nd Bomb Group pilot:

'We'd taken off before first light. It was dark and the forming-up altitude was around 10,000 feet, solid overcast and the Group kept moving the assembly altitude up higher and higher, indicating to me that the top in the overcast was going up too. There were many, many planes in those clouds, hopefully all going the same direction. The exception would be the British bombers coming back from their night raids – at about right-angles to our flight path. We often saw them. Everybody wanted to come out of the war whole, but especially no one wanted to get it in a mid-air collision.

'As we climbed out, there were several sets of eyes aboard looking ahead. I was on the gauges. If I could express myself like a writer of quality, I could say what happened next literally made goose bumps on your arm. In a period of two or three seconds there they were, at about eleven o'clock high but not real high – two red lights on a collision course to our track. It was another plane, probably a B-24 which had reversed course and was continuing to climb. We couldn't make out the type of plane, but we could clearly see the red light on the left wing tip and the red passing light in the leading edge in the wing between No 1 and No 2 engines. How close to us – no one could tell.'

Sometimes even a near-miss could bring disaster to an overloaded bomber struggling up through the clouds. Stan Staples experienced this one winter's morning over Italy:

'We had taken off and had to climb up through a cloud layer before forming up on top. We entered the cloud base – the overcast – at around 5,000–6,000 feet. We went on the gauges and continued the climb. Some minutes into the climb someone broke radio silence to announce he had encountered severe turbulence, was out of control and bailing out his crew. A few minutes later, almost ready to top out of the cloud layer, patches of blue would sporadically appear momentarily, the ship shook and shuddered violently, a condition I'd never before experienced. First thought was that we had struck something, but that passed when the ship began to roll and the instrument panel went absolutely crazy. The directional gyro began to spin, the flight gyro (artificial horizon) flopped to one side, the altimeter began to unwind, but the airspeed just stayed there. The needle ball indicated a spin but nothing responded to the controls. Unknown at the time we had crossed right behind another B-24 without even seeing it and had caught the "prop wash".

'My engineer was between the two seats, with the rest of the front end crew on the flight deck: navigator, bombardier, nose turret gunner. The remainder were in the aft end of the ship.

'Things were going nowhere fast so the prudent thing to do seemed to get the blazes out of there. I had the co-pilot hit the bail-out alarm button, then with my right hand and thumb I motioned those on the flight deck to go. After they had vacated the flight deck I motioned the co-pilot out and as he left his seat I unbuckled and followed him. The going was right tough, we were held against the floor and it was most difficult to crawl. The thought in my head at the time was, what a heck of a way to leave an airplane.

'Then, just as I'd cleared the seats I looked back over my shoulder just as the plane broke out of the bottom of the cloud cover – the ground was right out the nose. Somehow, some way, we both got back into our seats and regained control, coming level just a few hundred feet above the ground. The airplane had stayed together, the bomb load was still in place and two thoroughly scared young men, wet with sweat and just perhaps a little else, tried to regain their composure. In a few seconds one of the crew from aft came up front to enquire as to what had happened. Because of the apparent centrifugal force in the rear they had been unable to move and didn't leave the ship. This whole action probably took place in less time than it takes to read this, but the time interval at that moment was interminable.

'We were still over land but had no idea as to where we were with respect to our base. Flying around the area we tried to spot the chutes of those who had gone out a few minutes before but had no luck. In due time we worked out an approximate position, which must have been quite accurate because we were able to head for home and land without further problems. A few hours later all the missing had been returned back to the base with nothing more serious than a sprained ankle. Of course, as pilot, I was called before the Group Commander to explain the circumstances. Also had to take a rather extensive instrument flight check by one of the higher group officers. With a satisfactory check ride behind me, I was returned to status as an airplane commander and mission pilot.'

In trying to find a formation in clouds, some pilots became lost and eventually had to abandon the mission and return to base. Bob Boyle was more determined than most pilots to find his group formation:

'We took off as usual, but when we climbed to altitude and broke out of the overcast it seemed that the clouds built up higher along with our climbing, so that visiblity was poor. I flew back over Buncher 8, but could not find our Group which should have been forming there. As it turned out, the 489th had been recalled but for some reason no one on our plane heard the message. So, not knowing why we could not find the rest of our group, I headed south as I knew that we were to leave England over Beachy Head and cross the Channel to France. I figured we'd find the 489th as it left the English coast as the upper weather seemed better in the south. As I headed there we kept looking for B-24 formations. Each time one was spotted we "poured on the coal" and changed altitude, as necessary, to catch up, only to find it was another group. After doing this a few times we were nearing the southern coast, so I decided we'd attach ourselves to another B-24 unit instead of returning to base.

'We pulled in position as a "spare" of the low element of the B-24 formation we were chasing at that moment, fired the appropriate identification flares, and we were on our way. Our mission had been briefed to be a short one but this group went much further so that I began to worry about fuel. I even imagined that we had latched on to a group going on a shuttle-mission to Italy. Because we had chased around the sky over England we wasted some fuel and now we were going further than we had planned. We plotted fuel consumption and at one point decided that if we didn't come to the IP in ten minutes we'd have to turn back and return alone. Before that time passed we did come to the IP so we stayed with our adopted group and, after bombing, headed with them back toward England.

'Fuel consumption/conservation was the big thing on our minds. As soon as we left the coast of France I left the formation to begin a gradual let-down. I called "Darky" and asked for a heading to the nearest landing field that could handle a four-engine bomber. This was given and in a few minutes I was told I was over the field. I really could not see any runways and radioed for clarification. The response was to the effect that they would fire a white flare. I saw it, but it was a grass field and I radioed that I could not land as it would be too soft. I was advised by their reply that it would definitely handle our plane so we completed our let-down and landed.

'We enjoyed lunch with the RAF at Church Norton and then took off for

Halesworth after being refueled. Thus an uneventful mission, but one that had a lengthy period of greater than usual anxiety, was ended.'

Occasionally, in certain weather circumstances, large formations of aircraft actually made their own clouds. 453rd Bomb Group pilot Louis Wust's diary:

'Feb 14, 1945 . . . The weather for take-off was fair and we did not run into any trouble until we were crossing the coast of Holland. At this point we ran into a thick haze and the planes began to stir up heavy persistent contrails. Under these conditions formation flying became extremely tedious. The contrails, on many occasions, became so dense that it was practically impossible to see the plane on whose wing we were positioned. The only visibility was a fleeting glimpse of the other planes as the contrails whisked by. After almost an hour flying under these conditions, we broke into the clear a short distance from the target.'

Two days later, on return from a tiring mission, Louis Wust faced a situation in which all of Britain was covered by dense cloud almost down to ground level:

'February 16th, 1945 . . . Upon arriving over England we were still on top of a solid undercast. Our base advised us that the ceiling was extremely low and that ground haze existed all around. These conditions prevailed all over England and we found ourselves without a diversion point. The only remaining alternative was to make an instrument "let-down" into the congested haze-covered area. All planes received a final warning regarding the high towers and buildings of the Norwich area before they proceeded to "let down". We prepared by descending to the top of the clouds. At this point we turned out over the North Sea and began descending into the clouds. We held this reciprocal homing course until we had descended to the estimated midpoint of the thickness of the cloud coverage. We then made a 180-degree turn and began to "home" on the airfield while losing altitude at a constant rate. This procedure was to allow us to break through the clouds while still over water and in sight of the coastline. As we cleared the base of the clouds the altimeter barely indicated 50 feet. We found ourselves in heavy haze with visibility extremely limited. Maintaining our heading with the little altitude we had, we strained to see the coastline. Suddenly, in rapid succession, there appeared the coast and the buildings and towers, some extending well above the altitude at which we were flying. We had to avoid them by flying to the side, since their proximity prohibited our attempting to gain enough altitude to fly over them.

'Several minutes later we found ourselves over the airfield in the company of many other planes trying to find the landing runway. It became quite a tedious job trying to orientate the plane for a landing and still avoid a collision. On our attempt to land we found that we lost sight of the airfield on the downwind leg, even though the runways were brilliantly lighted with flares. At this point it became obvious that we were going to have to fly a pattern of timed headings, starting directly over the runway, in order to come close enough to the runway for a landing. After several attempts, we finally approached the runway almost in line and were able to skid the plane into position for a landing. Although the actual mission was a "milk run", the weather was the most severe so far encountered.'

Fog was an even greater dread for the lone fighter pilot, his own navigator. There were several instances of pilots having no other safe option than to bale out when caught in such conditions on return from operations. In bad weather the prudent fighter pilot put down on the first airfield seen. In the north-west European winter, weather conditions could vary considerably within a few miles and being able to see one airfield was no guarantee that one's home base a few miles away might not be obscured in cloud. 'Stubby' Stubblefield's anecdote gives some indication of this variability:

'England was fogged in on return from a mission and, separated from my squadron, I decided to put down on the first base I saw, which was Boxted. Next morning when I was getting ready to leave, the tower operator said that another P-38 from my squadron had buzzed the field not long after I'd arrived. The P-38 was seen to circle the field with gear down but then disappeared in the murk and was never seen again. The Boxted tower man thought the P-38 might have crashed but there were no such reports. When I got back to Honington I found that the missing P-38 was flown by Steve Welch. When he circled Boxted it was momentarily lost from view in the fog and when he landed he found he was on another base a few miles away.'

Perhaps the most feared of natural hazards was the sea, or more correctly fear of having to ditch or to parachute into it. The Mediterranean and Adriatic could be warm in summer but they still took a toll of airmen's lives. The North Sea was the real dread, so cold in winter that once submerged in its icy embrace life expectancy was just a few minutes. Many fliers were plucked from the sea by British Air Sea Rescue launches and amphibious aircraft and, in the later months of the war, by USAAF flying-boats. Such a feat, so vividly described by Francis Glasser of the 5th Emergency Rescue Squadron, leaves little doubt about the grasp of the sea:

'On the afternoon of 3 February 1945 three Catalinas went on what was to be a sightseeing flight to locate landmarks, particularly in the Lowestoft, Yarmouth and Cromer areas. These three "Cats" had members of other crews on board and some took their ground crew chiefs along for the ride. I went with Lt Combs' crew, for our plane was hangared for some minor ailment and I wanted to get a look at the countryside. The lead plane of the three Cats had a P-47 pilot with them to show us around and this was the only plane that had direct contact with "Colgate", Channel B, Air Sea Rescue Base. We had radio contact between the three but it didn't carry very far. It so happened that on this day the Eighth put over a thousand planes up and messed things up pretty badly around Berlin in particular.

' "Colgate" called our lead plane to report a ditching by the crew of a B-17 seen in rafts and they wanted to know if we could pick these people up. Evidently the P-47 pilot in the lead plane was given the okay to go on search; he contacted the other two Cats and out over the North Sea we went, three abreast and spread pretty far apart. We didn't even have a map on board covering the areas we started out to look at, we had no "flimsy" to give us the reply we would need if we were challenged and these challenges changed every four hours; last, but not least, we didn't even have a raft on board. We weren't supposed to be out over the North Sea – this was strictly a sightseeing trip, uh huh!!

'Conditions over the North Sea were "eerie" this day, the sea was a dark gray with lots of white caps showing; from the deck up to about a thousand feet or so the sky was a ghostly gray and above this area it was as clear as a bell. I was sitting in my favorite spot in the port blister and in the gloom I could barely see the Cat that was off to our side. Spotting a Wellington bomber circling above the haze several miles away with landing lights on, I reported to Lt Combs what I had seen. He tried, to no avail, to contact the other two planes so we took off toward the Wellington by ourselves. When we reached the bomber we saw that it was circling two rafts lashed together, both with survivors in them. It was late in the afternoon and Lt Combs wanted to get down as quickly as possible, rescue these people and get off of the water before it got dark; what he didn't figure on were swells of 20–25 feet high – we never saw anything like this in the Gulf of Mexico. We dropped a smoke bomb to get the wind direction and went in for a power landing, hit the water, shot off a swell and were airborne again. We went around again and this time we full-stalled onto a swell, staying on the water but the swells were so high that we couldn't do much maneuvering for fear of dipping a wing. With the men in the rafts working their butts off trying to get to us, and our trying to get to them, we finally got close enough to throw a line and haul them into the plane.

'Nine scared and wet men from a B-17 were happy to be on board. The bombardier didn't survive the ditching. The navigator was in deep shock, I had never seen anything like this before; he had a grip on his Weems plotter and just stared straight ahead, oblivious to where he was or what was happening. Now, with seventeen men on board and dusk rapidly setting in, Lt Combs tried to get off of the water. Each time we would get up on a swell and get up a little speed, water would come crashing into the engines and kill our take-off attempt. After about three of these hair-raising attempts, Lt Combs decided to try it once more and if he wasn't successful we'd try to ride it out until the sea calmed down or help got to us. The last attempt we made was a "dilly", we got up speed and then were hit by a wall of water that broke the front end of the plane open. No choice now, for water was pouring into the plane so Lt Combs fully opened up the engines and pulled the Cat off the water. The plane seemed to hover for an instant before the engines grabbed and kept us from going back into the sea and certain death. When the nose had broken the water soaked everyone and everything up front, including our main radios. We all shook hands with the Almighty this day but he wasn't ready for us yet, thank heavens.

'We were in the air, but far from being safe. Not having a map, the navigator estimated where we were at and gave the pilot a heading he thought would get us somewhere close to our base. I turned on the IFF and remembered something I had read in an Air Force pamphlet about a crew that had its radios knocked out and was in more or less the same sort of bind we were in, and what they had done to overcome this problem. I had the radio-operator hook our trailing wire antenna up to the "Gibson Girl" transmitter we retrieved from the B-17's rafts before we sank them. While one of us cranked it, another keyed SOS PBY, SOS PBY, SOS PBY, over and over so the shore batteries could get a "fix" on us and hopefully identify us as a friend. The English didn't take kindly to lone planes coming over their coastline, especially at night, but it worked as we were not fired upon. When the navigator thought that we were near land we put on a fireworks display with our Very pistol that must have been something to see; no doubt about it, we did everything that we could to let the English know who and where we were. We approached a field that had fire pots lining a runway and to our amazement it was Halesworth.

'Funny thing, but while we were on the water actually fighting for our lives I never was scared; however, after this episode was over and I sat down and thought about what had happened, and what could have happened, it got to me. Every February 3rd I give thanks for being alive.'

Not a few crews became lost in the course of a mission, particularly in inclement weather. The lucky were saved by the lifeline of a radio directional steer; others blundered further into enemy territory; yet others just disappeared, probably victims of the sea. Good navigation was essential to keep clear of the known areas of anti-aircraft defences, as well as to avoid wandering and depleting fuel supplies. Formations tended to rely on the navigation of the leading aircraft crew and following navigators and pilots were often unprepared when they suddenly found themselves forced to go it alone, a situation observed on more than one occasion by Wilbur Lewis, a 359th Fighter Group pilot:

'During a mission, now and again a bomber would have an engine fail, couldn't keep up, and its pilot would decide to turn back. Instead of flying a reciprocal course back to England, you would often see them taking a heading that was way out and on occasions I'd switch my radio to "C" Channel and warn them. I got the impression some navigators were not doing their job properly, relying on the navigator in the lead bomber of the formation. When there was an emergency situation they were caught out.'

Navigation was a precise art and no more so in 'pinpointing' to a target. When cloud obscured the ground it was a matter of calculation and luck for the bombardier. In the final months of the campaign he had radar to help him locate his target, but it was still a fraught business. Harold Smith:

'On 11 December 1944 we were given the task of knocking out a river bridge between Ludwigshafen and Mannheim. I was flying lead in the Low Squadron. The Lead and the High Squadrons had the aid of the new GH radar system while I had the old H2X ("Mickey") pathfinder equipment. As we made our turn toward the target area which was covered with clouds, I noticed the Lead and High Squadrons turning at least 10 degrees to the left of course. I called our Mickey operator and asked him if he was sure he had the target on his scope. He assured me we were OK. Minutes later the two other squadrons had turned another 5 degrees to the left of our course. I knew something was wrong and asked the pilot if we could turn and try to pick up a new heading as we certainly were off the target. He turned approximately 15 degrees and suddenly the clouds broke and there was the river and the bridge. At the same moment we ran into a heavy barrage of flak from Mannheim and Ludwigshafen. We were hit immediately and the number three engine was knocked out. I called to the pilot to attempt to maintain our airspeed and I told him I was going to drop visually. I clutched in the sight and was fortunate enough to be able to make what I thought to be an accurate sighting. We turned off the target and I called to the tail gunner to try to see where the bombs hit. He called back excitedly and said: "Right on the nose. Half the bridge had collapsed."

'When the photos taken were shown at a critique they showed the bomb strike. Colonel Lyle exclaimed "Great Job". There were no pictures of the other two squadrons' strikes. Suddenly the Intelligence Officer said: "Wait a minute. That's not the briefed bridge. That's a bridge that was under construction five miles up the river!" '

15
Not as Planned

The nature of the air war and the limits of both technique and technology made mistakes almost inevitable. Occasionally bad enough to jeopardize a unit's mission. Don Bevan:

'On January 27th 1943, the day of the first American air attack on Hitler's Germany, our 306th Bombardment Group, leading a four-group maximum-effort 54-plane raid at about 25,000 feet, flew along the string of coastal islands and, at a point approximately between Emden and Wilhelmshaven, the right outside wing plane in which I was flying right waist gunner, peeled off in a severe maneuver, banking sharply over the coast into Germany. The move was unexpected and frightening to me – but when we leveled off and I could look back another plane from our squadron was turning up and banking after us. The others began to follow more closely. Colonel Armstrong's lead squadron followed the lead of our 423rd right wing formation. It took many anxious moments for the group to catch up and close a tight rank with us again. When ranks were closed, bomb bay doors were opened. The time over Germany was short but busy. During the bomb run on Wilhelmshaven the bomb load from a plane to the left of us – from the formation flying in the hole – dropped away, prematurely, causing the bombardiers to doubt their own sighting calculations. Confusion reigned over the intercoms. Later, back at base in England, at our dispersal area – after our engines were cut and our crew alighted – the very first comment was, "Who was the son-of-a-bitch that did *that*:" *That*, referring to the prematurely released bombs.

'As the combat crews, being picked up, came together in the trucks the first comment, again, was: "Who was the son-of-a-bitch that did that!" And when all the crews from the trucks came together at the Spam sandwich table in the briefing hut, the first comments on the raid were the same. It was the number one reaction to the historic raid. The next day one of our mechanics approached me with, "You know who that so-and-so was that released those bombs – that Hollywood VIP friend of Armstrong's. A communications bigshot. He accidentally pushed the bombardier's hand off the control while his head was buried in his sights and toggled his bomb load!" The mechanic's account was more elaborate, scatologically speaking.'

Carelessness was a companion of error. Most flying perils could be precipitated or aggravated by human fallibility, triggered by a variety of circumstances. Expediency was behind the anecdote told by Irwin Pochter:

'A practice mission was set up on a rare sunny November day when we were stood down from combat. Together with my pilot and co-pilot I had been instructed to proceed to our B-17 "No Gum Chum" and that the enlisted men on our crew would meet us there. Harry O'Grady and Weyman Carver settled themselves in the cockpit and, after completing their checks, informed the tower that our enlisted men had not yet arrived. Although assured they were en route, O'Grady grew anxious. The other aircraft participating in the practice mission had already started engines and our pilot, impatient over the delay, started engines too and was cleared to taxy. I went back to the rear fuselage door to see the crew had all their equipment when they arrived.

'Up in the cockpit, co-pilot Carver looked out of his side window and saw the truck arrive and our boys spilling out. He informed O'Grady, who told him to let him know as soon as everyone was aboard. Carver took another look and saw no one was left on the hardstand. All aboard, he told O'Grady, who immediately had the B-17 rolling out to the active runway. Soon after take-off O'Grady discovered that one of "No Gum Chum's" main wheels had failed to retract. He instructed Carver to contact our engineer on intercom and tell him to crank it up. The engineer didn't respond. Carver tried the other positions and got no replies. Believing the intercom to be out, O'Grady ordered Carver to go back and see what was wrong. A few minutes later Carver returned, fell into the co-pilot's seat and gasped: "There's no one there!" Dumbfounded, O'Grady called the tower: "I've lost my crew." He was told to return at once to Mendlesham to collect his navigator and gunners who would be waiting in a truck at the end of the runway.

'What had happened was that when the crew arrived at the aircraft, I saw they had not got their machine-guns. Even if it was only a practice mission it was necessary to have armament and be prepared for any emergency. So I ordered the gunners to collect their weapons and jumped on the truck to go with them to the armory. Carver, seeing the truck had gone from the hardstand, assumed everyone was on board. Needless to say, for the rest of our tour we all took a lot of razzing about the incident.'

In the predicament experienced by Coleman Sanders it was a case of assuming the other guy had everything under control:

'In January 1944 the Ken Edwards crew was assigned to the 303rd Bomb Group at Molesworth. We took ground classes for a week and then went for an area familiarization flight with Tommy Quinn, an experienced pilot, and Joe Vieiera as radio-operator. We flew around the area so that they could show us the prominent landmarks. When it was time to return to base, the Group was returning from a mission, and Flying Control needed us out of the way while the planes landed. We flew around, climbing through the overcast to about 5,000 feet. As I'd finished my assigned duties for the flight, I didn't pay much attention to the instruments and didn't know that a 100-knot wind had developed at the altitude we were flying.

'When it was time for us to let down through the cloud, Quinn asked me for a heading back to Molesworth. I looked down as soon as we broke out and saw London below. Joe Vieiera, our radio-operator, heard my report to the pilot and came on intercom with, "London doesn't have an Eiffel Tower!" At first I thought he was joking, but sure enough it was Paris not London. What a shock. An unarmed B-17 flying around over enemy-held territory was unlikely to be ignored. Sure enough someone soon calls out that a couple of fighters were coming up fast. Quinn promptly took us back up into the clouds, but not before one of the fighters had taken a shot at us. We took a heading for England and finally got a steer from the radar people who had been tracking us and wondering what we were doing. When we eventually got back to base we all swore secrecy, hoping our stupidity would not be known. Next morning the ground crew found a few bullet holes in the B-17 so we had some explaining to do.'

Carelessness also danced with forgetfulness as in the tale Robert Strobell tells of near-catastrophe at the 495th Fighter Training Group:

'Gun camera training flights involved two P-47s in mock combat maneuvers, one chasing the other to bring his gunsight to bear on the "enemy" and, using his gun camera, attempt to "shoot" him down. The film was then evaluated in a special analytical machine to determine the effectiveness of the shooter, and a critique followed to let the pilot know what he did well or what he needed to do to improve his gunnery.

'Two pilots, whom I knew well, took off on such a flight and when at the agreed altitude communicated by radio to commence mock combat. The "shooter" flicked the camera switch on, got on the tail of his buddy, the "enemy", and pressed the trigger on his control column. He not only photographed the "enemy", he put a burst of bullets into his target. Imagine his surprise. He had flicked the arming switch down for guns and cameras instead of up for cameras only. And imagine his buddy's surprise to hear bullets rattling through his aircraft. The "enemy" was not hurt and the airplane continued to fly. But it had taken some damaging hits, one to the hydraulic system. After flying around Atcham airfield taking instructions from the tower, he managed to lower the landing gear manually by cranking it down. This solved part of the problem. No hydraulics meant no flaps and this required him to land "hot", or faster than he normally would with speed-reducing flaps. He put down on the runway but rolled off the far end, went across the overrun strip, ploughed into some soft dirt with his wheels locked, flipped upside down, straddling a deep ditch, resting on tail fin and nose. The tower received a transmission from him to the effect that he was off the end of the runway and upside down! He was unhurt until he reached down and unlocked his safety belt and fell into the bottom of the ditch where they found him unconscious. But he was back flying two weeks later.'

16
Facing Flak

There was a marked difference in outlook between the men who flew in bombers and those in fighters. The former were usually the attacked and the latter attackers; a difference of having to steel oneself to assault by enemy anti-aircraft artillery and fighter interception as against the aggressive thrill of being the hunter. But for all, the most haunting memory was the fall of comrades, often a transient scene, distanced by the roar of engines and the screen of Plexiglas. Louis Wust recorded his reactions in a diary entry:

'November 2nd 1944 . . . I didn't suspect for a moment that I was about to see one of our ships disintegrate before my eyes, then it happened; there was a brilliant flash and the entire plane was enveloped in flame. The flaming mass slowly fell from the formation and began to disintegrate into bits of flaming wreckage that twisted and turned dizzily toward the earth. I strained my eyes toward the ghastly sight in the hope of seeing parachutes of survivors, but there were none. It was hard to believe that men I sat with only a few hours before were riding that blazing inferno to the ground. It's difficult to express my exact feelings at witnessing that sight. Although impossible, I imagined that I heard the crackling of the flames as the wreckage fluttered earthward. Perspiration covered my face, although I shook, chilled to the bone, and my stomach felt that it had shrunken to half its normal size. I promised myself that, should I ever get back and have the opportunity to stay on the ground, I would never look at an airplane again.'

The helplessness felt by onlookers in such situations is made plain by Bob McMath, a 447th Bomb Group pilot:

'The most traumatic experience of my combat career was watching two B-17s from my squadron collide. Our target that day was Merseburg oil plants, probably the most heavily defended place in Hitler's Reich at that date. I was flying the right wing of the lead element in the low flight of the Group's low squadron, directly between the two aircraft involved. We were about an hour from reaching the target when I suddenly noticed the ship high on my right begin to drift left. My co-pilot had the controls so I could watch with some apprehension as the Fort continued to slip right across above and in front of us. I couldn't see what was wrong; all engines appeared to be running.

'The pilots finally seemed to have arrested the drift but the ship was now positioned over that of Lt Moses flying the left wing of our element. The troubled Fort was sort of wobbling and going up and down. I could see that the ball turret gunner had positioned his guns pointing straight down and must have had an awful view of what was to happen. The higher ship started slowly sinking towards Moses's. I wanted to shout a warning but even if it had been possible I doubt if I could have done it; I was momentarily struck dumb with fearfulness, waiting for the two machines to come together. I was in perfect position to observe this horrible scene unfolding just 100 yards away. Finally the No 2 propeller of the descending ship sliced through the aft end of Moses's radio room. There seemed a hesitation before the front section of Moses's Fort nosed down. It seemed that the rear half momentarily remained attached to the higher aircraft before it too disappeared from my sight. I was then aware of fragments of torn aluminum from the impact and there in the middle of the debris the radioman slowly spinning through the sky, separated from his parachute pack by about ten feet. It is not possible to describe the feelings such a sight engenders, a helpless human being going to certain death five miles and two and a half minutes below, and probably knowing it. The drama was played out in just a second or two to my vision but remains an indelible slow-motion print on my mind. Moses and his whole crew were killed. The other ship managed to crash-land in Holland with no casualties. The pilots said they were having trouble with a runaway prop when the collision occurred.'

Few combat airmen feared fighter attack more than flak – the popular name for anti-aircraft artillery fire adopted from the German Fliegerabwehrkanone. When the Air Corps planners conceived high-altitude precision bombing, it was assumed that the bombers could fly above the effective range of anti-aircraft guns. In the event, flak proved deadly: 88mm and 105mm calibre shells could reach the bomber's optimum altitude of 25,000 feet with accuracy. Flak became the bomber crew's dread. For John Zima, a 448th Bomb Group co-pilot, the introduction to the reality of being a flak target more than lived up to the reputation:

'Spotting the air above our target, off to the left, was easy. It was awesome. Without exaggeration the sky was filled with small black balls . . . FLAK!! To my uninitiated mind it was inconceivable that we were to fly through it. I started to pray. As we flew south outside the flak area it seemed my prayers had been answered. Had our leader decided the target was too heavily defended? But then we started to turn straight in to the holocaust.

'The bomb run began with what was called the IP. This was some feature on the ground that could easily be identified from over 20,000 feet. This helped the bombardier pick up the target. In this case we were flying south toward the IP and the target was to the east. Upon reaching our IP we made a 90-degree turn to the left and headed on our bomb run. With our bomb bay doors open we flew straight for that obvious spot in the sky, black with flak.

'I grew more horrified as we approached our target and my Hail Marys were coming fast and furious. I wondered how anything, especially a four-engined bomber, could get through. Our nose gunner, who had the best view, said he couldn't stand it and cradled his head in his arms. As the formation ahead of us went through there was a sudden ball of fire, a puff of smoke, and chunks of airplane fell downward to earth.

'Then there was a lull, a suspension, followed by events unfolding faster than one can explain. The puffs were suddenly all around us, puffs of black smoke with centers of red fire, curling and twisting as each shell exploded. I saw a shell before it exploded. Suspended about three feet to the right, it exploded about five feet above us. It was just a blur as my eyes followed it up and watched it explode.

'And then time stopped as the plane we were flying formation with was hit. The intercom got busy as the crew cried out at what they saw:

' "He's hit!"

' "He's on fire!"

' "He's spinning down!" Crying out from the left and right, their voices were overlapping, cutting each other off.

' "He's on fire! He's on fire! He's going down."

'The plane was to the left, in front, and slightly above us when hit between the No 3 and 4 engines. As the plane rose and turned over on its back the co-pilot was clearly visible in his seat, looking as if nothing was happening. He was either hit or not able to grasp the calamity that had overtaken him.

'The huge plane passed over us before beginning its death dive. There was a flash of fire as the right wing parted and went over us. A piece of debris, I think it was the supercharger, came directly at us. We ducked our nose and the debris ricocheted off the nose turret, the navigator's dome, and then went over the cockpit. I thought that our nose gunner and navigator were dead. All the while shells were exploding all around us. It seemed as if we were being singled out, picked on, as if they were bound and determined to get our one aircraft. But surely other aircraft were attracting their share of attention.

'Then, quite suddenly, unexpectedly, we were in the clear. The beautiful sky ahead was completely clear of shell bursts, as though the war was left behind us. The sky was blue and peaceful. It was as if I had never seen a blue and peaceful sky before.'

Whether at 30,000 or 50 feet, flak was a torment. Indeed, ground fire at low altitude was an even greater hazard and bombing raids at 'zero' altitude by B-26s and A-20s were soon abandoned when the attrition rate among the attacking aircraft proved too great. A graphic description of a low-level raid was recounted in a letter from 319th Bomb Group's Ashley Woolridge to his parents in the summer of 1943 – long after the actual event in the previous December:

'My first mission was a tough one. We flew over the mountains and dropped down on the deck at Gafsa. We hedge-hopped from there to Gabes. The leader's navigator got off course and brought us in on the field on the wrong axis of attack. Instead of going over the field, the leader made a 270-degree turn to the right, then went across. That was violating all the ethics of low-altitude bombing. I wasn't worried about that, because in the 270-degree turn I was on the inside getting prop-wash plus almost stalling out. There were times in the turn that my wing was very near the ground. The scare I got in the turn was greater than I had anticipated getting over the target. We rolled out of the turn and pulled up to 300 feet as we went over the end of the field. We were headed NE. We were to hit planes, hangars and barracks on the NE end. As I crossed the SW end of the field a lot of tracers came up. It looked as if there were a bunch of guys down there squirting red water out of a hose. I squirmed in my seat a little, but nothing hit me; however, I had several holes in my wings and fuselage. After that things got rough. First I got hit with five 20mm shells – none exploded – one went through my tail gunner, but left the ship without going off. While we were getting hit, Ewald was dropping bombs – 100lb bombs dropped from 300 feet (instantaneous fuses – didn't have delayed fuses in Africa) just about knocked the wings off a ship. It was a hell of a rough ride. There was a lot happening in those couple seconds.

'On leaving the target we were to make a turn and dive to the left. For some reason, the leader did a 180 turn, right over the harbor. They were still shooting at us. In this 180 turn I almost stalled out, but got control again just above the water. I ran into more trouble there when they began shooting coast artillery shells in front of me, making big shafts. I barely missed two of them. Hitting a column of water like that would be worse than hitting a tree. I got back over land all right but my trim tab control rods had been shot away, making the ship very difficult to fly. When my tail gunner was hit, Cox, my radio-operator and waist gunner, called Irish on interphone. Irish left the co-pilot's seat while we were still over the target and went back to see what he could do. My trouble wasn't over yet. Kneen's bombs wouldn't drop over the target. Pewitt was his bombardier. When I headed west inland from the coast I was still trying to recover from the last turn and was almost under Kneen. Pewitt salvoed at a RR track and I was caught. I saw them coming and made a steep turn and climb to the left. Just about the time I started up, the bombs went off and I took on altitude fast.

'After that I got back in formation and took a rest. After the tail gunner got it, Cox had taken over his guns. We didn't have an escort, but pursuit didn't bother us much on the deck. My ship was laid up for two weeks after that trip . . . This low-altitude bombing in a '26 against well defended targets will make an old man out of you in a hurry.'

Ashley Woolridge endured in the pilot's seat to fly a record 106 missions and become one of the most distinguished members of the Marauder fraternity.

The metal fragments from an exploding shell slashed through the aluminium skin of an aircraft like a knife through butter and flak damage was commonplace over targets like Merseburg, Ploesti and Berlin. Flak jackets (body armour) were worn to deflect low-velocity fragments but flak still took its toll of men, if not the aircraft in which they flew. During the late summer of 1944 there was an average of approximately one casualty to flak for every 50 heavy bombing sorties to major targets; and one casualty in 50 was fatal. The other 49 lived to wear their Purple Hearts. Stan Staples:

'On February 22nd 1945 we received the usual early morning wake-up call, had breakfast, then were trucked down to Group Headquarters where the briefing room was located. Moans and groans followed the revelation that the target was in southern Germany. As we rode out to the flight line a strange feeling came over me. I can't explain it, a premonition of some sort. We had a high overcast to penetrate but this was accomplished without incident. This overcast turned to layers of clouds as we proceeded on course and by the time we had arrived for the various turning points, things were coming unglued. First off we lost visual contact with the main group and a while later our squadron lost visual with the group formation – we were just twelve airplanes up over Germany by ourselves. The squadron lead navigator, to his credit, didn't keep in one direction too long – every few minutes there was a course change.

'Apprehension in the cockpit was now pretty intense – where are we, where are we going, what are we going to do? The decision must have been made in the lead airplane to scrub the mission and head for home because the situation just was not tenable. Shortly after turning on a southerly heading for home all hell broke loose. Quite apparently we had been tracked by anti-aircraft radar because the first bursts caught us all right in the middle. The damn stuff was all around us, red centers and all. The pieces of flak hitting the plane sounded like rocks were being tossed at it. Then a close shell burst right out in our 11 o'clock position, just a bit below us. The ship rocked from the explosion and at the same time my left foot was very heavily knocked from the rudder pedal. Over the intercom came the anguished cry "I've been hit!" The plastic astrodome on top of the nose, about five feet in front of the cockpit, shattered and disappeared into a thousand fragments. At the same time the engineer, George Craig, located in his top turret, hit the "dead man" release of the turret seat and fell, stunned momentarily, in a heap to the flight deck. We thought he was dead but he came to, fully recovered, in a few minutes. A few horrendous seconds, then it was over – no more flak.

'The radio intercom call had come from the nose gunner, Charles Krause. A piece of hot metal had entered the side of his turret, passed down his flight jacket sleeve, opening it like a pair of shears and took his left thumb off just where it joined his hand. As the astrodome shattered, our navigator, Ralph Naven, was cut around the forehead and face by the flying Plexiglas. He and the bombardier, Don Kessler, pulled Charley out of his turret and gave him first aid. In a few minutes they had him laid out on the flight deck, morphine administered and covered with a blanket. In the meantime my left foot had begun to ache something awful – just as though several bricks had been dropped on my toes. Very gingerly I tried to move my toes and felt a warm, squishy sensation. Thought we'd better take a look, so I slid my seat back, pulled off my flying boot and found the end of my sock soaked in blood. The sock came off and what looked like a bloody stump appeared where my big toe should have been.

'We flew back to Italy, made an emergency landing at Foggia where we took our nose gunner to the hospital there for care. Doc looked at my foot and "figured as how" the squadron flight surgeon could patch me up. During the landing approach to Foggia Main we found our landing gear plumbing had been shot out, so two of the crew, engineer George Craig and George Boerger, cranked the gear down. We returned to the plane, sans our more seriously wounded mate. Our co-pilot took us off and brought us back to Torretto airbase, south of Cerignola. The squadron surgeon, Dr Dan Nathan, took a look at my foot and promptly sent me down to the field hospital at Bari where I remained for a month.'

Examples of adherence to duty among even the badly or fatally wounded were not difficult to find. The conduct of Hugh Walker's bombardier in such circumstances was later acknowledged with his country's second highest award for bravery:

'On the morning of D-Day our B-26 group was briefed to bomb gun emplacements at Grande Champs. The lead bombardier couldn't pick up the Aiming Point because of haze and, despite having been ordered not to make a second run, the group leader took us through a 360 degree. Seeing a formation of aircraft swinging out of Normandy towards the beaches, some Allied gunners offshore opened up on us. One shell splinter creased my bombardier/navigator's helmet, knocking him down, but he was able to release his bombs on the signal for the rest of the group. He then succumbed to shock. After bombing, the formation was confronted with a solid bank of cloud and our leader ordered separation. With no functioning navigator I wasn't going to risk being lost, so stuck in close to my leader all the way up through the murk although I'd never done anything like this before. It proved the right decision, for when we broke out on top at 12,000 feet there were no other planes in the sky and I followed the leader back to base.

'Two days later my crew was scheduled for a mission to bomb Valognes to create a choke point south of Cherbourg. I told my bombardier, a heavy-set man of Norwegian descent, named Gustave Kjesness (pronounced "Chess-ness"), that he didn't have to go. He replied he was okay and that "I should fly if I can fly."

'As we were on the bomb run, the Cherbourg flak got our range. One shell exploded directly beneath my plane and put 88 pieces of flak into it. One piece severed Kjesness's femoral artery in his thigh but he managed to release the bombs and close the doors. Although one of our crew got to him within two minutes he had bled to death and there was nothing we could do for him. When we landed the whole underside of the fuselage was stained with his life blood. The posthumous DSC was the only one awarded a member of the 391st Bomb Group.'

Flak inspired someone in the 15th Air Force to parody the tune 'As Time Goes By' which John Slothower, a 98th Bomb Group bombardier, delighted in singing. It also reveals the commonly held view in the 15th that 8th Air Force operations were accorded an unfair amount of publicity:

You must remember this,
The flak can't always miss,
Somebody has to die,
The odds are always too damned high,
As flak goes by.

And when the fighters come,
You hope you're not the one
To tumble from the sky,
The odds are always too damned high,
As flak goes by.

And then it's one-tens and two-tens,
Knocking at your gate,
Sky's full of fighters,
Got to kill that rate,
Bombs won't go away,
Salvo don't delay,
The target's passing by.

It's still the same old story,
The Eighth gets all the glory,
And we're the ones to die,
The odds are always too damned high,
As flak goes by.

A direct hit and detonation of an 88mm or 105mm shell was rarely survived unless at some extremity of the aircraft. The ignition or explosion of fuel tanks was likely following any hit on the wing. This was a particular dread to B-24 crews where the tanks in the shoulder wing were in close proximity to the fuselage and would quickly flood the rear with fire. Edwin Range, a radio gunner with the 454th Bomb Group, was one faced with this terrifying prospect:

'When we bombed Maribor, Yugoslavia on February 13, 1945 the flak nearly sent us to heaven or hell, or "such other punishments as Courts Martial may direct". We received a big hit in the right wing panel and 100-octane fuel from the ruptured wing tanks flooded the internal fuselage from bomb bay to tail. Those in the waist were quickly drenched. There were gas puddles in the bomb bay and in the ball turret. The plastic windows at the machine-gun positions were completely clouded over, so that none of us in the waist, tail and ball turret could see out to shoot; and had we done so the ignition of the vaporized fuel would have meant a fiery end. Because of the debris which flew off our ship into the other squadron elements, not to mention that we might blow up at any moment, my pilot was ordered out of the formation, which quickly left us behind and alone in the sky. Protective fighter cover was nowhere in view.

'The return from Yugoslavia was miraculously accomplished, but the landing presented more problems. The left gear would not lock and we had a wild ride in the waist while the pilot raised the left wing again and again, flopping it down hard, to try to get the locking device to show. Nothing worked and the tower told the pilot to bail-out the crew over the field. We all refused to jump. Secondly, we had no flaps, no brakes, so the pilot told us to rig parachute brakes out both waist windows. And on the touch-down, the chutes were opened and that is how we stopped our roll.'

17
Messerschmitts and Focke-Wulfs

Enemy fighters did not engender the fears that most men had for flak. With flak it was a case of 'sit there and take it'; against fighters most men in a bomber crew, except the pilots, had a gun with which to hit back. In the later stages of the air war when mass fighter assaults were made on formations, these proved far more lethal than anti-aircraft artillery in destroying bombers. A fighter attack was usually fast and furious, as 466th Bomb Group tail gunner Melvin Robinson describes:

'After bombing troop and supply concentrations near Prum on Christmas Day 1944, we were about two minutes from the Belgian border when I noticed a few bursts of red flak at 6 o'clock level. I had forgotten what this meant but a few seconds later was quickly reminded when I noticed a series of small bursts in a horizontal line coming directly at my tail turret. Following this line back I saw an Fw 190 at the end, cannon blinking. At the time we were flying under a long cloud bank and perhaps 30 or 40 Fw 190s were using this as cover to launch a surprise attack on our formation. There was just time to warn the crew, throw the main power switch to my turret, take my guns off safety and start firing as the Fw 190 came into range. I gave him one long burst as he closed from about 800 to under 100 yards. He broke away to my left and repositioned on the tail of a lower B-24. As the Fw 190 rolled he briefly gave me a full side view and I opened fire again, observing several pieces of metal fly off his plane. As the 190 faded out to my left the tail of the B-24 he had been firing at came into the outer edge of my gun sight and I instantly released the trigger but the right gun continued to fire due to rounds "cooking off" in the overheated barrel. I pulled the charging handle back, holding the breech of that gun open while I swung the turret back to the 6 o'clock position. I was just in time to catch a second 190 coming in at our ship. I levelled the guns down on him and started firing. His bullets were hitting all around me, knocking out the turret Plexiglas. The fighter broke away at about 75 yards and went to my right, coming into firing position on another B-24. Again I had a good view of his side and in opening fire once more observed pieces of dural come away as the 190 faded out of my sight. Instinctively I brought the turret round to 6 o'clock and was confronted with a third Fw 190 coming in at me. I started firing and immediately saw strikes on his cowling. A line of 20mm bursts were coming straight at me and I prayed I would get the 190 before he got me. The next thing a 20mm hit the armor plate at the base of my turret and another exploded against the armored glass. The blast shattered the heavy glass and lifted me off my seat and clear out the back of the turret, temporarily stunning me.

'When I came round my eyes were filled with blood and rapidly swelling shut – shards of glass had penetrated my eyeballs and other exposed areas of my face. I motioned to the waist gunners for help but they seemed frozen with fear and did not come. Dragging myself back into the turret, I reconnected my intercom and called the pilot to ask if no one up front was hurt could he send someone back to help. The pilot called the bombardier and asked him to take a look at me. Meanwhile my eyes were rapidly swelling and I was blind to what was going on but knew we were still under attack because of the sound of exploding 20mms. All I could do was move my turret around and flag the guns up and down in the hope of making the enemy pilots think I was still in action. Then I passed out again. When I revived, a waist gunner had reconnected my oxygen mask hose and put me on a walk-around bottle and was in the process of trying to haul me back to the waist. Lt Halls, the bombardier, bandaged my eyes and at my request connected my intercom set to I could talk to Lt Moore, our pilot. He told me he was going to land at Brussels to get me to a doctor as soon as possible. I tried to talk him into going back to England but he set the ship down at Brussels anyway.

'I spent six days at the British Edith Cavell Hospital where they operated on me to remove the glass from my eyes. Then I was evacuated by air to the US 192nd General Hospital in England where I spent three weeks. I eventually got back to my Group at Attlebridge on 25th January 1945 but my combat days were over and I was soon shipped back to the ZI.'

On both the Fortress and the Liberator the gun position with the best field of fire, and the reputation of being the most effective defence point, was the so-called ball underturret. The gunner was stowed in a foetal position, sighting between his spread legs. Statistically gunners in the ball received fewer wounds than in any other position but to ride in this small sphere slung under the belly of the bomber required strong nerves. Harold Harding of the 91st Bomb Group:

'Having failed to get selected for pilot training I came overseas as a mechanic. There was a shortage of gunners on our base and I had the opportunity to volunteer for this duty after gunnery school in England. I was assigned to operate the ball turret. Scared me to death the first time I had to enter one during flight. When the hatch was opened up in the fuselage and you climbed in, there was nothing below but Plexiglas between you and the ground. Real eerie. Once I knew it was safe and got the feel, I didn't wish to fly in any other position. The only worrying thing, there was no room to wear a parachute in the turret or take it in with you. A very small man could wear a chest chute unhooked on one side, but it was bothersome. The turret's K-4 reflector sight was the best on the B-17 and no other gun position could be turned through 360 degrees in azimuth and 180 in depression, all with a clear field of fire. My problem at first was knowing in what direction I was facing relative to the aircraft's flight, unless I could see other planes in the formation. Pretty soon I learned that there was air pressure on my legs through the trace link chutes for each gun. When the air pressure was on the left leg the turret was swung to the left and when on the right leg the turret was thataway. It was snug – if your electric suit worked okay – and the only personal problem was urinating. I took condoms to fill. Apprehension about getting out if ever the plane was hit was always my major concern. I reckoned it would take a good half minute to swing the turret into position so that I could open the hatch, disconnect my straps and climb into the fuselage to get my chute. When it happened for real I didn't get a chance to bail out as we were too low and finally crashed in a field near Munster.'

The mass firepower of a bomber formation brought another hazard which was not uncommon during extensive air battles. Earl Wilkinson of the same group recorded this in his diary:

'April 29, 1944 . . . After landing and looking the ship over we found that the holes were caused by two .50-calibre slugs from another formation. Some dumb gunner had hit our ship while tracking the Me 109s as they came through the formation. When the two bullets hit the left trim tab it caused the left flap to drop down and our ship to go straight up. The bullets went through the fuselage, passed through a main spar and just missed our Tokyo Tanks. Getting shot up by our own planes gives us something else to worry about besides flak, 20mms, propeller wash, fog, mechanical failure of engines on take-off, frostbite, anoxia, mid-air explosions and collisions.'

Inevitably, stray shots led to more serious consequences. John Howland in his diary entry for 20 February 1944:

'Our spirits were high as we returned to the base and landed, but the red flares being shot from a ship in front of us indicated "wounded on board" and he was requesting an ambulance. Our hardpan was right next to them and we walked over to see what had happened. The top turret gunner was dead. The top of his head had been blown off. But it wasn't enemy action that killed him. A careless gunner in our Wing had accidentally fired a round, probably while clearing his guns. The .50-calibre bullet caught him right in the forehead.'

The fighter pilot's contact with the enemy was even more fleeting than that of bomber crews. Rarely was fighter–fighter combat a prolonged twisting and turning dogfight. The majority of combats involved a single pass and the successful were those where the victim did not see his attacker coming, or was too late to evade. If seen in time, the chances were that you would live to fight another day. Sharp eyes and quick thinking saved Cary Salter of the 354th Fighter Group:

'My assigned P-51 was unusual in that instead of having a letter of our alphabet as an individual identification it had the Greek letter π. Certainly the only one in our 354th Group and probably in the whole 9th Air Force. I named this Mustang "Charlotte's Chariot" for my wife. On April 16th 1945 I was flying it as No 4 man in one of two four-plane flights on patrol ahead of our ground forces in Germany. We were at around 13,000 feet when we saw several Fw 190s below us and rolled over to the right to go down on them. I had just started my turn to follow my element leader when I saw two 190s above and to the front of our original heading coming down on us. I quickly pulled back to the left and brought the nose up to face the attack head on. Here I made the mistake of firing too soon and also right at the first 190 instead of slightly above. I saw my tracers falling just under him and tried to pull the nose up more, but he had already pulled up and I guess must have passed right over me. I could not follow as I would have had to loop and did not have the speed to do this. So I pushed back down with the intention of firing at the second plane. This 190 had rolled over on its back and was evidently firing at me because a 20mm shell exploded on the upper leading edge of my right wing just where the landing gear pivots. My earlier loss of speed and the resulting hole in the wing caused the Mustang to snap over and head straight down. I'd stalled, for a fleeting glance showed the IAS down below 90mph. I let the airspeed pick up to around 125 and pulled out level.

'An Fw 190 passed in front of me from left to right and I instinctively fired at him although there was little chance of a hit. All this had happened in just a few seconds. Taking a look at the hole in the wing, I decided my plane was in no condition to be in an air fight and headed for home. The pieces of wing skin pushed up by the slipstream took 50–60mph off my airspeed at the usual settings. The gauge was only registering 185 instead of the normal 240–250mph. On reaching our base at Mainz I realized I had lost hydraulic pressure – a line must have been cut – and knew there would be no flaps and wondered if the gear would lower. The wheels extended when the handle was put down and I kicked right and left rudder hard to try and lock them into position. The guys in the tower said the gear looked okay so I came in as slow as I dared. At first it seemed the main gear was holding then, as I dropped the tailwheel, the right main leg started to fold, letting the right wing tip and prop hit the ground, bouncing me fairly gently off the right side of the runway. I hadn't been shot down but that German pilot's shooting had put another P-51 on the junk heap just the same. In the fight I was the only P-51 hit and the other seven pilots claimed a total of 13 Focke-Wulfs. For me there was the consolation that if I hadn't turned back into the two coming at my element leader and myself we would probably have both been clobbered.'

Most fighter pilots would agree with the observations of Royal Frey:

'When you had pulled in position behind an enemy aircraft ready to fire it was the most exhilarating of experiences. It was impersonal; you were intent on clobbering the plane; you didn't consider the guy inside. When the position was reversed it became a highly personal situation, sheer terror. I've been both places. My conditioning came on January 5th 1944. Our Group, the 20th, was to pick up the bombers near Kiel and cover them over the target. We arrived early and, as there were no bombers to be seen, started a wide turn. Lt French, flying No 4 (I was No 2) in our flight, called in that he was having engine trouble, whereupon our flight leader turned us west toward England. I happened to glance up and see two lines of aircraft approaching high from the west and called over the radio that the P-51s had arrived. Because I always came out top in the aircraft recognition tests we had, the rest of the squadron pilots tended to rely on my assumed expertise (but never again after this episode). Our flight leader then turned east again and then north, and as I looked over to see how French was making out, the whole of his P-38 lit up with sparkles. He was being shot at! Swinging my head back I saw an Fw 190 sitting off his tail. The immediate reaction was to transfer my sight to my rear-view mirror and as I did, French appeared to stall out and go down trailing smoke. To my horror, framed in my mirror was a head-on image of a 190; I could even see the pilot's head he was so close. My reaction for self-preservation was to pull up right into a full power climbing turn just above stalling speed. As I did I saw tracers coming at me off to the left. Why the enemy pilot had delayed his fire I don't know, but that fraction of a second probably saved my life.

'I continued the tight right climbing turn and the 190 hung on behind briefly but then flipped off to the left due to torque. Other 190s followed and flipped over, while I continued my climbing spiral until, suddenly, at around 28,000 feet my P-38 also flipped over to the left and fell away. As I recovered, the Fw 190s seemed to jostle each other to get behind me. Once more I pulled my plane up into a climbing spiral and again it flipped out to the left when I reached 28,000 or 29,000 feet. What I did not know was that a rubber connection on the intercooler pipe to my left engine had ruptured and I wasn't pulling full power with that one and thus had problems of my own, not only with torque, but also with asymmetrical thrust. At first I had been frightened to near panic but in this chase my mood gradually changed to one of humiliation and anger, plus the determination that if they were going to get me I would try and take one with me by ramming it, if necessary. I was suddenly aware that another P-38 was in the melee as it came towards me, firing at one of the 190s as I was pulling out of my dive. Once more I attempted to out-climb my tormentors, only to flip out for the third time.

'When I recovered the sky was empty; as if by magic everyone had been made to disappear. I was all alone in the sky; I did not see another plane, friend or foe, anywhere! The combat must have continued for at least five minutes but I felt it had just been a matter of seconds. The funny thing about air combat was that everything seemed compressed in time.'

The image of the fighter pilot as a gung-ho, devil-may-care individual is not necessarily a true picture. In some respects the stress on this lone combatant was greater than with the occupants of a bomber flight deck. There was no sure answer to how an individual might react in combat, as Don Clark observed during an engagement between Messerschmitts and P-47s of the 362nd Fighter Group over France:

'We came up behind this Me 109 and I watched my element leader – I was flying wingman – just sit there behind this Jerry's tail. Kept waiting for him to fire but he didn't. Presently the 109 pilot must have looked in his rear-view mirror for he suddenly broke away hard to the left and we lost him. When we landed back on our strip I asked my element leader what happened, why didn't he fire. He just looked at me, shrugged his shoulders and said, "Don't know. Guess I just got buck fever." '

There was little room for hesitation in the fighter business. The successful fighter pilot had to have an aggressive streak. No qualms about his quarry. He understood it was a business of destroying or being destroyed. He was, above all, an opportunist and a good example is the following account from Walter Konantz, flying a 55th Fighter Group Mustang:

'On January 13th 1945, the 338th Fighter Squadron was circling Giebelstadt airdrome in preparation for strafing it – the second time in a week. I noticed a couple of planes taxying on the ground, then saw one take off. I watched him while he made a climbing 180-degree turn to the left, passing under me in the opposite direction. I did a tight 180 and got behind him. It was an Me 262 jet not yet accelerated to high speed. We had the new K-14 gyro sight installed a week previously and I'd never fired the guns with this sight. It worked perfectly and I clobbered him with over 40 strikes, setting his left engine on fire. He made no evasive action whatsoever, even after the first hit. He then spiraled into the ground and exploded.

'Since I still had some ammo left, I picked out a parked Ju 88 and started a strafing pass. Just as I got in range of my target I saw that it was a burned-out hulk from our previous strafing visit, so did not fire. However, the hornet's nest was stirred up and light flak was coming up from everywhere. A single 30-calibre bullet smashed through from the left, cut a groove in the sleeve of my jacket and then hit the radio control box on the right side of the cockpit.

'When I climbed away not another P-51 was to be seen. My radio was inoperative because of damage to the control box so I was unable to call for a DF steer back to England above the undercast. Luckily I found a lone P-47, joined up with him, signalling by hand that my radio was out and that I wanted to land with him. He took me to St Trond, Belgium, where I spent the night, returning to England next day. Meanwhile, back at home base my barracks mates had assumed the fiery crash at Giebelstadt was me and were in the process of dividing my personal belongings as I walked in the door.'

The foregoing highlights the dangers of ground strafing where a single rifle bullet could spell demise. In the last year of hostilities the majority of fighter losses were to enemy fire while engaged in ground-attack. Strafing fighters became a very effective offensive weapon, especially against road and rail transport, and were feared and detested by both military and civilian travellers in enemy-held territory. Walter Konantz again:

'On February 21st 1945 I was leading Blue Flight on a target of opportunity search after departing the homeward-bound bombers. I had already clobbered four locomotives when I spotted a German soldier zooming down the road on a motorcycle. I maneuvered into a position to come down the road behind him for a strafing pass. The rider, spotting me, constantly looked back over his shoulder to see where I was. He also appeared to have opened the motorcycle up to top speed. Turning around to look at the wrong time, when approaching a curve, he simply went straight off the road through bushes and small trees, then end over end off a 30-foot embankment. Doubt if he survived. I never fired a shot so I guess you could say I scared him to death.'

18
Members of a Crew

Fighter pilots of a squadron were dependent upon one another in combat but there was never the close camaraderie that developed between the members of individual bomber crews. The reason for this is made clear by B-17 flight engineer Robert Custer:

'I was only 20 years of age and the main thing was to stay alive and do our job. My crew was from ten different US states; two fellows were Catholic and one a Mormon. We got along good and trusted each other with our lives. Pilot Harold Miller was one of the coolest men that I ever knew and deserves a lot of credit for getting us through our missions. I survived 34 sorties, three to Berlin, three to Munich and two each to Leipzig, Hamburg, Bremen, Koblenz, Frankfurt and Warsaw.'

There was a certain feeling of security to be had from being a member of a crew that worked well together. In such circumstances no one wanted to be separated from his crew and some individuals, like George Rich, went to great lengths to ensure that they were not:

'I was the top turret gunner for the Dempewolf crew. We had already received our orders to ship out overseas. However, my ankle had developed a boil and the swelling was considerable. I did not want anyone to know it for fear that I might be hospitalized. The night prior to our leaving, the inevitable happened – I couldn't walk on the infected leg. My crew members had to literally force me to the hospital by carrying me and left for overseas without me.

'When the doctors had taken care of the infection, I reported to the CO's office. They really didn't know what to do with me as they didn't know exactly where the Dempewolf crew was – much less how to get me there.

'At the time I was only about 250 miles from home – so I requested a weekend pass until a decision could be reached. The CO said only the Flight Surgeon could give me a pass because I was on orders to ship out – so I went to see him.

'He said he couldn't issue me a pass. However, I reminded him that he was reponsible for my mental condition as well as my physical condition – which he had already taken care of – and if I had to roam around this airfield for the weekend – being only 250 miles from home – I would go NUTS!!! With this explanation he gave me a pass and told me to report to him personally upon my return.

'When I arrived back at the base – September 5th – I enquired as to what I was to do. The Flight Surgeon handed me a copy of the orders given to the Dempewolf crew. He said go, find your crew. I replied how? Where are they? With a rather wry smile he said, "They are in England somewhere. If you were smart enough to get a pass out of me while on shipping orders you will be smart enough to find them. There are a lot of planes leaving for England. Go find one!" I packed my B-4 bag, stuck my orders in my pocket, and went down to the flight line.

'Every time someone would come along with a packed bag, I would enquire as to their destination. Finally some fellows ferrying a C-47 said they could get me to Scotland. We flew to Newfoundland, got snowed in at Greenland for several days, and then Iceland.

'Upon arrival in Scotland we parted company and I continued my hitch-hiking to England. People along the way were most accommodating. In the evening I would search for a military base or hospital. Finally, after roaming about England for several days, a CO at one of the installations suggested I go to General Doolittle's headquarters. They arranged the transportation and there they located Dempewolf's crew, with the 453rd Bomb Group at Old Buckenham. The General's adjutant even arranged to have a box lunch prepared for me and had me transported to the railroad station.

'When I reached "Ole Buck" and reported to the Officer of the day, he informed me that the Dempewolf crew had not returned from a mission. I was stunned to hear this after hitch-hiking 3,000 miles to join them. Happily the crew hadn't gone down, but showed up that evening after surviving a mid-air collision.'

Often the comradeship was such that crew members were protective of one another, should there be trouble with the unit or base authorities. They would also cover for an individual's misfortune, as in Harland Little's crew:

'When our crew was formed, Corporal Emory "Hap" Arnold was assigned as the ball turret gunner. If the authorities had taken a look at Hap they would have known he was no way going to get into a ball turret. He was a really big broad-shouldered guy. Lt Hipple, our pilot, re-assigned him to waist gunner. From the very first training flight until the last ride home in 1945, he got air-sick every time we flew. The other enlisted men covered for him even on combat flights. He was also assigned extra duty as one of the Group's aerial photographers to take pictures on combat missions. Corporal Weiss, the tail gunner, would take them for Hap, for all Hap ever saw was the bottom of an ammo' can. We always got a big laugh when the officers in HQ complimented him for his great pictures. We never gave him away.'

Flying with strange crews was anathema to most men and where possible was resisted. Apart from fill-ins brought about by illness and incapacitation, the experienced were often detached to be despatched with novices. Earl Williamson's diary entry for Friday, 24 March 1944 indicates why the latter duty was particularly unpopular:

'The schedule was so arranged that I was to fly with a new crew – an idea that I contested bitterly, with no results. According to the Operations Captain they needed at least one experienced man to help in case of oxygen failures and other difficulties that the new boys might not pick up. I laughed sarcastically at his explanation but it did no good. I told the Captain it was hard enough to finish 25 missions with your own crew, but when you have to complete 30 with mixed crews it's rough.

'We got to the ship, put our guns in and began to check everything. I found that the engineer hadn't even checked out an extra parachute. We finally got another and then I saw the ball turret man stripping his gun and wiping all the oil off. I told him to leave that oil on there – he might wish he had. After all it isn't one man's life, it's ten and those guns are the most important thing on a ship when engaged by the enemy. As I had feared, I was in for a day of that sort of thing. We took off, formed over the base at 18,000 feet and started on our journey. Everything went well until we got halfway across the Channel and began to test-fire our guns. All worked except those in the tail, the most important. I was half scared and angry – I had my ideas about any gunner who couldn't get either of his guns to work from the start. I asked him on interphone what he thought was wrong and he gave me several unthoughtful answers. First he suggested the guns were frozen. I told him that couldn't be because I had flown with temperatures nearly 60 degrees below and my guns had never frozen. And this day it was only 30 degrees below. Then he said he thought the firing pin was broken. He hadn't yet fired a round so I told him to forget that idea. After more discussion I told him to loosen the headspace on the guns. He did and the right gun worked. This helped considerably as one gun would be enough to get by. A hundred things could have been wrong with those guns. And then too, working at altitude with that monotonous oxygen mask, the heavy flak suit in such a small space, while trying not to pull out the two interphone wires and the heated suit cord was no picnic.

'A little while later the bombardier made his regular oxygen check over the interphone but there was no answer from the tail gunner. I unplugged all my cords, got a portable walk-around oxygen bottle and started back towards the tail to see what was wrong. Either his interphone cable plugs had become disconnected or, worse, his oxygen line, and he might be unconscious from anoxia. The first thought was right and I soon had him plugged in again before crawling back to my position.

'When we were about 25 miles inside France, I noticed No 1 engine was smoking and notified the pilot on the interphone. He continued to have trouble with it and eventually feathered the prop and turned out of formation back towards home. The bombs were dropped at the French coast but then the bomb bay doors would not close. They can be cranked up by hand but before this is done, it is advisable that the fuse be removed from the electrical motor that normally closes the doors in case it suddenly starts and injures the man hand-cranking. The fuse is located back in the fuselage near the tail turret and the engineer came back to take it out. He got the plate off the fuse box but he couldn't get the fuse out. Luckily I had a pair of pliers so I got another walk-around bottle and went to help him. He removed the fuse and I told him I would put it back after he had cranked the doors up and thus save him another trip. Everything then went all right until we reached our base and prepared to land. When we were on final approach I noticed the ball turret man still trying to crank his turret around. I asked him if he had the guns up in the landing position and he said he hadn't time to crank them up. There we were about to land on three engines and the ball turret guns still sticking straight down where they would strike the runway. He wasn't going to do anything about it. So I ran to the waist, plugged into the interphone and told the pilot not to land. The pilot abandoned his approach and pulled up to go around again – not a desirable situation on three engines. We got the guns up and next time the pilot made a good landing. Gosh, I was glad that trip was over but we didn't get a mission credited.'

That a man faced a greater risk when flying with a crew other than his own was probably exaggerated, but the order to do so was viewed with foreboding by many. Richard Boucher, a 445th Bomb Group pilot, tells of an instance when such apprehension was justified:

'There were people who made their own luck. My original tail gunner, John Goan, was one. Our crew wasn't scheduled to fly but they needed a fill-in tail gunner for another crew and picked John. No one was happy about flying with another crew and John was no exception. He had a feeling things were not going to go well. He approached me and asked if he could use my back-pack parachute. At this date only pilots of B-24s were being issued with this type which was incorporated into the rear of the harness. The rest of the crew were issued chest packs which could be quickly clipped onto the harness. The tail gunner did not have room in his turret to stow a chest pack and it had to be left outside in the fuselage. If there was an emergency it might take vital seconds to turn the turret to a position where the tail gunner could climb out and clip on the chute. I readily agreed to John's request and he took my back pack on this mission. His apprehension proved justified. The B-24 took a direct hit in the fuselage and broke in half. John was temporarily stunned and when he came round he was still in his turret and the rear of the plane was tumbling end over end. If he had had a chest pack it would have probably gotten thrown out when the fuselage broke. He managed to get free and open his chute, but a heavy landing knocked him out again. He was revived by a French woman throwing wine in his face. The Maquis underground fighters took him in and he stayed with them until liberated.'

There were, however, some men who actually looked to fly with other crews to increase their tally of missions. Al Jones:

'Our crew was a very close-knit group. We got along swell and tried to look out for each other, officers or e.m's. Our pilot had flown a mission with another crew prior to taking his own crew into combat so he was one ahead of the rest of us. We all wanted to finish up our tour together so each individual looked to pick up an extra mission flying with another crew. We four officers of the Henry crew took a 48 pass to London together and while walking down a street were nothing short of astonished to meet our tail gunner Ed walking towards us in his flying clothes with his 'chute tucked under his arm. Unbeknown to us, while we were away from base, he had taken an opportunity to fly a mission with another crew who were short of a tail gunner. The B-24 was shot down over Holland and Ed had to jump, luckily to an area taken by the British. When we met him he was on his way to the rail station to go back to base.'

It would be wrong to imply that crew camaraderie was not without its detractors in the heat of battle, as Milton Lipa discovered:

'The January 11 1944 mission was one of the hardest my group ever undertook. Coming off target things began to get really rough, we were under heavy fighter attack and a lot of Forts had been hit and were going down. I decided it was time to put my chute on and reached down to pick it up, only to find it wasn't there. A nasty feeling to realize I'd left it in the Communications shack back at Deenethorpe. I called the tail gunner on the intercom, an Irishman and former prize-fighter. "Malloy, you're the biggest guy on the crew and if we have to jump you're gonna have company. I haven't got a 'chute. You'll have to give me a piggyback." The reply was, "Like hell. This is going to be all for one and everybody for me, you damn Czech." Our plane came through, but I was a very worried guy for the rest of that mission. Didn't look as if anyone was going to give me a helping hand if the worst had happened.'

The failure or carelessness of one crewman was not always easily forgiven by his buddies. The team spirit of a crew could be disrupted by the errant activities of one member, and if this was brought to the attention of the unit's CO the individual concerned was replaced. If such antagonisms went unrecognized, extreme situations could arise, like that encountered by John Kirkpatrick:

'After my first tour was over I decided to stay in England and fly another one. This decision was slightly ill-conceived because instead of being assigned to a regular crew they used me to fly as a gunner on any crew that was one man short. I soon learned that some of these new crews did little to instil confidence. There seemed to be more than the usual abundance of foul-ups; errors of judgment in all crew positions were frequent and there was little mutual confidence among the crews.

'One morning I was scheduled to fly ball with a crew who were noted for frequently "aborting" when the target was a tough one. I suspected the pilot might have chickenitis or two left feet. As I prepared my turret, the co-pilot, a total stranger to me, walked up and astounded me with the following proposition: "You know we're going to Munich and it's liable to be a bad one and neither you or I want to fly with this pilot. For instance, when you get into the ball you might just accidentally smash the gun sight or break off the intercom wires with your foot. In that case we'd have to turn around and come back." I replied that I had been doing my job for some time, was extremely careful and was damn sure that no such damage would ever take place. He turned and indignantly walked off.

'What should I do? I honestly didn't know how to handle this situation. To suggest sabotage to any aircrew member, stranger or not, was cowardly and unacceptable. If I went to the squadron CO or the group CO, it was going to be my word against the co-pilot's. Finally I decided to say nothing but the incident troubled me more than a little during the mission and I was extremely happy to feel us settle onto the runway when we returned. That was one crew I made sure I never flew with again and I've thought about that SOB co-pilot many times over the years.'

There is some evidence that lead crews (those selected to lead formations) were more likely to have disgruntled members. Composed of the talented, an individual had higher expectations of those who flew with him than would be found on a regular crew. Frequently lead crews had supplementary specialists or air commanders assigned to fly with them whose expertise was not up to the standard expected in lead crews. This is evident in the following entry from John Howland's diary:

'At interrogation I was chewed out for not recording "bombs away" time and also for not noting the time we passed that airfield in Holland. However, by this time I just didn't give a damn. I was disgusted with lead teams that couldn't lead properly and lead navigators who couldn't follow navigation instructions. I failed to see why the S-2 interrogation officers were so concerned about "bombs away" time and an airport in Holland that had probably been photographed a hundred times by reconnaissance planes; and no interest at all in the poor performance of the lead team who, against instructions, led us through the concentrated flak areas of "Happy Valley". I was also disgusted with frustrated co-pilots who couldn't run a decent oxygen check and knew less about SOP let-down procedures than the navigator.'

At one period, before radar bombing became generally available, radar lead crews would be located at specific pathfinder force (PFF) bases and despatched as required to groups assigned to head task forces. That PFF lead crews were not popular is highlighted by John Howland's diary for 18 and 19 May 1944 when his crew was to lead the 381st Bomb Group with whom he had originally served:

'Our preliminary briefing in the evening was for Berlin. We landed at Ridgewell about 0030 and got two hours' sleep before breakfast. But who can sleep under such conditions? In addition, our reception at breakfast is becoming a depressing ritual. When we walk in through the door of the mess hall there is an audible groan as the men recognize the PFF team members and realize, for the first time, that the scheduled mission will be a Deep Penetration. Old friends and acquaintances that we lived with and flew alongside just two months ago now shun us like we have the plague. There is no compassion in their voices and no consideration that under Plan A Deep Penetration or a Plan B Milk Run to occupied territory, they get to go on the Milk Runs, but we don't. I try to tell myself that it is nothing personal; but it is hard to get a lift when the greeting is: "Here come those Poor Fuckin' Flyboys. Why don't you PFF guys stay home in Bassingbourn?" '

Undoubtedly some units were more efficient or had more pleasant regimes than others, but only a man re-assigned might become aware of this. Wayne DeCou was a Liberator pilot who felt unhappy about many aspects of one of the three groups he served with:

'I flew nine missions with the 489th Bomb Group. When in October 1944 this outfit was selected to go back to the States to convert to B-29s and take on the Japs, my crew was broken up and I was sent with a make-up crew to another B-24 outfit to complete my tour. Despite our experience we were seemingly treated like a rookie crew and outsiders by the new group. On two-thirds of the 24 missions flown with them we were the low left plane in the squadron formation, the most vulnerable position to fighter attack, generally referred to as "coffin corner". It was here on one mission we were shot up by an Me 262 jet. My feelings towards this group were not good for several reasons. With one or two exceptions, I was never happy with the leadership. The take-off and landing procedures were poor and the attempts to make them better, ridiculous. They devised a plan that would have had B-24s landing ten seconds apart. Happily, there weren't too many pilots stupid enough to get that close to the previous plane.

'On one occasion we were ordered to fly a mission in a beat-up, war-weary B-24. We lost one engine and then another through oil starvation and after throwing out all loose equipment just managed to keep going long enough to make it back to base. The engineering people must have known about the condition of those engines and the way they drank oil. The plane should never have been scheduled for a mission in that condition. Just one more incident that reinforced my feeling that there was a "couldn't care less" attitude with a lot of the people in this group.'

19
Fear and Fortitude

'The fear of loss of reputation and pride, letting someone down, was much greater than the fear of death. A bomber crew was a team and I think we all worried that we might be the man who let his pals down.'

These words of 96th Bomb Group gunner John Kirkpatrick would probably be endorsed by the vast majority of those who flew combat in the USAAF. One hid personal fear of death or injury, for the greater fear was letting the team down. The burden of combat was greater on some than others and each man had a way of dealing with the strain. Walter Bergstrom of the 351st Bomb Group found solace in solitude:

'Ashton Woods with its singing birds and butterflies and the large canopy of oak trees offered a sanctuary and place of comfort after a rough mission. I could return from combat and lose myself in the sanctuary of these woods. There I could let down, sob if necessary, without fear of losing that veil of "bravado" that a man was supposed to maintain. The birds of Ashton Wold could care less, they would scold but not criticize.'

For many, if not most, the hours before take-off were a difficult time. Navigator John Greenwood:

'For me the worst part of any mission was after being woken by the CQ, the knock on the door and the light from his flashlight. It immediately hit me with a sinking feeling that stayed through breakfast and briefing. This apprehension was engendered by the unknown dangers that lay ahead. Once in the air, that passed, there was work to do and one became resigned to whatever fate had in store that day.'

Bob Doherty, 96th Bomb Group radio-operator:

'Most of us smoked; it helped relieve tension. I know I smoked the most when we were in a situation when the weather conditions were in doubt and it was a case of are we gonna go or are they gonna scrub the mission. That was when you really became stressed.'

Tension and fears did not subside for everyone once a mission was on its way. P-47 pilot Bob Strobell:

'We were at combat altitude, well over 25,000ft, headed into France and crossing the flak belt along the coast. Bursts of 88mm shells suddenly appeared all around us. It probably caused all of us to do some elevated pulsing but one pilot was extremely frightened. His personal stress at this moment caused him to grip the throttle handle so tight that he unconsciously mashed the radio transmitter button, transmitting his rapid and labored breathing over the air. It sounded like an asthma attack; wheezing and gulping. We all listened for a few moments, feeling for the afflicted pilot, hoping he would realize what he had done. Finally it was more than some pilots could stand and though they knew the offender would be unable to hear them – as while you transmitted the receiver was automatically cut out – they mashed their transmitter buttons, shouting, "Get off the air," "Knock it off," and someone said, "Who's breathing?" Immediately a low, mischievous voice came on the air and said, "We all are!" I guess the quip certainly helped relieve the tension.'

Previous experience aggravated one's apprehension. Everett Shue, 386th Bomb Group turret gunner:

'On previous missions I had been on aircraft that had battle damage. I had also seen some of our aircraft shot down. One of them had a wing burnt off from an engine fire, which impressed me very much! It sure went into a tight spin. On this mission, just after we dropped the bombs and turned to head home, I saw what I thought was light smoke from the left engine. Just as I reported it the whole cloud of smoke caught fire. I did several things in rapid succession. I shouted over the intercom, "We're on fire!" I never waited for an acknowledgment but dropped out of the turret, snapped on my parachute pack and headed for the escape hatch. The waist gun was swung back out of the way and the tail gunner and waist gunner were looking at each other over the open hatch. I slapped the waist gunner on the fanny and yelled, "Jump, we're on fire!" He shook his head and yelled something that I never understood. I answered saying, "You follow, I'll go first!" and started out the hatch. They both grabbed me by the seat of my pants and pulled me back inside the aircraft and shouted, "The fire is out!" It finally got through to me what they were saying. I looked out, the engine was feathered, the gear was down, and there was no sign of fire or that there ever had been a fire. While I was looking the gear started to retract.

'It was the first time we had made a single-engine return home. When we got back and looked the plane over, we found only one hole in the aircraft. It was right by the exhaust stack and inside a bullet had cut through the pressure fuel line before it entered the carburettor. The smoke I had seen was vaporized fuel and when it ignited there was a heck of a lot of flame. No wonder I got excited. The aircraft was easily repaired and was ready for the next mission. As a result the crew also had more confidence in single-engine operation of the Martin B-26.'

Flight Engineer Irving Shapiro of the 94th Bomb Group quelled fears arising from his experience by seeking a practical solution:

'I was in my turret when a flak burst below our B-17 sent a shell fragment up under my seat where it was deflected by the metal superstructure and prevented a permanent case of haemorrhoids. The same burst caused a fire in the cockpit and I quickly attended to that with a fire-extinguisher without fuss or panic. The shock didn't catch up with me until the next mission. As soon as taking my place in the plane I found I was shaking; a subconscious fear allied to the narrow escape I'd had. The morning after we got back from that next trip I got up very early, went to the field, and collected one flak mat out of several B-17s and put them down on the floor of my engineer's compartment. That helped to overcome my anxiety about a hunk of flak coming up from below.'

As the largest proportion of splinters from an exploding flak shell blasted upwards, concern about the vulnerability of one's lower regions was justified. For some men it became a fixation; as Earl Trull, a 397th Bomb Group armament officer, observed:

'One of our pilots was having trouble with his B-26 flying tail heavy. On investigation he found the tail gunner had packed the floor of his compartment with filled sand-bags. Turned out this gunner had an obsessive terror of getting hit in his reproductive organs. I decided I could help him overcome this fear. Took the sheet of armor plate from a wrecked co-pilot seat and bolted it to the floor under the tail gunner's stool. The pilot said this had little effect on handling and the gunner's apprehension was soothed. Hear he produced a pretty large family after the war.'

Some men concealed fear with bravado, while a few seemed genuinely able to sublimate it with ease. The majority might control their fear but were not ashamed to admit it. Henry Heckman encountered an explicit example of this last:

'When the B-17s landed after having been attacked by fighters on the first mission our squadron participated in, we asked one of the tail gunners: "What was it like, Mac?" He held up both hands, with the tips of his fingers repeatedly opening and shutting, and said: "This is just the way those shells were coming, and that's just the same way my ass-hole was going!" '

However well a man might steel himself against combat fears, his constitution could be broken down by a harrowing experience. And fate often placed one individual in a succession of such incidents, as Harold Smith relates:

'Fate plays a strange part in the experiences of some flyers. A co-pilot named McMann from Florida had more than his share of tough luck. His first crew took off from Kimbolton in dense fog. The plane lost one engine as it climbed and then a second engine failed. The pilot bailed the entire crew out. They all cleared the B-17 and he followed. The crew landed in a row a few hundred yards apart and suddenly out of the fog came the plane, followed by the pilot. The crew screamed for him to watch out, but his back was turned to them and the plane and he drifted into the wreckage as it blew up. He was killed instantly. The co-pilot was assigned to another crew and one morning on a pre-dawn assembly over the field a flare inadvertently ignited the oxygen system of the plane. With the intense heat the pilot bailed out the crew. McMann said the heat was so intense he only managed to hook on one ring of his chest 'chute and thought he would be able to hook the other one on his way down. Unfortunately, as he left the plane through the bottom hatch, the slipstream took off his heavy flying boots and his civilian shoes. He said all the way down he attempted to hook the other ring but finally, when he realized he was very low, he pulled the ripcord. With only one ring holding he came down on an angle and bare-footed. He broke the bones in both feet and was hospitalized. He returned to the base after recuperating and said he had had enough and was going to request to be relieved of flying duty. We persuaded him to continue and he did. He was assigned to fly as a tail gunner in the lead plane to grade the formations.

'On his first mission, as the plane approached the field, he got out of his position in the tail but left his chest 'chute there. On the down-wind leg the pilot dropped a third flaps and as he did, fire came out of the number 3 engine. The waist gunners and the radio man jumped and were saved. McMann, who weighed about 180lb, ran to the tail position, grabbed his 'chute, pulled the escape hatch under the tail and got half way out when he got stuck. He could see flames coming back at him and he knew the only way to escape was to pull the ripcord, which he did. The 'chute opened and ripped him out of the plane. He almost broke his back, but he made one swing and went through the roof of a barracks. He went through up to his armpits. Mac went back to the hospital, but needless to say when he came back to the barracks no one dared ask him to fly again.'

Or again, Ken Kennard, 401st Bomb Group communications officer:

'Now and again you encountered men who were the victims of the most curious happenstance. There was a sergeant who enlisted and was accepted for flying duties, went through gunnery school and was assigned to one of our crews. We learned that in civilian life he had been in the merchant marine on coasters sailing up and down the Atlantic seaboard. Once he decided to jump ship in New York city, only to learn later that his vessel had been lost on its voyage, sunk by a U-boat with the loss of all the crew. Whether it was this knowledge that troubled him, no one knew, but he was a "goof off" in our organization. He sought to escape air duty on any pretext. He was the bane of the squadron flight surgeon's existence. Most times his tales of woe and reasons for being excused from flying duty were not accepted, but on one occasion they were, and he remained on the ground while his bomber crew went to their deaths. Another radio-operator/gunner had replaced him, the ship took off on a training flight on a fine day from Great Falls and blew up – a fuel leak being the suspected cause. This only unnerved the man more, but despite this he came overseas with our group.

'On one of the first missions he was flying the ball turret when the guns jammed. He left the turret and another member of the crew had to go down to clear the guns. While he was in the turret the B-17 collided with another and the ball turret was cut clean from the fuselage, killing the occupant. The sergeant who should have been there and wasn't became a virtual maniac after this incident and was permanently grounded.'

The men in the foregoing accounts endeavoured to carry on after the first traumatic experience. A very few fliers quit after perhaps the first or second taste of combat, like Stan Staples' co-pilot.

'On his first combat mission, when we flew as a complete crew, we had run into some flak. There were no hits or injuries but it was a bit unnerving. Right after we returned and landed at home base, the co-pilot hightailed it for the squadron CO's office, and told him he was not going to take any more, took off his wings and laid them on the CO's desk. He was gone from the squadron within a few hours. We never saw nor heard from him again.'

In other cases it was a gradual attrition, a mission by mission erosion of an individual's determination to control his fears. Lew Felstein, 96th Bomb Group:

'Some aircrew members had emotional and mental problems. It was hard to tell how individuals were dealing with the stresses of combat. Our crew had a tail gunner, an ex-coal miner. He was a pretty tough character and when he drank he would take a punch at anyone that disturbed him. Generally tail gunners see the fighters going away after frontal attacks, but on the Flensburg mission in May of 1943 we had attacks from the rear. For the first time he faced the blinking of 20mm cannons firing at him. On a couple of missions later our radio-operator came to me and said there was something wrong with our tail gunner. He was lying in his bunk absolutely rigid and when I rapped my knuckles on his forearm it sounded much like I was pounding on wood. I think the medical term for this condition is catatonic. He was removed from the crew and reduced in rank to private and given menial duties in the squadron. He took this situation very well and seemed happy to be grounded. He should never have been assigned to an aircrew as he just was not psychologically equipped for flight duty.

'Our left waist gunner was the type who did not seem to show any emotion whatsoever. He was a good gunner and appeared to have no problems. On our fourteenth mission we had a lot of mechanical trouble and crash-landed at the unfinished airfield of Little Snoring. Our pilot had ordered all the men in the rear to brace themselves in the radio room for this landing, but this gunner either did not hear the order or disregarded it and remained by his gun. When we hit he was knocked down and a full box of ammunition landed right alongside him. If it had hit him in the chest or head it would have killed him. He was obviously disturbed when he came up to me while I was checking equipment and said he would not fly any more. I asked him why he was quitting now after all we had been through and he answered that he did not think we were going to make it through our missions. I found out later from other crew members that he had said he did not think any of us were going to come out alive. He too was reduced to private and put on menial duties but, unlike our tail gunner, he could not endure the disgrace of everyone knowing he had quit. He subsequently begged us to take him back on the crew but we had filled his position. He completed his tour as a stand-in gunner as needed on other crews.

'So you can see people reacted differently to the demands of the kind of aerial fighting we were engaged in at that time. One could not tell what was really happening inside a person.'

Such was the supposed stigma of being seen to be consumed by one's fear, a victim was not always apparent to fellow fliers. But sometimes there were clues. David Tallichet, 100th Bomb Group:

'Often it was hard to tell when a man could not take the strain of combat. There was a guy in my hut who did his job, joked with the rest of us and seemed fine. I had a skin infection on my left hand and on mission nights prior to going to bed I would put water in a helmet, warm it up on top of our pot-belly stove and soak my hand in it. Then wrap the hand in gauze, put on a silk glove and jump into bed to get a few hours' sleep, but the pain often kept me awake. The rest of the barracks would be asleep except for this fellow lying in the top bunk. In the dark I could see the red glow from his cigarette and it seemed every night he was unable to sleep. I realized that this guy had a problem. Sure enough after his twelfth mission he psyched out and was taken off combat.'

A man who broke was not good for other fliers' morale and hence the victim was quickly removed from the scene. The incident seen by Bob Doherty must have had a demoralizing effect on those who witnessed it:

'There was the odd guy who cracked up, couldn't take it. We were always anxious, wondering if this was the mission when we wouldn't be coming back, but you kept your fear under control. Right after briefing for a mission we gunners were outside climbing onto the 6 × 6 trucks which would take us to the planes, when there was a commotion among another crew. A waist gunner was refusing to climb into the truck; he'd broken down and was crying. The MPs came over and tried to force him to go but he resisted. Someone had sent for the man's pilot and when he arrived he raised holy hell with the MPs. He didn't have any time for the gunner but he wasn't going to fly with a guy who'd cracked up and might endanger the whole crew. They took the man away, to the hospital I guess, to see if they could straighten him out. There was a policy for the psychoanalysis of combat stress victims.'

Medical staff watched for any signs of extreme combat stress and would periodically send sufferers to rest homes for periods of a week or two. In cases of breakdown special psychiatric treatment was prescribed and in many cases the patients were successfully returned to combat. The medical decision on sending a man for hospitalization was usually straightforward. In the case recalled by Arthur Bryant of the 486th Bomb Group the cause of the doctor's diagnosis was unusual:

'Our Nissen hut was occupied by the officers from two crews. The other crew's aircraft crashed on take-off but fortunately the bombs were unarmed and the gasoline did not ignite. Everybody escaped, a little shocked but unharmed. Later that day one of the "gravel grippers" sent the co-pilot out to the wreck to retrieve the crew's parachutes, which the co-pilot had checked out and for which he was responsible. The experience of going back to the wrecked plane caused the co-pilot to become "Flak Happy"; he returned to our hut quite unable to speak. The pilot sent for the Flight Surgeon. When he came he observed the co-pilot and decided it was a case of delayed shock and that the man did not require hospitalization.

'As he was leaving our hut the doc noticed a small structure beside the co-pilot's cot and inquired what it was. He was told it was a model aircraft the man was building. The Flight Surgeon asked why it had no propeller and a long brass tube attached and was told that the co-pilot had said it wasn't going to have a propeller but would be powered by a jet of hot gas. This really puzzled the doc who remarked, "If he has been thinking an airplane can fly without a propeller, he's worse than I thought." With that it was arranged for the co-pilot to be hospitalized. I've often wondered when that Flight Surgeon first learned about jet propulsion.'

The chance of becoming a casualty varied considerably depending on the type of unit. For a heavy bomber crewman flying in the ETO there was only a 36 per cent chance of surviving the required tour of duty during the winter of 1943. A year later this had improved to a 66 per cent chance, even though a man was required to fly an additional ten missions to complete a tour. The loss rate of individual combat units varied considerably, but few men were aware of exactly what this was. Roger Armstrong of the 91st Bomb Group had an inquisitive nature:

'One day I walked down to Operations for something to do, as we had not been flying for two or three days due to weather. I looked over the various items on the bulletin board. I noted at that time the 8th Air Force was averaging 2 per cent losses per mission. It did not look too bad until I started adding up 2 per cent on a daily basis. That way it looked like the 8th was losing all the planes about every 60 days until I thought about all of the bad weather and the days that the Groups did not fly. At least things were not so bad as they had been during our Group's first year of combat. From November 1942 to November 1943, 41 per cent of its combat personnel were missing in action and only 32 per cent completed their tours.'

Earl Williamson of the 323rd Bomb Squadron in the same group was not aware of the percentage rate, but the facts recorded in his diary after some six months of operations show that he was well aware of the high attrition:

'When we came to this base during the latter part of December 1943 there were eleven replacement crews altogether, a complement of 110 men. As things stand, we are the only crew left out of the eleven and three members of our original crew are war prisoners as a result of flying with other crews. Of course, there are two or three men who were in the eleven who were grounded at different times and have been lucky enough to finish. We sleep in bays and at one time I saw a whole bay get wiped out with the exception of two men on the end. Once eight crews from our squadron went down over a period of eleven days, leaving the outfit with only twelve crews and a few spare fliers.'

The scale of losses was evident to parents, wives and relations back home through newspapers and radio broadcasts. In letters each combatant chose ways to lessen the concern of loved ones. At one extreme some made no mention of combat, while at the other little was hidden. William E. Smith, a 392nd pilot, believed his parents should learn of the missions he flew, although in the following letters describing the crossing of the Rhine and prior events he conveys a decided air of confidence that must have been reassuring to the readers:

'Dear Folks: Well, a lot of big stuff is in the wind. It will have happened by the time you get this, I think. What it is, I can only guess, but it is a new role for heavy bombers and I am going to get a shot at it tomorrow, for sure. I believe we will put up two missions tomorrow and they will definitely be different.

'Weather, as you no doubt can guess, is a lot better. It is often very sunny and I just eat that up.

'Went up today and checked the Auto-Pilot on a new ship and ended up buzzing the hell out of the countryside. It's a good way to get the steam off. Love, Bill.'

'Dear Folks: I wasn't wrong when I told you the heavies were going to do something different. Today we took supplies (gasoline, foodstuffs, medical supplies, mortar shells, etc) and dropped them by parachute from less than 500 feet. I guess Patton, or somebody, crossed the Rhine early this morning and a lot of glider troops, etc went in, and so the heavies took them supplies. We were never over 1,500 feet at any one time and, generally, less than 100 feet still flying a sort of formation. It was all fun at first. We were not bundled up nor on oxygen, just comfortable.

'We flew very low and crossed over the Cliffs of Dover (first time I've seen them) which, I might add, are very beautiful. In no time we were in France and damn, but that place is *ruined* plus. Terrific holes in the countryside, towns bombed and shelled out, pillboxes sitting all around the countryside. We flew up and down valleys and over and under the hills. The Frenchmen in the field stopped ploughing and would wave at us. We were really going along to beat all hell. It was most tiring as we were at a very low altitude and had to be careful, besides the air was very rough. As we got to the front, things on the ground were more unsettled and we could see more widespread destruction, field hospitals, etc. Also burnt-out towns, houses and woodlands. Even closer to the front we could see tanks and a lot more activity on the ground.

'We finally hit the big smoke screen and started seeing the ships coming back from the target. We really dropped down on the deck, then (if a haystack was in our way it got blown all to hell) in a minute or two we hit the Rhine and on the other side, fires, black smoke and utter confusion was all we could see. In a minute or more we saw a lot of parachutes on the ground in the trees and fields. Gliders were all over the place and most of them smashed up like little wooden matchboxes. We saw a little light artillery firing at us and we knew a lot of small-arms fire was being directed at us, for sure. In a second more we hit our dropping area or target. We released all the bundles and I yelled "bundles away" while the lads in the back kicked out their odd parcels. The most dangerous part of the trip was the very low turn away (and back into the wind) from the target (and German lines). It exposed much of our undersides and offered a slower target to shoot at. I kicked the old SOB in the ass and got even lower and got the hell out of there. I was really sweating. We passed right over a blown-up B-24 which was burning like mad, and a lot of small (20mm and 40mm) stuff was hitting us all over. We got spray on our propellers crossing the river again (almost).

'Then we came on home. When we got here two ships of the other two squadrons, which had gone in before us, had cracked up on two different runways. Both ships had extensive battle damage and had had to come down. We landed, counted quite a few nice holes (mostly from small-arms fire) and took a look at a friend of mine's ship who really got shot up. He had two direct hits by HE shells and had an engine knocked out and a hole in the fuselage a foot around. The navigator's chute stopped a .30 bullet which would have gotten him for sure. So ends my 19th mission. Gotta fly again tomorrow and then one week off to loaf (and fret and stew, in general). Love, Bill.'

Many of the survivors could look back to an occasion when because of some simple action, some minor happening, their lives were saved. Not untypical is James Knaub's experience:

'When I reported back for duty on November 4th after two weeks in the base hospital, the crew list for the next mission was already posted. It was the practice to stand down one squadron of the group every four missions and also to alternate specialists within each squadron lead crew. I was a lead radio-operator and it was my turn to fly on the next mission posting. But due to some reason the crew list was not changed after the November 5th mission – when my squadron didn't fly – and the other lead radio-operator flew on the 6th. The B-17 received a direct hit in the radio room from an 88mm shell and he was killed. It should have been me and I probably owe my life to some duty clerk's oversight. I wouldn't know how to describe my feelings at the time, but they were far from good.'

A feeling akin to guilt, because you were alive when another had died, was a natural reaction. Such instances remain large in veterans' memories, as did all those cruel twists of fate that were encountered. George Brumbaugh of the 95th Bomb Group:

'On March 14th 1945 the B-17G I was piloting was the tail-end Charlie, the lowest and rearmost position in the group formation and often reserved for new crews like ours. On the bomb run for Hanover railyards the enemy radar appeared to have locked onto us and one burst wrecked No 3 engine. The prop windmilled, broke the reduction casing and the engine was afire. A 12,000 feet dive put out the flames, only we were now alone with No 4 engine also giving trouble. Turning west, a pair of P-47s appeared to shepherd us to friendly territory. Suddenly we again received the attention of flak gunners and it looked as if we would have to bail out. The ball turret gunner was badly wounded while vacating his turret. By evasive action we managed to get away from the flak, but with the damage sustained it still looked like we would all have to jump over friendly territory.

'Shortly after crossing the lines my navigator spotted a steel mat fighter strip dead ahead. I called for third flaps, low prop pitch, high rpm on the two good engines and gear down. We shot off red-red flares to advise the airstrip tower we were in trouble and landing. At 1,000 feet only the left wheel was down, so I had to abandon the approach and go around again, holding 110mph indicated airspeed, in a shallow turn into the two good engines for a large slow circle. We made it down safely in spite of having a ruptured right tyre. I rolled the Fort to a stop off the right side of the runway so local fighter traffic could resume. The ball gunner was quickly removed to hospital while we marvelled that no one else had been hit. The plane looked like a strainer and was beyond economical repair.

'We went over to the mobile flying control tower to thank the operator. If he had not cleared all other traffic for us during our approach we might easily have crashed. He had also ordered the ambulance and crash truck to stand by. We were most grateful. As we walked away towards the Operations shack, thinking what a close call we had had, a fighter came in to land. For some reason the pilot lost control, shot off the runway and crashed into the control tower we had just left. We ran back but pilot, tower operator and his assistant were all dead. How fickle was fate.'

And there were those individuals who appeared to anticipate fate through some action or statement upon which others would later reflect. Forrest Clark of the 44th Bomb Group ponders on one such case:

'We had a gunner in our hut at Shipdham who was always playing Black Jack. He was known to us as Alabama. He would bet his pay almost every time. One night we had an unusually long game with much arguing and contention among the players. Alabama was frantically trying to win with each new hand but he always lost. Finally, about 3am, he let out a shout, jumped up and reached into his pocket to pull out his wallet. He fumbled about in it and, seeing that it was empty, he threw it down. "I won't be needing that any more," he cried, and stomped off to bed without so much as another word to anyone. Two days later he went down on his next mission. We never saw him again. I remember thinking, did he have some premonition of what was to happen to him?'

But the majority of the young combat airmen were sustained by the inherent belief that it always happened to the other guy; despite the obvious attrition and their natural fears, each believed he would survive. Such was the innate confidence with some men that they returned for a second and even a third tour. A few flew over 100 missions in bombers and others 200 in fighters and became legends in their units. Many who survived a tour in the ETO or MTO went on to 'have a crack at the Japs'. Of these, few can claim the experience of pilot Harry Carroll:

'I flew my first eleven missions out of Foggia, Italy, with the 97th Bomb Group. Then, in the spring of 1944, when they were trying to standardize procedures used by the 8th and 15th Air Forces, my crew was exchanged for one from England and we were assigned to the 381st Bomb Group at Ridgewell. After my 26th mission out of England they told me I'd done enough and sent me back to the States. Liked the idea of flying the new B-29s and after training I was sent to the 73rd Bomb Wing on Saipan in the Pacific. Made eight missions to Japan before the A-bomb brought things to an end. During my time in combat I'd flown bombing missions over all three Axis capitals – Rome, Berlin and Tokyo.'

20
The Planes They Flew

Few fliers were indifferent to the aircraft in which they went to war. Most had strong feelings about the worthiness of the machine to perform the task for which it was built. Those men who safely completed operational tours tended to look more and more favourably on the particular model they flew as the years passed; a natural reaction of loyalty to the plane that had seen you through. There was also an understandable rivalry between those who flew in different makes of aircraft employed for the same mission. Nowhere was this more marked than in the realm of the heavy bomber and the advocates of Fortresses and Liberators. The B-17 Fortress, the earlier design, important in the development of the US Army Air Corps' doctrine of high-altitude daylight precision bombing, received considerable media attention. For this reason the B-24 Liberator was somewhat overshadowed, despite having slightly greater capabilities. While each aircraft had its advantages and disadvantages, operationally there was little to choose between them when it came to crew survival. However, the crews of one type never lost an opportunity to indulge in sarcastic banter or some action to highlight the supposed shortcomings of the other type. Bill Garrett, 453rd Bomb Group:

'I was pilot of the B-24H "Squee-Gee", a great aircraft that never let us down in 35 missions. We loved the Liberator and delighted in showing the Fortress guys how disadvantaged they were. We were always eager to show them our greater speed and were not above fudging a bit to drive this point home. One technique when "slow timing" (checking engines and equipment) over England was to keep a close watch for B-17s engaged in similar activity. When we spotted one we tried to maneuver into position several thousand feet above and behind our intended victim. We then dove down to build our speed up to near redline (the warning line on the indicator), perhaps 270 IAS, and then levelled out behind the B-17 – which was probably only going at 150 IAS – at which time we would feather one engine and roar past at fighter speed. We reveled in what we assumed to be the amazement and consternation of the B-17 crew who watched us speed by with one engine feathered. There were some bold spirits among B-24 pilots who claimed to pull this prank with both props on one side feathered. That was really living!'

The partisan attitude that prevailed was best recognized by the derogatory jingles or ditties aired by the other side. Ben Slowthower, a 97th Bomb Group B-17 navigator at Amendola, Italy, recalls the following chorus sung to the tune of 'Strawberry Roan':

Oh that B-Twenty Four,
Oh that four-engined whore,
The man who gets in it will certainly lose

At fifty-five inches she won't even cruise.
Oh that B-Twenty Four.

However much confidence and affection men might have for their aircraft model, all would admit that there was considerable variation in the flight characteristics, performance and dependability of supposedly identical machines. Pilots were particularly sensitive to this; like Ralph Trout of the 401st Bomb Group:

'During WWII there were probably many outfits in the US air forces that had airplanes with built-in eccentricities not put there by the manufacturer. We had one such plane in the 401st Bomb Group at Deenethorpe air base. It was a B-17G and had been flown on many missions. It had no name so I shall refer to it by the last three digits of its serial number, '876.

'Joe Cromer, our crew pilot, and myself, had flown several combat missions when we first came into contact with old '876. We were ready for take-off and waiting for the green flare when the plane decided it was tired and all four engines shut down at the same time! Since we were number three in line for take-off, we rapidly went through the starting procedure and got the engines started again. We ran the magneto check and every other check in the check list. Nothing was amiss. The engines purred like kittens. We should have pulled off the taxi area and gone back to our hardstand, but the engines were doing great and we simply hated abortions. We had never had one. The green flare fired and we were ready to roll. Too late to change minds then. We took off and flew the entire mission without a murmur from the old bird.

'Upon return to base Joe told the crew chief about the morning happening. He shook his head and looked at Joe like he didn't believe a word he said. He did say he would check it out.

'A few days later we flew another mission in old '876. We were returning from the mission and letting down over England when Joe eased in a little left rudder and left aileron for a left turn. The plane made a gentle turn to the right! You have never seen such a perplexed look on a pilot's face. Joe did not mention this antic to the crew chief, lest the crew chief would think that Joe had lost his mind.

'A week passed and we found ourselves again flying old '876. We were at 25,000 feet, Joe was flying formation and jockeying the throttles. My gaze swept over the gauges as all good co-pilots are supposed to do. Number three cylinder head temperature was running high. I cracked the cowl flaps on number three. The cylinder head temperature dropped to normal and on down to below normal. The engine began to backfire. Joe looked at me as if to say, "What the hell have you screwed up now?" I closed the cowl flaps, and the engine kept on backfiring. Finally it quit backfiring. I looked at the cylinder head temperature gauge and it was still below normal. Several minutes later I looked at number three again and the cylinder head temperature was normal. When we landed Joe wrote it up in the Form 5. The crew chief said he would check it out.

'On our last encounter with old '876 we were returning from the mission and had arrived back at base. We were in the landing pattern on the downwind leg when Joe called for "gear down". I hit the landing gear switch and the wheels could be felt rumbling from the engine nacelles. I looked out and said, "I have a wheel." Joe looked out his side and said, "I have a wheel." I checked the instrument panel. There was no green light. Joe said, "Pull 'em up and try it again." I repeated the procedure and once again the wheels rumbled out of the engine nacelles. We both visually checked, the wheels were down, but there was no green light! I called the tower and told them we were coming by low and to check the gear. We did and they replied that the gear was down and looked good. Joe then had the Engineer go back and get the crank and try it manually. The Engineer came back shortly and reported the gear was down. We advised the tower we were coming in and the crash trucks and meat wagons came roaring out to the runway. We came in fast and Joe made an airline grease job landing. After taxying to the end of the runway and unlocking the tail wheel we pulled off on the taxi strip. The green light came on! Joe faithfully wrote the problem up in the Form 5 and discussed it with the crew chief. The crew chief looked at us as if he wished we were glider pilots. Since glider pilots never came back, we got the message.

'That night the crew chief jacked the plane up and spent hours running the gear up and down. The green light never failed to come on!

'After the war ended '876 was flown back to the States in Operation "Home Run". Joe and I often wondered what nerve-racking experiences the pilots had in crossing the Atlantic in that crate!'

Other bombers and fighters did not induce the same sort of rivalry that existed between the B-17 and the B-24 boys. There was nevertheless a general faith in the aircraft flown, an important factor in morale. The P-47 Thunderbolt is one notable example. Intended as a fighter interceptor, it did some of its most valuable work in the dangerous business of ground-attack. Don Clark, 362nd Fighter Group, reflects a confidence that was fairly general among Thunderbolt pilots:

'For the low-level job we had to do, where you couldn't keep out of the light flak and small-arms fire, there wasn't a better plane than the P-47. It would keep going with damage with which other types would have fallen out of the sky. I was lucky and only got shot up bad once. We were strafing a patch of woods in which there was supposed to be some Jerry armor. I was flying the CO's plane which suddenly started to shake and smoke. When I landed at base I found a string of holes about 2 inches apart that stopped just behind the cockpit armor plate. In a crash a pilot had a good chance of being able to walk away. The most extraordinary case I saw was when the group was flying out of Metz, taking off from a Pierced Steel Plate runway. One kid drifted too far to the side, went into the mud, flipped over and skidded along upside down with two 500-pound bombs riding along with him. We all thought the pilot had been killed, but when men got to the wreck they heard a voice call, "Hey, get this thing off of me." He just had a few scratches.'

Much of the confidence in your aircraft came from the work of good instructors. Indeed, the flying and technical training organizations in the ETO and MTO excelled in devising the best operational techniques, extracting that extra performance, then passing this know-how to newly arrived aircrew. A good example was the 495th Fighter Training Group, OTU for both 8th and 9th Air Forces, where Robert Strobell went through its course for replacement pilots:

'The base was equipped with P-47s and experienced instructors who had some combat experience. To me, the most impressive part of this training was the fact that the P-47 had far more capabilities than we were led to believe during our Stateside training. An example was the relationship between the turbo-supercharger, the manifold pressure and water injection, not to mention the engine rpm under varying conditions from sea-level to 35,000ft. In the States we were taught not to exceed the red lines on the instruments. In England we were taught to use much higher red lines and to ask the airplane to perform under maximum stress as a means of saving the airplane and ourselves if the need arose – and it did in combat. Slow engine rpms and high manifold pressure would keep the P-47 in the air much longer, using less fuel. It permitted me to fly back to England on several occasions, with so little gasoline left that on one landing the engine quit, out of gas. The difference was that here in England the flight safety record was a few points down the essentials list.'

In a few cases there was a loss of confidence in the aircraft model flown; not so much due to the aircraft itself, rather the manner of its employment. One was the Curtiss C-46 Commando, a cargo airliner adapted as a troop transport and committed to a combat environment. Sheldon Witt was one of the pilots of the Troop Carrier Group destined to discover the hard way the shortcomings of the type:

'Early in 1945 our group, the 313th, converted from C-47s – the DC-3 – to the C-46. The powerful Pratt & Whitney R-2800 engines were great but the fuselage set-up looked vulnerable if ever exposed to enemy fire. The flight control lines were hydraulic and we thought about what might happen if these were cut. Also, we found the deep fuselage and very large tail made handling difficult in cross-winds. The main advantage of the C-46 was that it could carry 34 fully equipped paratroopers and had loading doors on each side which allowed faster exits, whereas the C-47 took 24 paratroopers and had only one door.

'An evening before the big cross-Rhine assault on March 24th, Axis Sally came on the radio and said they would welcome a look at the 313th's new aircraft. This was a shocker to say the least, but we passed it off as propaganda. However, we decided to polish our shoes just in case we paid them an unexpected visit. Sally was right, their 20mm flak raised all kinds of hell for the C-46s. Our ship was shot down. Flak hit the hydraulic lines to the tail so we had no control and the right engine took fire.

'Our navigator was killed, two other crewmen sustained broken legs and the crew chief and I were captured by the Wehrmacht. They moved us back to a farmhouse but a little later a British patrol came along and got us out, taking the Germans prisoner. Back at our base, B-54 at Achiet, next day we found our squadron, the 48th, had only two of its eighteen C-46s flyable. The Group had sixteen aircraft shot down and another three were beyond repair. The experience of the 313th convinced high command the C-46 was not suitable for a combat situation. They took the C-46s away and we got our C-47s back.'

21
Those Who Maintained

For every man in the air there were some 20 on the ground in their air force of assignment. On combat airfields there were nine ground men to every fighter pilot and three or four to every bomber crewman. For the combat crews the most important were their ground crews on whose care and diligence their safety could depend. The risks of combat were high but flying in the mass-produced aircraft of the times was, in view of the large number of non-combat related accidents, quite dangerous. Mechanical malfunction could and did result in the loss of aircraft and often their crews. There was no room for sloppy maintenance and repairs. The ground crews literally held the lives of the flight crews in their hands. The skill and dedication of the average ground crew was of a high order and it was important that flight crews trusted them implicitly. Those who had doubts offended. Carl Gjelhaug of the 446th Bomb Group:

'I was 20 when sent over as a replacement to the 446th Bomb Group late in 1944 and found I was the youngest first pilot in the 707th Squadron. After our first five missions my crew was assigned to a Liberator named "Going My Way" which was looked after by a crew chief of around 30, just off the farm in Nebraska, who could fix anything. An old-timer when it came to experience for the job. He must have noticed me walking around the aircraft and seeing I was a little nervous checking on things before our first mission, he came over and said, "Lieutenant, there's one thing you don't have to worry about and that's the condition of this aircraft. It's been pre-flighted for you and always will be. You take my word on it." Somehow he seemed to bestow confidence and I agreed to put my trust in him. From that day on, until we finished our 25 missions, when we flew in that aircraft I never had to pre-flight it and never experienced any mechanical problem. At the end of the war we took him and the ground crew on a sightseeing tour of bombed-out Europe. He must have had confidence in me as well because we flew this B-24 back to the States with all our ground crew on board, another safe flight.'

It was a matter of pride with many ground crew chiefs that their particular charges suffered no mechanical or equipment failures that would cause a pilot to abort – turn back without completing the assigned mission. Many crew chiefs only left their aircraft in order to eat and sleep, devoting the rest of their time to administering to the demanding machine in their care. Such devotion did not go unobserved or unacknowledged by the fliers. Barky Hovsepian:

'There couldn't have been a more conscientious and dedicated crew chief than S/Sgt Haberer, the little fellow who looked after our B-24, "The Joker". He rarely went to his barracks and lived out on the field beside the airplane in a wooden hut he had made from old packing cases. It was fitted out with a stove which he fueled with the waste oil drained from aircraft engines. As far as I know he never went to the mess hall, either getting the other ground crew men to bring him food or he cooked his own. Never went to ablutions either by the look of him and the smell inside his shack. But he sure was good at his job and kept that B-24 in perfect order. The day after we flew our last mission we decided to take him to town. We took up a collection and purchased some toiletries for him. He didn't want to go so we held him down, shaved off the stubble he always seemed to have, washed him and got him to change his clothes. He gave up resisting and enjoyed himself.'

Although a ground crew had a limited role in repairs, they often undertook work which would have tested the skills of those in major depots. This was particularly so in North Africa before adequate support facilities were available. Jack Ilfrey tells this tale of the 1st Fighter Group:

'On December 2 1942 my P-38 got pretty badly shot up by Me 109s while flying on the deck on one engine. I only made it back thanks to the timely intervention of my flight commander and his wingman. The left fuselage boom had been pretty badly damaged and the repair crew had to replace it with another scavenged from a junked P-38. When they came to connect the control cables that passed through the boom to the tail, these wouldn't quite stretch enough to make connections, no matter how they tried. So they backed off and cut and spliced the cables so they would reach. The CO came by to inspect the plane and said to get Jack Ilfrey to test it. The crew told him they couldn't guarantee their splice job as it had been made under difficult conditions and without proper equipment. His response was to tell them not to worry as "that damn fool's going to kill himself anyway".

'Now I'm not told anything about this; not even to take it easy; just told to go ahead and make a test flight to see everything works okay. Off I go and start wringing the P-38 out over the field – rolls, loops, buzzing and all the rest. Everything's fine. The repair crew are down there watching with deep apprehension and mighty relieved when I put the fighter down safely. I'm still not told about the splice job and continued to fly the plane with no problems. I'm sure the ground crew made an inspection after that test flight and probably kept a regular eye on it – but a case of the less said the better when it came to telling the pilot. As for the CO's comment, I know I was one of his headaches but I think he knew that the repair people could be relied upon to do a good job. Didn't get to know about all this until 40 years later.'

On a combat station there were no set hours of work for a ground crew; it was a case of carrying on until the job was done. Tiredness and discomfort were the frequent lot of the ground crew. Gene Venezia of the 479th Fighter Group:

'When there was a lot of combat flying mechanics often got little sleep. The P-38s needed a lot of work and most of this was tedious. Ground crews were often up at three in the morning and out on the hardstands and flight line until near midnight when things were busy. We had an assistant crew chief, a curly-headed Jewish guy, pre-flighting a P-38 one morning for an early escort mission, engines going full out, when it suddenly started to creep forward, brakes locked on, just sliding slowly on the slush. The Lightning went across the hardstand and started chopping up a shack made out of belly tank packing cases. There were a couple of guys inside and they took off like startled rabbits. Luckily no one was hurt. The shack checked the plane but the engines were still going full out. I ran over, climbed up onto the back of the wing and went to the cockpit. Looking through the canopy I could see this guy's head pitched forward and I thought he was ill or dead. Releasing the hood and letting in cold air he suddenly springs to life. With the canopy closed he'd dropped off to sleep – it was warm in there and he was mighty fatigued and comfortable for a change.'

The inclement weather, particularly in winter, made conditions for servicing and engineering difficult, to say the least. To which were added such irritants as the like described by Robert Auger:

'Working on the planes out on the field was rough at most times but at night it was made more difficult because of the blackout. We were trying to change oil coolers for the engines one night and had a big cover over our heads to keep off the rain and to shield the beam from the dinky little flashlight we were using. We were about frozen stiff. Suddenly a Jeep comes roaring up and someone yells, "Put that goddam light out! We can see it from way across the field." So I shouted back, "How do you expect us to change these things if we can't see?"

' "Too bad," comes the reply, "just keep that light out." Then this MP roars off again, showing far more light from the beams of the Jeep headlights than our little flashlight. This sort of stupidity made you mad.'

The armament and ordnance men who loaded ammunition and bombs tended to do much of their work in darkness, almost exclusively so on bomber bases. Not unusual was the order to unload and return the bombs to the store or to replace with a different type of ordnance. The loading crews developed ways to lessen their labours akin to those described by Bob Bennett of the 861st Chemical Company:

'Planes which had aborted or been recalled on a previous mission and were still carrying bombs often had to have them removed. It could take five minutes or more to remove each bomb by the use of the crank assembly. Sometimes there would be about 44 100lb or 150lb bombs in a B-17 and there was no time at 2.30am to defuze, unload, reload and fuze the other bombs. We learned that we could cover our bomb trailers with the British biscuit bed mattress before moving them under the bomb bays. After removal of the fuzes, they were individually toggled off with the aircraft's release system, one bomb at a time. They would drop 4–8ft onto the soft mattresses and the fellows on the ground would roll them clear. We were doing this one night when the Safety Officer drove up in his Jeep. He didn't wait to chew us out, he put his foot down and the Jeep was gone.

'In another situation an untrained man was removing a plane load of anti-personnel (fragmentation cluster) bombs in broad daylight. They already had arming wires through the bands which held the six 20lb bombs per cluster. A temporary wire should have been threaded through the holes, but the arming wire had been pulled out too soon. The aluminum band came apart, at least one fully armed bomb struck, exploded, and 27 men were killed or maimed.

'One night I found one of my men fusing 44 Napalm 100lb bombs, surrounded by 2,800 gallons of high-test aviation gas all by the light of his Zippo lighter as his flashlight was dead!'

There were a number of bomb loading accidents which killed many of the handlers, in the majority of cases due to carelessness, a case of the old adage 'familiarity breeds contempt'. Human fallibility was a natural part of any scene, but with high-explosives and dangerous material, catastrophe was highly likely to result. Young men given duties they were not much interested in compounded the likelihood of such happenings. One of the most common causes of personal injury among ground men was falls, usually off aircraft. Another was road vehicle accidents. Edward Anthis discovered another killer, although happily not so in his case:

'In the States we have a two-wire electrical system, 110 watts, usually harmless. I found out about the British system the hard way soon after my outfit moved bases to Abbots Ripton or, as we soon called it, Rabbit's Rectum. We had to set up a new bomb-sight repair shop with the electrical plugs and sockets we needed. Some wise old sergeant said, "Be careful. You can touch this wire to this wire but don't touch that wire to that wire. Got it?" An inattentive 19-year-old, about 30 seconds later I sure got it: 220 volts when I touched the two wrong wires!'

The inventiveness of ground personnel was well known and a veritable flood of innovations were forthcoming from units in both ETO and MTO, many being adapted as standard by the USAAF. Most of these ideas were born of the necessity to overcome some shortcoming in equipment that was not highlighted until brought into general use. Harley Stroven, Armament Officer in the 486th Bomb Group, was confronted with one such problem:

'The nose and tail fuzes on every bomb had propeller-type vanes which, when the missile was dropped, were turned by air pressure to arm the fuzes so that the bomb exploded on impact. To prevent the vanes turning while the bomb was still on racks in the aircraft's bomb bay, they were secured by a springy wire looped through a ring clipped in a spring snap on a short cable attached to the bomb station. When the bomb was released the safety wires were pulled out as they were anchored to the aircraft, allowing the vanes to turn and arm the bomb as it fell. The wires remained on the rack but my ordnance sergeant was often reporting that the wires were missing, indicating that some bombs were being released unarmed. At first the thought was that our personnel were failing to hook the ring on the wires onto the snap but the frequency was far too often for that. I took a ring and snap and jiggled them about for a while, eventually discovering that if the springy wire caused the ring to lay in a certain position it could be pulled out of the snap without resistance. Obviously this was what was happening on missions.

'A solution would be to replace the spring snap with something from which the ring on the wires could not escape. I began looking round for something suitable and realized we had just the thing needed in the special securing cable for clustering incendiary bombs. This cable had a metal T-bar on one end which, when passed through the arming wire ring, became a fool-proof latch. Group Armament approved the idea and, using this device, we lost no more arming wires. A few weeks later Major Bornstein, our Group Armament Officer, asked me to go to a Divisional meeting which for some reason he could not attend. Neither I nor my driver had been to 3rd Division HQ before and got lost, consequently arriving late. The HQ was an ancient country mansion. I was ushered into a great room where the meeting was well underway and, not wishing to interrupt the proceedings by introducing myself, I sought a chair on the side and sat down.

'There came a point when the Division Armament Officer informed the gathering that Major Bornstein's group had licked the problem of lost arming wires which had troubled many units. He further instructed everyone to use the T-bar clustering cable in place of spring snaps to prevent loss of arming wires. I was elated and wanted so much to stand up and say to the assembly of Majors and Colonels around what was the largest table I'd ever seen in my life: "Hey you guys, did you know that was my idea?" I did not, of course, and so the meeting ended. I signed in for Bornstein and left. Even so, I had experienced, if only to myself, my place in the sun.'

22
Missing in Action

Total USAAF casualties for the ETO and MTO were 94,565, including dead, missing, wounded and prisoners. Aircraft losses for the two theatres of operations came to 25,022. Overall, one in four aircrew became casualties although chances were higher for those engaged in some types of operations than for others. Men in heavy bombers commanded an overall 32 per cent chance of becoming a casualty and, surprisingly, fighter pilots also suffered this same casualty rate, while the lowest casualty figure was in light and medium bombers at some 22 per cent. Of the total casualty figure, approximately 55,000 were fatalities. The casualty figures would have been higher if several thousand airmen in crippled aircraft had not been able to reach friendly territory, most to fight again. Bob Vickers of the 392nd Bomb Group:

'It was always going to happen to the other guy and when it doesn't you can't believe it's happening to you. Other members of the crew told me two engines were shot out, we're dropping out of formation, and over the radio another pilot reports a B-24 going down . . . and I still couldn't really take it in that it's ME. This situation brought a feeling of annoyed disbelief. We bailed out over liberated territory and came back to base to fly another day. Strangely, the event gave me a confidence I had not previously known. I was less apprehensive on missions from then on and completed our combat mission tour without further major misfortunes.'

The airmen who landed in liberated territory invariably received a warm and generous welcome from the local people, despite the deprivations of wartime. Such provided Arthur Fitch, 457th Bomb Group navigator, with his most memorable wartime experience:

'It was cold – it was dark! The date was January 10, 1945. It was England – it was wartime. We had been awakened about 5.00am and our crew had to report to the briefing room for orders for our first combat mission!

'I would say that I was nervous, apprehensive, excited and scared! Looking around at all of the men making up the bomber crews, getting ready to go to war five miles up over Germany, I suspected all were feeling varying degrees of the same emotions while trying to act as if we might be going for a short, enjoyable flight in our B-17 bombers.

'I thought we had a great crew. We had all originally met in Sioux City, Iowa, about four months earlier and gone through our transitional training in a professional manner, completing our requirements and developing a comfortable feeling with each other knowing that each person did his job well, and that we just had a great all-around team!

'After briefing I went to get my equipment. The parachute issued to me that morning, a back pack, did not seem to fit very well. I couldn't adjust the harness so I asked for, and received, another chute which seemed much more comfortable and easy to adjust. Along with an extra oxygen mask, I brought my GI shoes, which was a recommended procedure.

'We were closing in toward the target area and up until then I had not seen any enemy fighters and very little flak. The first trouble seemed to start when the left outboard engine (No 1) suddenly stopped. Shortly thereafter, No 3 engine stopped and we began to fall behind the formation.

'I stepped up on the navigator's table to look back through the astrodome toward the flight-deck and could immediately sense the pilot and co-pilot were concerned.

'Suddenly, as I looked out, No 4 engine was ablaze and fire was streaming back over the wing and beginning to burn part of the tail section. The pilot announced over the intercom that he would try to dive and put the fire out. We made a turn back away from the target area, back toward friendly territory, but the flames did not die.

'Because we had hoped to make an emergency landing, the crew in the back of the ship had left their positions and removed their earphones and had not heard the order to abandon ship. However, the pilot had pushed the bell which was the signal to bail out and I had gone as far back as the bomb bay and because all of the compartment doors were open, I motioned to the crew and watched as they went out the waist door in tandem-like fashion.

'By the time I returned to the escape hatch in the nose, it was open as the co-pilot had already left and the pilot was coming off the flight deck preparing to go out behind me.

'I remembered to tie my GI shoes on my harness at the last second and I estimated we were now down to nine or ten thousand feet. All I remember was a flash of the tail section over my head and my GI shoes swinging through the air and hitting me square in the nose. I don't remember pulling the ripcord – but there I was, after the noise, seeing the fire, the confusion of what was going to happen next and then all of a sudden the silence while floating in the winter air.

'Thud! I hit hard and fell backwards, cushioned somewhat by the new snow. The chute continued to fall in front of me. All was quiet; I was in a valley and in a pocket of fog. Where was I?

'I sat in the snow, released the harness and the chute and covered it with snow. Now, which direction will I go? It really didn't make much difference. If my calculations were correct, my location was about 15 to 20 miles west of the fighting and somewhere in the vicinity of Louvain, Belgium.

'So I started to walk and probably went only a quarter of a mile. I was going uphill and out of the local fog and into the sunshine. Then I began to hear voices – very far away – like children playing. I could see a part of a small village and the voices were real – children playing games – probably at school recess. Soon, two of the small boys saw me and started to run toward me – shouting. They escorted me to the nearest house at the edge of the village and into a bright kitchen. By this time there were over a dozen excited young people all talking at once and though none spoke English, I could tell they were giving me a warm welcome and certainly understood right away how I had "arrived".

'Next, a bottle of cognac appeared from a cupboard and put before me – for me only! Needless to say, by this time I felt the need of a drink and while not familiar with cognac, it sure warmed and relaxed me in a hurry. After a while an older person came and said to me, "Military Police!" and then, "Follow me!"

'Out we went into the warm afternoon sun – made even warmer by the amount of cognac I had consumed. The children were all dancing around me. Shortly, we came to a halt as the man who asked me to follow raised his hand and indicated for me to enter his house. He introduced me to his wife who immediately went to her kitchen to make a plate of ham and eggs. "Great American dish," she stated as she brought out the welcome food.'

When his 17th Bomb Group Marauder was shot down over Toulon, George Moscovis had a miraculous escape from death and was saved from the enemy by an audacious ruse:

'We had dropped the bombs and while the bomb bay doors were still open, we received two direct hits, one to the fuselage and another completely severing the right engine. McCluskey, the radio gunner, didn't move. He was pinned down by flak jackets and the gravitational pull caused by the B-26's spiral, so I shoved him out the waist window. Tried to follow, but it was some time before I could get clear. Before jumping I couldn't find the ripcord on my chute which appeared to have been torn. When I came out of the plane I hit the tail and it knocked me out. As far as I know my chute never opened. McCluskey says he watched that plane spin in, hit the ground and explode; he never saw another chute. I had almost free fall from about 1,000ft. From what I could gather, I either hit a tree or house top that broke my fall. I was unconscious and all smashed up with a broken leg, arm and shoulder.

'The Germans thought I was dead; they took my identification tag off. Then they told the French to go ahead and dispose of the body. The French took me to a little shack and got a doctor to come down. He thought I was dead too; he couldn't feel my pulse. They pulled an old ammunition box close and were going to put me in it. That's when I came to and opened my eyes. I'd been in a deep coma for four hours. They were crying and kissing me. They put my clothes on a dead Frenchman and his on me and took me to a hospital occupied by the Germans. A French and a German doctor fixed a cast on my leg. I passed for a Frenchman! Stayed in a French house until the Americans arrived.'

It seemed that every successful evader had an exciting tale to tell of hiding places and narrow escapes from capture by the enemy. In their various disguises it was not uncommon for airmen to almost brush shoulders with German troops. In this respect Ralph Patton, a 94th Bomb Group pilot, tells of the audacity of his befrienders:

'Having evaded capture and been sheltered by the French underground people from January 5th 1944 until March 16th, they moved us to the town of Guingamp in northern Brittany. We were put into the home of a gendarme which was only a block away from the local German headquarters. During the day troops often marched up our street and madame allowed us to sit by the window and watch them. Even though these were elite troops, we got to realize that they were no different from our guys. Hitherto we had been conditioned that they were supermen. It somehow gave us a new perspective on the Germans, eased our minds and gave us the confidence to pass by with ease.'

The majority of evaders in western Europe passed along the escape lines, either to cross the Pyrenees into Spain or to be taken off the French Atlantic coast by boat under cover of darkness. Those coming down in Italy or the Balkans were often befriended by partisan units who arranged their return. Others who could not contact an escape or patriot organization remained in hiding until liberation. There were a few who, finding themselves in liberated territory, were in no hurry to return to military control. One such adventurer was Ernest Kelly, a 91st Bomb Group pilot:

'The French Resistance hid me, with three other members of my crew, in an underground room that was part of the Maginot Line defences that the Germans didn't know about. We had the company of two Russians who had escaped from work camps and had been looked after by the French for over a year and had learned to speak the language. As I could speak French, we were able to converse and I discovered they had some mighty strange views of Americans and America. They insisted, quite seriously, that the B-17s we had flown had all been made in Russia and loaned to the US as we were such a downtrodden and poor country. So instilled was this Soviet propaganda that I could not convince them otherwise. Even so, when we were liberated they were disinclined to go back to Russia and we heard they tried to hide out in the west.

'We stayed with the French for thirteen days until the US Army advance liberated us. We then hitched a lift into Paris where we found instant popularity. At that time it looked as if the war would be over in a matter of weeks and I had no desire to be in a hurry to return to military control for a few days. I told the other three that as we were still officially missing we might as well enjoy ourselves. Having a French grandmother, I was fluent in the language. Now, when I bailed out I was wearing my Class A uniform (the best) under my flying coveralls. I had been preparing to go to town when we got the mission alert and the old hands said the weather was too bad and the mission would be cancelled. Well, it wasn't and my ship was shot down. As luck would have it, due to an oversight, in the pocket of my uniform I also had my officer's AGO identity pass, which would see me okay with any MPs. With the aid of this pass I requisitioned hotel rooms for each of us and meal tickets at an officers' mess, without turning ourselves in for interrogation.

'Paris was still in the throes of liberation twelve days before, with thousands of Allied servicemen and Parisians socializing day and night. I talked to American soldiers who were going AWOL for a couple of days before rejoining their units and, as many hadn't been paid for a few months, I went in with them and signed their pay books, claiming to be their commanding officer on detached service from the air force to the army for air support. For this service, most gave me a percentage. One sergeant, seeing my AGO pass, suggested I accompany him to a supply depot and requisition supplies which we could sell to get some French money. We did this twice, offering soap and K-Rations on the street near the Eiffel Tower until a Frenchman warned us the MPs would catch us. He then offered to buy anything we brought him. But the bombardier, worrying about his wife getting a missing in action telegram, turned himself in, meaning that we all had to go to a headquarters and do likewise. I'm not proud of my stolen days in Paris and worried about it for years, but excuse is due to youth and relief at surviving.'

The crews of several battle-damaged or malfunctioning aircraft sought sanctuary in neutral Sweden and Switzerland when they knew there was no hope of regaining friendly territory. All arrivals were supposed to be interned for the duration of hostilities but some individuals, like Stewart Goldsmith, were not prepared to wait:

'My B-24 was damaged on the May 11th 1944 mission and we decided to try and make Switzerland as we knew we'd never make it home to England. We had a fuel tank blow before we could land and had to bail out. The bombardier and myself survived and were interned by the Swiss. Got to know a sympathetic Swiss Army officer and he, with a woman rumoured to be the mistress of a high-ranking Nazi, agreed to help us escape into France. They provided peasant clothes for a man and a woman. I wore the woman's! We went with a party of mushroom-pickers who regularly were allowed to cross the border to search the meadows. This was near the resort town of Darbos. Walked right by the border guards without any problems. Once in occupied France, we contacted the Maquis and lived with them until liberated by the US 7th Army in October.'

One of the most unusual happenings to an internee concerned Penrose Reagan, a 401st Bomb Group gunner:

'Due to heavy damage we had received over our target (Munich) on July 31st, 1944, we had to put our B-17 down in Switzerland where we were interned. One day a notice was put up in the camp from a film company which wanted someone to play an American flyer in a movie it was making. My waist gunner, a good-looking guy, decided he would like to go for the film test and, as this was an opportunity to get out of camp for a while, I put my name down too. There were 41 volunteers and I was the last to take the test. Apart from it being an interesting experience, I really didn't give it much thought. To my amazement, three weeks later I was told I'd been selected for the part. I had to give my parole with United States Government approval not to escape, and for six months I was allowed to live in Zurich. The movie was an anti-Nazi film about two British officers and one American sergeant who were escaping from a prison camp in Italy. Along the way they picked up many fleeing refugees. Nine different languages were used by the various nationalities appearing; 90 per cent real counterparts. They used me, an internee, because they couldn't locate an American who had escaped from a PoW camp.

'There were several British people involved in the film, including Lord Montague's sister, the Honourable Elizabeth Montague, who was the assistant director. The title of the film was "The Last Chance" and in the States it was voted best foreign film of the year in 1945. The experience didn't give me a desire to take up an acting career; although it was a lot of fun. The best thing for this 20-year-old was all the lovely Swiss maids around. I tried to sort through them as best I could, but in the end just let them overwhelm me!'

During the final year of hositilities, as the Soviet forces pressed westward, the territory they had liberated was sometimes a closer haven for badly damaged bombers. It was fairly general for the Russians at front-line bases to be in no hurry to be rid of Allied airmen who 'dropped in'. If the stay was restrictive, it could also be entertaining. David Patterson, a 445th Bomb Group co-pilot:

'After a mission to Zossen near Berlin on March 15th 1945 our B-24 was in trouble and we decided to head for Russian-held territory. We had two engines out when we were met by Yak fighters which circled and led us to an airstrip where we made a successful landing. The Russians treated us well but seemed in no hurry to ship us out to a US base. We had been briefed that if seeking sanctuary with the Russians, it was a good idea to pretend the whole crew were officers as the Red Army tended to be pretty hard on enlisted men. With that knowledge the officers on the crew traded pieces of insignia with the gunners so we would all be kept together. This worked although I think the Russians had their suspicions they were being hoodwinked. During our two-week stay at this base we were able to communicate a little by using school-book German, but most of the time it was by sign language.

'We discovered that there was only one woman on the base, a nurse named Tanya, who we observed was a very close friend of the doctor. Despite the language difficulty Tanya understood our youthful fooling and responded with like. She was short and thick-set with a huge grin and one large bright gold tooth. And her strength was something. One of our gunners, a big guy, kept kidding her with sign language and when she'd taken enough she just went over and picked him up as if he were nothing. I think she took a particular fancy to our waist gunner, Dick Nason. She'd hug him, pick him up and throw him in the bath tub, give him a soaking, lift him out and put a towel round him. Some girl. Eventually word of our presence must have filtered through to the US authorities and an ATC plane was sent to pick us up. If our stay with the Soviets taught us anything, it was that vodka is a way of life for them.'

Not all contacts with the Soviets were so pleasant, as when Wesley Bartelt arrived in a 453rd Bomb Group Liberator over a Red Air Force airstrip:

'Our target was the Wehrmacht headquarters at Zossen near Berlin and we took a direct hit from flak on the bomb run. Two engines were knocked out and I had to dive under our formation. We called fighters for help and were told to go for an emergency landing field in liberated Poland. Although we slowly kept losing altitude the co-ordinates my navigator had given were accurate and we eventually pinpointed the field. The waist gunners said they could see fighters on the ground with red stars on their wings, so I started on the base leg. As I made my wide turn the tail gunner called out that he could see four fighters taking off. I replied that I'd make a longer turn as they were probably going to escort us in. Meantime the engineer had set up the Very pistol and was firing the double red flares we'd been instructed to shoot as identification.

'I put the gear down, went through the check list and looked up to see Bell Airacobras go by. I concentrated on the landing approach when suddenly everyone was hollering on the interphone that they could see tracers hitting us. Somebody yelled, "Bail Out" and before I could countermand this the navigator and tail gunner jumped. We were only at around 800 feet and I assumed they didn't open their 'chutes in time as both were killed. We had taken hits and I decided to abandon the landing, pulled emergency power on the two good engines and managed to gain another 200 feet before ordering the crew to bail out immediately. I was the last to go and was picked up by Poles and taken to a little town where I found my co-pilot. After spending the night in the local lock-up, we were picked up by a Russian truck and driven to the airfield at Lutz. Our accommodation was a barn with a straw-spread floor and here the rest of the surviving crew members were reunited with us.

'We were treated more like prisoners than allies as there was a permanent guard with sub-machine-gun at the barn door and we were only allowed to leave to go to meals or the latrine. We could communicate through one of our gunners who could speak a little German, but still didn't get any satisfactory answers as to why their fighters had shot us down or what was going to happen to us. We were kept in the barn for several days and then taken to another base where a B-17 crew was being held. By this time we were more than a little resentful of our confinement and the guards with guns who were always in attendance. One night we were taken to dinner with the local Red Army Colonel and his staff where toasts were drunk. Somehow I offended the Colonel because I hadn't stood up and saluted Stalin and he took this as a deliberate snub.

'Next morning we were all ordered out under armed guard to a truck. "You did it now. We're probably being shipped out to Siberia," I was told by my crew. We were relieved to be taken out to the airfield and a Russian DC-3 which took us to the US base at Poltava. The Soviets had painted a white line across the runway of the airfield and we were told we had to stay on our side and not try to buddy-buddy with any of the Russians. From Poltava a US transport flew us out of Russia. The experience taught me two things about the Soviets. First, they were trigger-happy and it was too bad if they shot the wrong guy. Second, they didn't want us to mix freely with any of their people and were highly suspicious of Americans.'

23
Capture by the Enemy

The proportion of those who evaded capture in enemy-occupied territory was small compared with those who were apprehended by the German military and made prisoner. The chances of successfully evading depended very much on the area where the crash-landing or parachute descent was made. Near the front lines or certain coastal areas one was almost certain to be apprehended. Generally the Wehrmacht personnel acted correctly, in line with the Geneva Convention relative to the treatment of Prisoners of War (PoW). On capture each prisoner was quickly searched for material that might be used in escape or provide useful intelligence. This often gave the captors an opportunity to confiscate, and later enjoy, popular US cigarettes. Occasionally the contents of an airman's pockets were particularly puzzling. T. C. Gibbs, of the 93rd Bomb Group:

'On January 28 1945 our Liberator had been hit by flak while we were heading into the Ruhr Valley. With an engine throwing oil, our pilot properly turned back to the coast. Over Schouwen, one of the Dutch coastal islands, another engine was struck. Our gallant B-24 could no longer sustain flight. With no choice we hit the silk. Fortunately, all ten members of our crew survived the jump. Unfortunately, there was a German anti-aircraft battalion on the island. In a short time we were German prisoners of war.

'In short order I was stripped of all my worldly possessions, including several packages of cigarettes. (I always carried as many packages of cigarettes as could be stuffed into my flight suit. We had been told that cigarettes were excellent trading items in such emergencies.) Within minutes after arrival at Command Headquarters, it was evident that the German officers were enjoying my cigarettes.

'In due course I was called before two officers for questioning. On a desk in front of the officers were several of my possessions, four English five pound notes, a pocket knife, watch, a few cigarettes and an inhaler. Finally, one of the officers pointed to my inhaler. "Was ist das?" (What is this?), getting in return my name, rank and serial number.

'After what seemed an eternity to me, one of the officers used their intercom and in the crisp authoritarian German gave an order. Shortly after the order an enlisted man entered the room with a long pair of tongs. He very carefully lifted my inhaler from the desk, departing the room immediately with the inhaler held as far out in front of him as possible.

'I often wonder how many tests my little inhaler underwent before it was determined to be non-lethal and not a secret weapon.'

The fear of losing personal property was very real. Ira Weinstein was extraordinarily fortunate in his efforts to save a watch:

'Just before I went into the cadets, a cousin who was an aviator gave me his

Longine "Weems" navigator watch and admonished me to bring it back safely. I was shot down on the infamous Kassel raid of September 27th 1944 when my group, the 445th, lost 27 out of 36 B-24s. After capture I was taken to the Luftwaffe interrogation center near Frankfurt. Stripped of my clothes, I was told I was being taken to be deloused and showered. Walking through the halls, another group coming back from the showers said the Germans were confiscating all watches and jewelery. I quickly decided the Germans would not have my Weems so I took if off and handed it to an Australian who had already been showered. Never expected to see it again.

'A few nights later, with other PoWs, I was in a boxcar held up by a British air raid in a marshalling yard while being transported to prison camp in the east. Other boxcars full of PoWs were parked on the line alongside and by an extraordinary coincidence directly opposite mine I recognized the voice of the Australian pilot. He asked if I would like my watch back, but figuring just how to pass it was another matter. We tried stretching arms through the openings between the slats of the car but could not touch. Finally, I asked him to throw the watch and I just managed to catch it. The watch was worn throughout my internment in Stalag Luft I and returned to the States with me.'

The treatment of airmen on capture became less correct or sympathetic as the war progressed, particularly in the enemy homeland. The almost daily intrusion into German airspace from the summer of 1944 brought a heightened loathing of the Allied 'Terrorfliegers' and the death and destruction they caused. There was often little pity or help for the badly wounded as 453rd Bomb Group's James Martin discovered on 21 July 1944:

'Our group was part of a many-plane mission to Munich. The B-24 in which I flew as co-pilot was leading the high right element of the high right squadron formation; it was the crew's eleventh mission. There was an extensive undercast and the clouds extended so high we had to go to 24,500 feet to stay above. Climbing at this altitude, our heavily laden Liberators became less stable and difficult to hold in formation. I believe the number 2 ship of our element, flying on our left, must have stalled out and in trying to regain its place in the formation came up and struck the underside of our fuselage. The first I knew about this was when I glanced out my right window and saw the other B-24 the moment he hit us. With the impact I remember no more until regaining consciousness and realizing I was falling. I had one of the limited number of back-pack parachutes that had been issued to pilots that morning and my immediate thought was to pull the ripcord. When I did, nothing appeared to happen. My left arm seemed injured and in desperation I reached over my left shoulder with my right arm and tried to pull the 'chute out of the pack. Once I had managed to pull some, the rest came and the canopy filled out above me with a jolt.

'I then realized I was still strapped in the co-pilot's seat and wearing my flak suit. Pulling the red tab undid the flak suit and when I flipped the release on the seat belt they both sailed away from me. Wounds on my head were bleeding profusely and I wondered if I would bleed to death before reaching the ground. I prayed. Finally I hit the ground with such force I was knocked unconscious again. Coming to, I found I had a reception committee; three German farm men, one with a two-prong pitchfork which he pressed between my shoulder blades while another searched me. I was so dazed I did not know all that was happening, but some soldiers arrived and made me carry one end of a stretcher on which an American airman was lying. He was a stranger, not from our crew, and I thought he was dead until I looked at his dog tags, when he suddenly opened his eyes. His name was John Cowger and I later discovered he was the only survivor from the other crew. In addition to myself, my pilot and a waist gunner were the only members of our crew to live. The pilot, like me, had been thrown clear when the plane broke up. The seats we sat in had undoubtedly protected us at that moment.'

The hostility of the German civilian population towards Allied airmen was encouraged by Nazi propaganda, although the extent of this enmity – if known at the time – was never conveyed to combat airmen by the Allied authorities. The hatred was quickly apparent to those unfortunate enough to land among civilians. Carl Runge, 486th Bomb Group Navigator, baled out of a flak-stricken B-17 near Saaz, Czechoslovakia, on 17 April 1945:

'As I drifted down from about 5,000 feet, the sight was something to behold. A sky full of planes, bombers at high altitude and off in the distance some fighters strafing ground targets. I caught sight of our abandoned ship spiraling in descent and saw it hit in a muffled roar with a mushroom of smoke. I was soon able to judge where I would land and the same estimate was made by a group of civilians scurrying in that same general direction, and we both guessed right. The field was ploughed and I hit softly enough and stayed prone. A warning shot flicked up dirt a few feet from me and, seconds later, a pistol muzzle was pointed at my forehead. I was completely surrounded. As I lay there I pointed inside my flying jacket and they removed my .45 and several clips of ammo. They motioned to me to stand and I indicated I would disengage my 'chute harness.

'By this time a crowd of 40 or 50 had assembled in the field. They were chattering away, most of which I clearly understood, having a fair knowledge of German from my parents who both emigrated to the USA in 1913, but I played dumb. My 'chute was gathered up and I was made to hold it, resting on my head with both hands, before being directed to walk down a nearby tree-lined dirt road. One flying boot had been jerked off when the 'chute opened and now I had to walk through manure with nothing but a sock on that foot, while the accompanying crowd cursed and spat on me. One crippled old man let loose with his crutch and I caught the blow square in the back of my neck. Then I heard a familiar sound and a P-51 came roaring towards us, flipping his wings as he passed at tree-top height. I am sure the pilot must have seen me land, but I am thankful he didn't try strafing my captors as I am sure it would have given them the excuse to finish me. As it was, the P-51's pass only scattered the crowd momentarily and we were back on the move.

'Shortly we arrived in a small village and a woman who looked like the school-teacher started asking me questions in English put to her by a man who I took to be the village burgomaster. If I hadn't been so damned scared it would have been rather amusing, for when the question was asked by the burgomaster in German for the teacher to translate into English I immediately knew what the question was, my German being better than her English! Their fumbling attempt at interrogation accomplished nothing and I only gave name, rank and serial number; my knowledge of German remained a secret. They were all curious and several quite hostile, but I could determine that nothing drastic would happen. Still, I was somewhat relieved when a German soldier pedalled up on a bicycle and took charge.'

The initial encounter was the most dangerous time for the captured airman. Bombardier William Boyd did not learn how fortunate he was until after his release from captivity:

33. A Liberator dies over Berlin.

34. A steel helmet was no match for high-velocity flak splinters.

35. Colonel Ashley Woolridge (Chapters 2 and 16) being congratulated by the crew chief of the Marauder in which he had just flown his 100th combat mission.

36. Corporal Emory Arnold of the 451st Bomb Group (Chapter 18).

37. Sgt Earl Williamson (Chapters 18 and 19).

38. Cary Salter and his Mustang (Chapter 17).

39. Roger Armstrong, radio-operator on the 'Qualified Quail' (Chapter 18).

40. Milton Lipa (Chapter 18), aged 22 and with 27 missions completed. Aircrew were permitted to decorate their A-2 or similar leather 'flying jackets' but they were not allowed to wear them on combat missions.

41. It always happened to the other guy.

42. Buddies for life. In typical crew pose for the camera, Harold Miller's men. Standing, left to right: Paul Green (waist gunner); Dean Saul (waist gunner); Asher Brown (radio-operator); Robert Custer (engineer); Dale Maughan (tail gunner); Bob Fomby (co-pilot); and James Slye (ball gunner). Kneeling, left to right: Sam Marshall (bombardier); Edward Carey (navigator); and Harold Miller. Their B-17G went down on its 36th mission on 12 September 1944 with another crew (Chapter 18).

43. A very creditable 'Buzz Job'. A 457th Bomb Group B-17 'cuts the daisies' at Glatton, England, to celebrate the crew's return from the final mission of their combat tour. By the end of 1944 there were 26 B-17 groups in the UK and six in Italy. [*via J. B. Wilson*]

44. B-24 crews considered their charge was 'a real man's airplane'. It certainly required strong arms and steady hands to fly one in formation as close in as this 461st Bomb Group aircraft. The B-24 was the most numerous heavy bomber by June 1944 with 20 groups in the ETO and 15 in the MTO. [*S. Staples*]

45. The pilot came out little hurt from this P-47 (Chapter 20). Note the bombs still attached to their racks. At one time there were 22 P-47 groups in the ETO and MTO.

44

45

46. The Curtiss P-40 Warhawk did good work as a fighter-bomber in the MTO where four groups operated. It was outclassed in air combat and was eventually replaced by P-47s. This example served with the 324th Fighter Group in Sicily.

47. The most successful US fighter was the P-51 Mustang. The example illustrated is a camera-carrying reconnaissance version designated F-6. There were 18 groups of Mustangs in the ETO and four in the MTO by the end of hostilities.

48. Overall, the Martin B-26 Marauder groups produced the most accurate bombing of all US bombers. It also proved to be a very durable aircraft, but because of supposed handling difficulties it was phased out of production before the end of hostilities. There were eight B-26 groups in the ETO and three in the MTO. The aircraft depicted served with the 319th Bomb Group. [*Harold Woinonski*]

49. The North American B-25 Mitchell was a sturdy, uncomplicated medium bomber which equipped three groups in the MTO. The B-25J in the photo served with the 340th Bomb Group. [*R. Besecker*]

2107733
48

49
7A
327704

50

51

50. Of all Second World War aircraft the most enduring was the Douglas C-47. Many of those which took part in Second World War operations were still flying in a civilian capacity a half century later. There were fourteen C-47 groups in the ETO and three in the MTO by the end of 1944.

51. Sheldon Witt at the pilot's window of a C-46 (Chapter 20).

52. A C-46 Commando of the 313th Troop Carrier Group.

53. Carl Gjelhaug (right) and his co-pilot Arthur Evans, in the 707th Bomb Squadron barracks area at Bungay (Chapter 21).

54
13587
55

54. Changing the tail boom on Jack Ilfrey's P-38F at Youks-les-Bains, Algeria (Chapter 21). 'Happy Jack' is on the far right.

55. The death throes of the B-26 from which George Moscovis fell to earth.

56. Everett Lindley (Chapter 23). A photograph taken by an RAF friend shortly after liberation from prison camp. The plate contains his first fried eggs since capture.

57. Carl Runge of the 486th Bomb Group (Chapter 23).

58. Penrose Reagan as Ray Reagen, the character he played in the Swiss film 'The Last Chance'.

59. Basket Ball at Stalag Luft I. Sports were a popular means of passing PoW time.

60. Captain Robert Morgan (Chapter 25) parades for the generals with the crew of 'Memphis Belle' before returning to the US in June 1943. The crewman standing directly below the engine is Bob Hanson (Chapter 11).

61. RMS *Queen Mary* at Gourock in her grey wartime paintwork. Thousands of US servicemen arrived and departed Europe on one or other of the 'Queens'. [*via B. Robertson*]

60

61

62. 'White Flak' giving Holy Communion at Hethel.

63. Co-pilot McCafferty examines the flak holes in the wing of 'Stork Club' after the food drop of 2 May 1945 (Chapter 26).

'I took a chunk of flak in the shoulder when our plane was hit. The pilots tried to make Switzerland but we had to bail out over the Black Forest area. I delayed opening my chute until the ground was getting close and was lucky enough to land in a little clearing in the woods. The canopy was quickly hidden under some greenery and I also got rid of my fleece-lined flying boots. I then hid till dark and started walking. Although it was July it was bitterly cold in these mountains and at times it rained. By morning I was feeling pretty ill and sat down under a tree. An old man came by and I decided that in my condition I should try to get some bandages for my shoulder. He pointed to a house a little way down the forest track. There was a grandmother and granddaughter in the house. The man went off in the opposite direction.

'The woman gave me some warm water to wash my wound and some cloth to wrap around my shoulder. She pointed to a wooden bench behind a stove, indicating that I could lie down. I was chilled and exhausted and felt a bit of rest and I could continue walking. However, about this time the old man came back with a gendarme. Later I was taken by the military to Freiburg jail. My guard kept opening the shutters on each door trying to find an empty cell. At one I heard an American voice with a strong French accent and recognized it as that of the radio-operator, Roger Gagnov of the crew I was flying with. I had not flown with this crew before and did not know them, so I doubt if I would have been able to recognize any by sight but the radio man's voice was quite distinctive. The guard put me in this cell and in addition to the radio man there was the waist gunner, Irvin Hughes, and the engineer Ed Theed. The other five members of the crew never showed up and it was not until after the war that I learned they had all been shot, beaten and killed by German civilians. The thought remains I could easily have gone the same way if I had met the wrong people.'

Ronald Douglas, 100th Bomb Group tail gunner shot down on the last day of 1944, had a miraculous escape from death, only to experience some worrying moments when surrounded by civilians:

'Our B-17 took a direct hit from flak over Hamburg and sliced in half just behind the ball turret by another plane's wing. I managed to haul myself out of the tail gun position and hooked on my parachute. The rear fuselage door was gone, as was the waist gunner. With the angle at which the tail was falling, it took me a long time to reach the door space. When I looked out the first thing I saw was a man on the ground looking up. There was no time to reason that if I could see a man looking up it would be but a second or two before the tail struck. I was out of the door, pulling my ripcord as I went. The shroud lines went by my face; there was the sound of the tail crashing to earth; the jolt of the 'chute opening and instantly my feet struck the ground. Only later did I realize that the tail had fallen around 26,500 feet with me still in it and that there had only been a fraction of a second between living and possible death.

'The wind caught the 'chute, dragging me a short distance in the snow until I tried to undo the leg straps. They were frozen stiff so I released my chest strap and stepped out. I went toward the man I'd seen from the 'plane and tried to jump an irrigation ditch, only to land in the middle and get soaked to the waist. The man grabbed me by the shoulders and started kissing me on both cheeks, shouting "Americanish, Americanish". Oh boy, I thought, I'm among friends. I found out later he was a Polish forced labourer. My relief was short-lived for I was soon surrounded by a far from friendly mob. One man drew a knife and advanced towards me; the knife descended and I thought it was all over. Then I found he was cutting off my alpaca-lined flying trousers – the zip was frozen. He only had time for one slice when the circle of civilians was parted by a young girl and an old man, both in uniforms. The man with the knife withdrew and the old man – about 70 I guess – made signs with his revolver for me to move. I suppose he and the girl were members of the local Home Guard. I got the message and walked. I'd had too many narrow escapes for one day.'

More than 500 Allied airmen are known to have been lynched in Germany and many others listed as missing are suspected of having suffered the same fate. Everett Lindley, a 1st Fighter Group P-38 pilot, was close to being included in this grim total but for his fortitude and quick presence of mind. His story is extraordinary:

'For me, all hell broke loose in the middle of a strafing run at the Landshut marshalling yard on April 15, 1945; I was leading the 1st Fighter Group on a low-level strike from Munich to Regensburg to Linz.

'I was in a 45-degree diving approach at about 700 feet, firing at a long line of freight cars, when out of nowhere came a concentrated volley of 20 or 30 orange balls from 40mm flak guns. Too late to turn and fire into the nest of flak, I was forced to pull out. But before I could completely extricate myself, my plane was struck several times.

'The first shell, ricocheting off the two-inch windscreen, pulverized the glass. When it broke loose on the inside, the exploding glass hit me in the left shoulder. I could move my left arm but did not want to look at my shoulder. As I pulled out I could hear more orange balls striking my aircraft. Two hit the right engine, one the wing, and two penetrated beneath the cockpit gondola, making contact with the armor-plated bucket seat. I could hear and feel those malicious last two, and I knew that they could start a fire.

'As I climbed away to about 1,500 feet, flames appeared around the right engine. I tried diving to extinguish the flame, but this seemed to only feed the fire. I started the procedure to eliminate the No 2 engine, feathering the prop and cutting off all fluids and electrical power to that engine. Even so, the fire got worse. Heavy smoke and flames entered the cockpit by my feet. Rising quickly, the flames started to burn my face and eyes, between the oxygen mask and my helmet.

'When I could no longer see the instruments, I was forced to release the canopy top emergency panel. This momentarily cleared the cockpit of smoke and I could see again, but it also sucked the flames from the burning shells in the gondola. I glanced at the right engine, finding it and most of the right wing engulfed in flames.

'I was holding hard left rudder, having completed my single-engine procedure except for trimming, when the cockpit became a mass of fire. Fearing that the aircraft was about to explode, I rolled down the left window and evacuated, stepping out into the slipstream of the number-one engine, which was at nearly 95 per cent power. This movement pinned me back against the rear cockpit edge.

'I couldn't break loose, and the P-38 was in a right spin. My long headset cord was still connected as I fought the prop wash. I could hear someone yelling, "Red Leader, bail out! Bail out, Red Leader!" While I could not move, I realized the ground was close.

'The urgent call to bail out came again and I made another effort to free myself from the fighter, but failed. Why this P-38 did not explode with all that fire and fuel aboard I shall never know. Finally, with my right hand on the ripcord, I used all my might and broke loose, instantly pulling the ripcord.

'From a hot and noisy environment I suddenly found myself in a delightfully cool and quiet situation. I looked up at my chute but saw houses, trees and farmland. As I looked down at my feet I saw only sky. Obviously I was upside down. I remembered trainers telling us to manipulate the shrouds to stabilize a descent when oscillating in a parachute jump. My hands were only halfway up to the shrouds when I slammed into the ground on my right side, my head impacting the surface. I was knocked unconscious momentarily, my chute covering me. If I had landed on my spine it would have been the end. Instead, I was in the village of Stenging, just north of Muhldorf, Germany, with a broken right leg.

'When I came to, my squadron mates were strafing around me to provide an escape. As I freed myself from the chute, I saw two enemy riflemen approaching but my squadron had departed. I scrambled for the nearby woods, dragging my broken leg.

'But it wasn't much of a wood. It was only a narrow grove planted between two levels of farmland, so I soon ran out of woods and into another open area. My movement had aroused a lair of deer that also ran out in the open. What a telltale indicator the deer provided for anyone wanting to know my whereabouts!

'I retreated into the limited woodland and tried to swallow a wadded up "flimsy sheet" but my mouth was too parched to swallow anything. I quickly buried the classified document instead.

'A German civilian, whom I supposed was part of a posse, noticed the frightened deer and continued walking until he passed right by me. He said something but did not seem belligerent. It was obvious that he would tell others my exact location.

'Soon hostile forces surrounded me. I drew and cocked my .45 Colt automatic and pointed it at the area where many seemed to have congregated. I remember thinking that I had worn this weapon on 43 missions and it had its purpose: to protect in my effort to avoid capture. Now I needed to use it.

'Someone yelled "Hands up!" and I could hear weapons being put in their ready-to-fire state. Other soldiers approached from my rear; I immediately turned and pointed my .45 at them. I was too busy to stop to ask, what was I doing with this macho behaviour against some 30 enemies. Someone else yelled "Hands up!" and I stood there, confronting them for what seemed to be an eternity.

'I think I was ready to die, knowing I would get a few of them before they finally got me. It was an electrifying situation and I know – now – if I had allowed another second to elapse they would have opened fire. I guess it was discretion being the better part of valor, belatedly, that took over; I tossed the gun to the ground. With my hands up, I was ordered to lead my captors out of the woods. As I proceeded to the lower level of ground I could see and hear woman fighting over my silk parachute. I was put in a vehicle and, under guard, driven from Stenging to Muhldorf.

'As we drove along I remembered what the intelligence officers told us to do if we were shot down. Then, being shot down never seemed to be such a big deal. But if you knew what could really happen, despite what they told you, some airmen might have refused to fly combat.

'When we arrived at Muhldorf, I was taken into what appeared to be a public building and ordered to stand with my hands up, at the bottom of a basement stairway. Many people were living in this basement in makeshift compartments. My captors, two civilians armed with rifles, barked a command that sent the residents scurrying. I heard many doors being closed and bolted. I guess they told people I might attempt to escape and warned that shooting would result. But I could see that this was no time to think about escape, especially when one German was taunting me by periodically pulling a clicking trigger on his rifle.

'After standing at the bottom of the stairway for 30 minutes, I was ordered upstairs. Just as I reached the foyer, an enraged civilian flew into me, throwing punches and screaming German. I guessed that our strafing had disrupted his world. He knocked me down and the guards ordered me up, then pushed me back into him with their rifles. A blow to my temple floored me a second time; I saw stars and felt dizzy. I was ordered to stand; rifle probes helped me. The civilian beat me until he was exhausted, hemorrhaging my nose, cutting my eye and driving my teeth through my lips.

'I was then put on display on the main floor for 45 minutes, again with my hands up. My white silk scarf, used as a buffer between my neck and the flight suit collar, was hanging out and saturated with blood that dripped from my nose and lips. Some Germans were pleased with this sight. Some spat at me. Others just glared; a few looked me straight in the eye and showed compassion.

'All of this vengeance was only a holding action – something for the civilians to do as they waited for the officials who were responsible for dealing with enemy airmen. A vehicle finally arrived with two German storm troopers. They were Obersturmbahnführer (Lt Col) Mathias Zeirhut and his aide, Feldwebel (Sergeant) Yohann Gilch. They took command of the situation and ordered me into their Volkswagen.

'I was directed to the front seat with the Sergeant; the Colonel took the back seat. We drove swiftly out of Muhldorf and into the countryside; I assumed they were saving me from the wrath of the German civilians and transporting me to a PoW camp. We soon came to a stop in the boondocks. An irate Colonel tapped the back of my head with his pistol and told me, "Grouse mitt you!" I obediently got out of the car with my hands up and faced him. I noticed that the Sergeant had gotten out and walked in front of the left headlight. With his back to me he seemed to be fiddling with his fly, so I assumed he needed to answer a "call of nature". Instead, he was loading his pistol.

'When Zeirhut got out of the back seat, I got a good look at his eyes. They were glossy and he appeared to be nervous. He walked around me with pistol in hand; it looked like a Mauser. In front of the vehicle he raised his right arm and fired. I had sensed his intention when I noticed his eyes and I winced when the shot was fired. Somehow it missed me and Gilch pointed his weapon at me. Zeirhut then walked completely around the car and came up from the rear to within six feet of me before firing again.

'This time, despite my ducking, the round struck me in the left shoulder. It felt like the kind of straight-arm hits made in football. It pierced the bone area and spun me around and into the ground.

'Rather than be shot to death on the side of the road I decided to run for it. I ran across the pasture, like a broken-field runner, hobbling on my broken right leg. Both Zeirhut and Gilch fired at me and I could hear bullets whizzing by my head and ricocheting off the ground. They must have fired at least sixteen times.

'My right leg was in pain; to this day I can still see blood pumping out of my shoulder through my flight suit at every accelerated heartbeat. I wondered, "Oh God, how can I live through this?" and yet, I lived by the 23rd Psalm: "Yea, though I walk through the valley of the shadow of death, I will fear no evil." I wasn't scared – there was too much going on; I was looking for salvation.

'I was also very thirsty, when I noticed a small river ahead. My mouth was foaming white, dry saliva; the only moisture I could get was from my bleeding nose. Again, I was ready to die, if only they would first allow me a drink. I ran zigzagging and favoring my right leg. My good leg stiffened and I finally tripped over myself. I was totally out of sync when Zeirhut approached, kicked me in the head and yelled once again, "Grouse mitt you!"

'Then, I felt a profound desire to live. I was really angry for the first time in my life and realized that only drastic behavior would save me. When I stood up he pushed me toward the river and I again had this terrific desire for a drink of water.

'However, I decided to make my move. As he shoved me with his left arm, holding the pistol in his right hand, I reached over with my right hand and grabbed his right wrist. With my left hand I jammed the muzzle of the pistol. I wasn't concerned about another gunshot wound. I don't know where the strength came from, but I picked Zeirhut up with this grip and swung him around, knocking Gilch to the ground. As I fought for his pistol, he finally let go and I pointed it at both of them as they ran away. I was going to shoot when I noticed they were running toward of group of people, including children, standing behind a dense hedge. I decided not to shoot for fear of hitting an onlooker.

'I saw a small bridge that spanned the river and headed hastily for it. It was open all around me. When I got to the high point of the bridge, with no place to hide and feeling totally naked, I stopped to gather my wits.

'An elderly German farmer approached, beckoning me to go with him because, as he said, I was "kronck" (sick), meaning I was bleeding. Although I felt his appeal was genuine, he knew I was an injured animal and therefore dangerous. I raised the pistol at him and he backed off. He tried another time, begging me to "komen sie here," but I stayed. On his third effort his son, Wehrmacht Feldwebel Joseph Kettner, accompanied him.

'I finally acquiesced when I could see from their eyes that they were really sympathetic. As we walked off the bridge I noticed a man behind some bushes, getting off a bicycle and removing a telescopic rifle from his back. I called out his position to the Kettners. The father screamed some words at the man who quickly put the rifle on his back and cycled away. This further boosted my confidence in the Kettners.

'Even so, this was still a critically dangerous situation. I felt completely lost and desperately sought any indication of salvation. By the time we arrived in the Kettners' yard all of the people I saw before were there – old folks, children and some my age. Their eyes said they were opposed to what had happened to me. Zeirhut and Gilch seemed to be hiding in the background. I think they hoped the Kettners would disarm me and turn me over to them.

'My immediate attention was drawn to the Kettners. While they exhibited great courage to attempt to assist me as I levelled a pistol at them, they were aiding an armed enemy, a violation of a national war principle.

'Suddenly, young Kettner yelled something in German and everyone except his father ran into the house. I assumed this meant the Kettners would try to kill me and that they did not want the others to see. I rapidly raised my pistol at the father and son. They backed off and begged me not to shoot. All the onlookers who had disappeared came running out of the house with hot water, bandages and medicine. One lovely girl, who was perhaps 16, came over and looked compassionately into my eyes. I melted. If this was a trick I would have been willing to die!

'But it wasn't a trick. The people surrounded me with help to stop the bleeding. Sergeant Kettner rolled back my flying suit, swathed my shoulder with hot compacts, sprinkled sulfa powder on my wound and applied a tourniquet and bandages. His father sat next to me and urged by to give up my gun. "Give me sie gun, comrade," he said repeatedly. I knew that this might be a trick but I finally gave it to him. These people were from a culture unlike any I had known. How was I to know to what extent they would respond? My religious faith strengthened me and their recent actions further confirmed my belief.

'Kettner put the weapon under his shirt and thanked me. The onlookers shook their fists in Zeirhut and Gilch's faces to harass them. I learned that during this melee, Kettner had dispatched a lad to the local Luftwaffe station for assistance.

'A Luftwaffe Hauptmann (captain) finally arrived to mediate the argument between Sergeant Kettner and Colonel Zeirhut. Kettner stood at attention, red faced, while Zeirhut walked back and forth, making his point to regain control of me. Kettner's family and neighbours stood in a line with him. During a 20-minute debate over my fate, two of the largest police dogs I have ever seen were directed to approach and sniff me. One order from their master and they would have torn me apart!

'Zeirhut was very unwilling to give me up because of his anger at my disarming him. However, a standard Third Reich procedure was that the Luftwaffe processed all enemy airmen. The Hauptmann accepted this responsibility and ordered me to follow him toward what appeared to be a large farm complex. The dogs and a guard were behind me. When we were about halfway to the farm, I saw two high-ranking Luftwaffe officers about 100 feet away. They wore long black leather coats with a lot of braid and were looking at me and talking as though they knew what I had been through.

'As I approached the farm I noticed a man in coveralls, standing on a stool and working on some machinery. When I got closer I was astonished to learn that he was servicing an airplane. And there were many! They were camouflaged Fw 190s, tailed into a dugout revetment. This farm was a cleverly disguised fighter base which utilized the nearby autobahn as a runway.

'The dogs' keeper, a private in the Luftwaffe, guided me to the station hospital. A Lieutenant Colonel doctor examined my injuries and told me, in English, "You are a good sport." As I lay on my back a pretty German nurse stared and waited to help me. The doctor asked me if I liked women. Thank God, I thought, I must be in at least a latently civilized society!

'A Feldwebel was assigned to guard me when I left the medical office. He ordered me to walk around the central area of the military base. He had a game right leg and screamed invectives at me. Evidently a very bitter warrior, he threatened me several times and waved a club. An officer eventually came and took me to my overnight prison cell.

'I was soon in a deep sleep, but at about 1am, two apparently beer-laden Luftwaffe pilots opened the door and seemed to study me, making comments without being hostile.'

Airmen prisoners of war were the Luftwaffe's responsibility and generally handled correctly, probably due to the appreciation that German airmen PoWs were well treated. In contrast to the rough reception so many American airmen received on capture, the transfer to the custody of the Luftwaffe was a relief. Judging by the amount of intelligence gained from interrogating newly arrived prisoners, an unguarded relief in many cases. In fact, the Luftwaffe intelligence agencies had extremely good and accurate cover on most USAAF activities and units. Walter Konantz' anecdote underlines this fact:

'In February 1945 I had just completed my combat tour when I got a phone call from a depot in northern England. It was my younger brother, Harold, who had just arrived as a replacement pilot. At my request the CO managed to get Harold assigned to our group, the 55th, where he eventually took over my trusty P-51, retaining my name on the canopy rail.

'The day before I was scheduled to leave for the States Harold got shot down by a B-17! This as a result of moving in close to try and identify the markings to see if the Fort belonged to the formation the 55th was to escort. He bailed out successfully and was captured as soon as he touched the ground. Taken for interrogation, Harold was asked his name. He answered "Konantz", whereupon the Luftwaffe officer shuffled through some papers, picked one out and studied it, then said to Harold: "We thought you had finished your tour and were on the way home?" The Luftwaffe certainly had some very up-to-date data on me!'

24
'Kriegies'

Over 32,000 US airmen became prisoners of war of Germany and her allies. One in two US airmen shot down survived as prisoners, a higher percentage than in RAF losses. This was particularly so in heavy bombers where the facility to escape from B-17s and B-24s was much better than in the RAF's night bombers. There were four Luftwaffe-operated prisoner-of-war camps, Stalag Lufts, most of which contained a mixture of RAF and USAAF captives and were all situated in eastern Germany to make it difficult for escapees to reach the west. Additionally, the Wehrmacht camp, Stalag XVIIB at Krems, Austria, became an airmen's camp and many US fliers were incarcerated in Stalags for soldiers.

For some US airmen their major experience of the Second World War was an enemy prison camp; for the early captives, a period of nearly three years. Albert Clark, a Spitfire pilot and Headquarters Officer of the 31st Fighter Group, was one of the first:

'The worst part of my imprisonment was the five months I spent not knowing if my family knew I was alive. It was a month before my wife knew I was alive, but a long time before I knew she knew. My letters and cards brought no response. I was shot down in July 1942 and did not get a letter from home until December. The Germans had it for months and held it back deliberately as I was the first senior USAAF officer they had captured. I think they were interested in seeing what effect the long silence had on my morale.'

The trickle of PoWs of 1942 and early 1943 had become a flood by the following year when US air operations got into full stride. The German guards at Stalag Luft IV, Grosstychow, probably had good reason to believe the tale they told Donald H. Jones of the 452nd Bomb Group:

'In the spring of 1944 B-17s and B-24s were sent into battle in their natural metal finish. The German guards told us the reason our bombers were not being painted was because they were shooting us down so quickly that we did not have time to paint them any more.'

Living conditions during 1942 and 1943 were reasonable but in 1944 the waning fortunes of the Third Reich brought pressures on prison camps, notably reducing food rations which, by early 1945, had become severe. In many camps men were near starvation. George Klare, who had flown with the 100th Bomb Group, recalled the effect this had on him and others:

'The major topic of conversation in the PoW camp was food. People talked about food, thought about food and even dreamed about food, because we got so little. The usual morning ration was two half slices of German bread and I learned to be there when it was given out. The one occasion I wasn't, when I returned to my room they had become the smallest half slices you ever did see! Sometimes we'd get dehydrated soup (vegetable only) or boiled rutabagas or potatoes for the evening meal but bread was the main item of our diet. To improve its taste (if there was heating in the room) we crumbled the bread into a pan, added water and re-baked it. Came out with the same consistency but looked like cake and this seemed more palatable. The Red Cross parcels were our life-savers. If we were lucky enough to get one, it usually had a tin of coffee and we'd open it up and pass it around just for the smell, it was so good.

'Such was my preoccupation with food that I would try and make up recipes using all the ingredients we didn't have – burnt sugar, marshmallow, ice-cream, nuts, chocolate and so on. On several occasions I took a poll on what the men in my part of the camp considered were the ten best restaurants in their area, the United States and the world.

'I had two memorable dreams. In one I was walking down a street eating a candy bar when two girls whom I knew well, came up. I offered them a bite but they ate the whole bar and I was so mad I woke. In the other I had been tramping through a forest and found myself on a balcony overlooking a medieval feast in a castle hall. There was everything on that table – roast pig with an apple in its mouth, pie, fruit, you name it. The people called for me to go down but I was so ashamed of my dirty, smelly, unshaven person that I couldn't force myself to go, the frustration eventually waking me. When you're near starving food becomes an obsession.'

In these circumstances Red Cross food parcels became the lifeline. By early 1945 there was no room for the diversion of contents to such unapproved use as Herb Schlicker remembers at Stalag Luft I:

'Red Cross parcels often contained prune and raisin packages. Some of our more inventive people constructed a secret still and produced what they called Pruno and Four Raisins wine. They found a way to jack up the alcohol content and the stuff could be quite potent. The Germans found out when some of the men became drunk enough to run outside at night to chase the astonished guard dogs. Luckily, the Germans realized the PoWs were drunk and just having a good time, so no one was shot, fortunately.'

After food, the preoccupation was when liberation would come. As a morale-booster the 'Kriegies' of Stalag Luft I devised slogans for the year of release. Howard Hamilton says these were:

Through the door in '44
Home alive in '45
Standing dicks in '46
Home or heaven in '47
Through the gate in '48

'We were reasonably certain we would be out by '49 so no slogan was formulated for that year.'

Speculation as to the date of liberation afforded an opportunity for another common pastime, betting. Stephen Simpson was one who indulged:

'Betting was one of the favorite pastimes in prison camp, particularly after D-Day when everyone was speculating on when we'd be out. I made a bet with another fellow we'd still be there when it snowed. He gave me ten to one odds we wouldn't, for in the late summer of 1944 it really looked as if the war would be over before the end of the year. Well, it wasn't and winter surely came, a little snow at first and he wouldn't admit he'd lost. Then one night we got eight inches and he conceded I'd won and that he owed me $100. He wrote me a cheque on the back of a cigarette pack. Guess he thought I'd never try to cash it. Well, I kept that cigarette pack and when I got home took it to the local bank; and they paid out, no problem!'

Donald Overdorff, a 95th Bomb Group navigator, remembers a more outrageous stake:

'People were always speculating on how long we would be held in captivity. Apparently one over-optimistic man bet another, "If we're still here at Christmas I'll kiss your ass". Christmas 1944 came around and the man lost his bet and was not allowed to forget it. On the afternoon body count, when our compound commander and his staff, together with the German guards, were preparing a head count, the two betting "Kriegies" marched out to the front of the assembled ranks. They were accompanied by two other men carrying hot water, soap and towels. Our leaders and our captors looked puzzled, particularly when the man who had won the bet dropped his trousers and bent over. The loser's second proceeded to wash one buttock cheek, then dried it and stood back, all in military fashion. The loser then advanced, made an inspection, and requested a towel be draped over a certain area of the other man's rear end. Finally, after further inspection, the loser bent and bestowed a kiss on the right cheek. The whole assembly was in a state of uproar and even the German guards could not contain their laughter.'

The need to sustain morale was well recognized by the PoWs but, with near-starvation levels of the 1944–45 winter, this proved difficult. Even so, there were occasions when spirits were raised. Edward McKenzie, a 92nd Bomb Group flier in Stalag XVIIB, cites Christmas Eve 1944:

'As darkness fell on Christmas Eve we watched our last two briquettes of coal turn into gray powder in the stove and we looked in vain for something else which might burn and provide some heat. Eternal cold seemed to have crept into our bones. We hardly noticed when the door at the end of the barracks opened, there were so many cracks in the walls and holes in the windows that one more cold draught made little difference. A voice hollered, "Hey you guys, no curfew tonight and we're going to have a Christmas service over in the next compound. Come on and join us."

'Covering as much exposed skin as possible with material at hand, my room mates and I forced our reluctant bodies outside. It was freezing and our breaths left trails behind us looking strange in the beams of the sweeping camp security searchlights. A few inches of new powder snow squeaked under our feet. We joined the parade of groups from other barracks who were heading in the same direction and trudged along until suddenly we realized that everyone had stopped. They were all staring up at the sky and for several minutes we did also, not making a sound. What we were seeing was a heaven full of stars so bright that the scene was breathtaking. Dim waves of Aurora Borealis were passing amongst the constellations, adding to the display. A nightly curfew had denied us a true view of the night sky and now we were exhilarated by a sight we once would probably have taken for granted.

'After the service and the singing of carols, as we headed back, our spirits were higher and the cold seemed less harsh. The only one who expressed it out loud was my friend Ace, who said, "Ain't felt so good since I tripped 'n fell into a watermelon patch." '

Don Overdorff noticed the same uplift at Christmas:

'Twice every the day the whole compound was required to fall out by barracks and stand in rows, five deep, to be counted. On Christmas morning,

1944, the men of our room stayed in the barracks until the last moment so that we could run out and form up in the front row facing our compound commander and the German guards. On a signal each man held out a card with a large letter on it spelling the message, "Merry Christmas from Block 3, Room 6" '.

Boredom was a major sap to morale and the Allied seniors did their best to arrange educational and sporting activities to keep people occupied. Other outlets for boredom were various stupidities that brought amusement. Howard Hamilton:

'A morale-boosting pastime at Barth was "Gangplank Drill". A "Kriegie" would pack his belongings, be blindfolded and had to march up an inclined board simulating the boarding of a ship. It was real fun if the participants had been drinking "Four Raisins" '.

Pranks at the expense of the German camp staff were ever popular and if successful did much for morale. Herb Schlicker relates this leg-pull occasion of Stalag Luft I:

'One of the men who spent a lot of time in the camp sick bay told me of a trick they pulled on the German guard there. He was a friendly guy and they kept him in cigarettes, but were always kidding him a lot. One day a patient was opening a medical Red Cross parcel and removed a small packet of ascorbic acid (vitamin C) pills. The guard saw the packet and asked what it contained. The patient kidded him along and said they were nothing important but at the same time made as if to hide the pills away. The guard became more agitated and demanded to know what purpose the pills served. So the patient said, "Okay, if you promise not to say a word, I'll tell you. These pills enable us to see in the dark." Of course, the guard laughed and didn't believe a word of it. Now this same guard was responsible for switching off the light in the sick bay each night and when he did this he delighted in never giving any time to tidy up and put away the projects or games. He'd just shout "Lights out" and flip the switch. That particular night the guard came round as usual and abruptly switched off the lights and walked away. But the talking and laughter continued just as if nothing had happened. So he turned back, listened for a bit, then opened the door and abruptly switched on the lights. There everyone was, still doing just as they had been, playing chess, writing letters, reading and whatever, as if nothing had happened. The guard was shocked and went running off to get his officer to tell him about the secret pills he had discovered. Naturally, when he returned with the officer, everyone was fast asleep.'

An effective way of irritating the guards was to laugh at them. One almost feels sorry for the unfortunate in the episode related by William Deane who had flown with the 388th Bomb Group:

'In the open compounds of Stalag XVIIB at Krems, Austria, a network of air raid trenches were dug for PoW protection. There was heavy snowfall during the winter of 1944–45, sufficient to completely cover and hide the trenches in the compound behind my barracks, 37B. A German officer, newly assigned to the camp administration, chose to go for a walk in our compound and, unaware of the trenches, suddenly fell into one. He quickly crawled out, brushed himself down and continued his walk only to disappear from sight again after a few more steps. Once more he climbed out and set off in another direction, only to fall into yet another hidden trench. By this time PoWs who had seen his first fall had called others to the barrack porch. Before the officer could safely clear the trench area there were more undignified descents through the snow, each acknowledged with a growing chorus of laughter and applause. The bedraggled and embarrassed man eventually made a hasty exist from our compound and I don't remember ever seeing him there again.'

Laughter was not always one-way, as Don Wassner observed at Stalag VIIA, Moosburg:

'I was playing catch with a fellow "Kriegie" who had been a prisoner longer than I and whose mind was somewhat affected. The rest of us tried to keep an eye on him to prevent his getting into trouble. He missed the ball, which rolled under the camp's warning wire (about 20ft from the fence) and although every PoW knew the consequences of going beyond that wire he went after the ball, paying no attention to my yells. I looked up at the guard tower, saw the guard raise his rifle and take aim, and shouted, "Nicht scheissen . . . nicht scheissen!" I thought I was shouting "Don't shoot . . . don't shoot!" but actually I was shouting "Don't shit . . . dont't shit!" It was a fortunate mistake. The guard doubled over with laughter and by the time he recovered, the rest of us had hustled our friend away from the warning wire. I soon learnt the the German word for "shoot" is "schiessen". Very similar, except that the former word is pronounced with a long "i" and the latter with a long "e".'

A more subtle sense of humour among the camp staff was revealed at Stalag Luft III. Albert Clark:

'The people in the German garrison, who we never saw but had almost intimate contact with, were the censors of our mail. It was an intelligence operation from their point of view and they worked under the direction of Dulag Luft. For that reason we PoWs had our own censors monitoring all letters received and sent. The closest we ever came to knowing that one of the German censors was human was the time a note was appended to an incoming letter. There was a PoW who always got complaining letters from his wife – the kids were sick, she couldn't pay the rent, the roof leaked, that sort of thing. It seemed like she only wrote about her troubles. The same censor (Kaprof) always checked the same man's mail and so they got to know particular PoWs and their families. One day one of these terrible complaining letters arrived and down the bottom, in fine print, was a little message. It said, "Dear Lieutenant; I have come to expect these letters. May God soon bring you home to this woman. Gepruft 63." '

Every camp had an escape organization and no shortage of men determined to tunnel or bluff their way to freedom. Very few were successful and those that managed to escape beyond the barbed wire of the retaining fences were usually recaptured. Albert Clark was involved in one of the most ingenious escapes:

'We once had two escapes lined up for one day. They were getting ready to open the American compound and it was plausible for a group of senior US officers to be escorted there to see where to put their offices, select quarters and things like that. I was one of six officers selected to be escorted by a bogus guard, a Dutchman, who spoke fluent German and would wear Luftwaffe uniform we had made, and carry the correct papers – forged of course. The other escape plan arose through the camp authorities having supplied some old beds which were found to be full of bugs. We were outraged and they agreed to take parties of a hundred men at a time out of the camp to a de-lousing building where they would clean our clothes while we took a shower before being escorted back. This became very routine, going on day after day, each party escorted by two "goons". So the idea was to try to take our own party out with our own escort who were German-speaking and wearing fake uniforms and carrying the necessary forged passes.

'Roger Bushall, Big X, decided that the senior officers' party would be sent out directly behind the bogus de-lousing party so if this failed – as it seemed likely to do – in the confusion created the other might successfully get away. On the appointed day we watched casually as the de-lousing party got through both gates without any trouble at all and marched down the road in the direction of the de-lousing centre. Then we started out. We got through the first gate all right, but were stopped at the second gate. Apparently the day before the Germans had put a new secret mark on the back of the gate pass and our escort didn't have it on his. There we were standing arguing and looking out of the corner of our eyes while a hundred guys ran off through the woods. It was 30 minutes before the Germans missed them, they were so busy jumping up and down and screaming at us. It was real turmoil when they realized what had happened. All the escapees were eventually picked up, although one guy got as far as the Swiss border. My punishment was the usual two weeks' solitary, but in this case it wasn't solitary as there were so many of us we were two or three to a cell.'

Had there been an opportunity, the majority of prisoners would have been very willing to escape. On the other hand, there were those prepared to endure the frustration of confinement in the belief that it was the sensible thing to do as liberation could not be far away. Then there were the odd individuals who took quite a different attitude to captivity, like the B-17 pilot encountered by Don Wassner at Stalag VIIA:

'One day when B-17s were attacking Munich a group of us were making remarks such as "I wish I were up there instead of here" . . . "You bet" . . . "Me too." Except Wilson who said, "Not me. I'm glad I'm right here!" Everyone stared at Wilson, and not a few muttered that he must have become a little goofy from being cooped up too long. Later I asked Wilson if he had said that just to be different. He replied, "I really meant it. I'll explain it and you'll understand." Seems that Wilson, like some other errant pilots, ignored repeated warnings not to buzz friendly airfields or anything else. He said he couldn't resist making some very low passes at an RAF base . . . so low and so many that it was easy to get his plane number. A complaint from the RAF base went up the chain of command to RAF HQ, then the 8th AF HQ, then down the American chain of command to Wilson's unit, with a note to Wilson from General LeMay. The message was strong and clear and ended by indicating what he might expect if it happened again. Wilson admitted, "Like a damn fool, I did it again." He couldn't resist the urge to make a few passes at the *same* RAF base.

'Wilson had some source of information at that base and was told the British got his aircraft number again and, worse still, one fellow scrambling down from the tower slipped and fell, injuring a leg. The base commander got off a hot complaint immediately to RAF HQ and Wilson, comparing the time it took the first complaint to go through channels to his unit, figured that he had one more day, possibly two, 'till he got the dreaded second message from General LeMay. Before it arrived he was shot down. He said, "It was almost a relief when I got shot down. I'd rather be here as a PoW than face General LeMay." '

That danger lurked outside prison camps was made plain to many of those PoWs who were moved west during the closing months of the war. Don Jones was one with no illusions in this matter:

'When we were captured the Germans told us "For you the war is over". No, it wasn't; for the inmates of Stalag Luft IV the worst was still to come. In February 1945 the Germans abandoned our camp and marched us west to escape the advancing Russians. The march lasted 80 days and covered around 600 miles, during which time we were strafed by American and British fighters, bombed by US B-26s, caught in the cross-fire of German and Russian ground forces, frost-bitten and starved, losing from 25–30 per cent body weight. I personally had shrunk from 140 pounds to 90 pounds by the time we were finally liberated by US troops on 26th April 1945 at Bitterfeld, Germany.'

This is echoed by Albert Clark:

'When the prisoners at Sagan were moved to avoid the advancing Russians there were a great many opportunities for escape. Those who did found the greatest menace to their safety was not the Germans, but strafing Allied fighters who shot up anything and anyone that moved on the roads. Guys who were recaptured and brought into our new camp said, "Hey, it's dangerous out there!" '

Even under extreme duress of those forced moves, an element of humour frequently asserted itself. Kenneth Maeran, who had been shot down in a 97th Bomb Group B-17, recalls the following incident:

'We were moved from Stalag 7-A at Merseburg to Stalag 17-B in boxcars. Naturally friends wanted to travel together but the Germans, with their usual efficiency, wanted a precise number of PoWs in each car. One very large German guard came to the open door of our boxcar and demanded one of us volunteer to move to another in order to even out the desired numbers of persons. As we all wanted to stay with friends no one volunteered. The repeated demand brought no response so finally the exasperated guard leapt up into the boxcar. Most of us anticipated what was going to happen and quickly got as far away from the door as possible. A guy called Perry Goldstein didn't move fast enough and was grabbed by the seat of the pants and scruff of the neck and literally thrown out by the guard. As he sailed through the air, arms thrown wide in expectation of a rough landing on the steep rock and debris-covered embankment below, Perry was heard to holler, "I volunteer". For months thereafter, whenever one of us encountered Perry in Stalag 17-B's exercise yard, we would throw wide our arms in greeting and holler, "I volunteer".'

Douglas Bowles, ex 306th Bomb Group:

'In early April 1945 the Jerries marched the "Kriegies" from Stalag XVIB through Austria to the Inns River at the fork with the Salzach. Soon after the start of the march, which was to last 17 days, we were quartered overnight in an Austrian farmer's barn. We arrived cold and tired as darkness fell and scurried about to find any spot to iie down. I scrambled up onto a large pile of hay. Burrowing down I yelled, "There's lots of room over here and it's fucking warm!" It really was.

'In the morning I awoke to see prisoners sprawled everywhere including on top of my pile of hay, which steamed in the chill mountain air. Then I noticed the odour. The hay was steaming because it was really old bedding from the animal stalls and was filled with dung. I had my best sleep of that whole march in a pile of shit!'

And Edward McKenzie, from 92nd Bomb Group, a prisoner since April 1944:

'In April 1945 the half-starved PoWs at Krems were marched east. Several days into the march we were halted in a large farmyard. I wondered if our state of exhaustion was finally being taken into consideration or whether there were other reasons for taking us off the road. It was still cold and damp and we immediately began establishing our living spaces in the area around the farmhouse and its outbuildings.

'Near the spot where my group had settled was a small fenced area. On looking closer I made out what seemed to be the top of a turnip poking up from the earth, perhaps left there from the previous fall's harvest. While my friend Vern shielded me, I wriggled through the fence and began excavating with my PoW dogtag. Gradually I uncovered not a turnip but a fat, white sugar beet, rimmed on top with purple. After I had crawled back out with it we melted back into the group to show off our find.

'Suddenly there was shouting out by the road and I could see a large open automobile had stopped. Three men leaped out and came striding into the yard, knocking men over and kicking campfires and equipment aside as they advanced. Little doubt of their identity now as their uniforms and intimidating manner had all of us whistling "SS" under our breaths. As they seemed to be heading right for where I was standing, I quickly dropped the sugar beet down the front of my pants, keeping my legs pressed together so that it would stay lodged in the crotch. Even though anyone who did not move out of the way fast enough was struck or kicked, we PoWs and our guards were trying to act calmly, hoping that the SS Lugers would stay in their holsters. After a quick survey of our numbers, it was a great relief to see the SS men climb back into their big touring car and roar off down the road. Immediately they were out of sight, Vern lifted my arms up in the air and yelled, "Hey, you guys, they were after our sugar beet, but the bastards didn't get it!" There was a burst of laughter and cheering as I fished the bowling-ball sized vegetable up out of my pants. We carved it up and passed pieces around. It made a fine supplement to the next-to-nothing we were existing on during the march. Later, one of our guards explained that the SS had not stopped just to kick people around but were looking for deserters from the Wehrmacht. Had they found any they would have been shot on the spot.'

25
Personalities and Eccentrics

Every man who served his country during the Second World War recalls individuals encountered or served with whose behaviour or distinctive personality elevated them to prominence in memory – characters. The United States Army Air Force was rich in characters. It is difficult to categorize them; they remained in memory for a variety of reasons, mostly the amazing or amusing. Despite the rigours of combat flying, there were those who appeared to treat it all with nonchalance, veterans like the man in the 384th Bomb Group that Bill Barnett remembers:

'My crew was made up of "Odd Balls" – we were all men who for some reason or another had become separated from our original crews or missed out on the normal assignment procedure. One of the oddest members of these Odd Balls was the togglier. While flying with us he turned up his 80th combat mission – more than anyone else in the group. One day, coming back to base, he suddenly came through on intercom and asked permission to bail out over the field, just for the hell of it. I was pretty sure he was "flak happy" after so many missions, but bailing out for fun was going too far.'

Then there were the eccentrics, those who did not conform to accepted practice. George Meshko advances his co-pilot:

'Our co-pilot, Jay Buttermore, always wore the same pair of pajamas under his flying gear when we went on missions. He wouldn't have them washed as he insisted that would wash the luck out of them. Didn't work; he was shot down on his last mission.'

As if combat flying was not risky enough, there were men who would take a calculated chance at any time. Those who endured were apt to become legend. Jim Verinis of the 91st Bomb Group:

'We had an engine go out while on a raid and we put down on an RAF base for more gas. Our pilot, Bob Morgan, said he is going to take off on three because it could not be repaired that day. The RAF had offered to feed us and give us beds for the night so, I asked Bob why can't we wait and get the engine fixed next day. Turns out he has a heavy date in London that evening and isn't going to stand her up. The crew tells him that we're not going to risk our lives in a three-engine take-off just so he can get back to base and meet some girl. So, while the rest of us stand and watch, he taxies out with Hal, the engineer, in my seat and starts the take-off run. He's going down the runway on three engines with the prop on the bad engine windmilling and it suddenly catches and runs. So Bob takes off and comes back in to land and pick us up. Nobody said a word!'

There were the one-upmanship characters, those who wanted to assert their individuality. Fred Hollien, a 392nd Bomb Group flight engineer, tells of one he encountered:

'It was common practice for flight crew members to decorate the backs of their flying jackets with the name of the bomber they usually flew, the number of missions they had completed and victory symbols for enemy aircraft claimed shot down. For security reasons these jackets were not allowed to be worn on missions and it became a tradition that a man only decorated his jacket once he had completed his tour. It was quite common to see men with each completed mission represented by a bomb symbol and each enemy aircraft claimed was either a swastika or a German cross. One day I happened to see a tail gunner walk by with 30 bombs, two Maltese crosses and two baby carriages painted on his jacket. When I asked him about this he said that all the other members of his crew had painted up the 30 bombs and two enemy planes that had been credited to them, but as he had married an English girl who had just produced twins he felt he had the right to show he was two up on the other guys!'

It was not unusual to find a man with an extreme pet aversion. An unreasoned hate for something or someone. Paul Reeves had such a friend:

'Jeremiah Sullivan, a buddy who had gone through pilot training with me and was assigned to the 55th Fighter Group at the same time, was a rabid Republican. He could see no good in Democrat politicians and, particularly, President Roosevelt. When I got near completing my 300-hour tour Sully was about 20 hours behind, so I asked our people to leave me off the operations schedule so he'd catch up and we'd both be able to go back to the States together. This way we both flew our last missions on the same day. When we left the Group our Squadron Flight Surgeon ferried us to an airfield near Stratford-on-Avon, a town we wanted to see. The airfield was some way from the town so we went out on the road to hitch a lift. An English truck driver stopped and picked us up. After we climbed into the cab he asked, kind of solemn, if we had heard the bad news from our country. "What's that?" says Sully. "President Roosevelt has died." "Good!" exclaims Sully. The driver looked a little taken aback but continued: "I'm sure it's as great a loss to Britain as it is to America." "I'm sure it is!" says Sully. The driver changed the conversation after that. As soon as we were dropped off in Stratford, Sully starts dancing a jig in the street. Thinking it's time to dampen his celebrations, but knowing better than to start arguing politics with him, I said: "The war has been going along pretty good under Roosevelt. You don't know what Truman's going to be like – and he's a Democrat." Sully stops dancing around and ponders awhile. "You're right," he says. From then on he never missed an opportunity to jump on Truman.'

Sometimes it was the losers, or those put-upon, who were the characters. Robert Powell, a 352nd Fighter Group pilot, remembers one who objected:

'Several Brits were assigned duty with the 352nd during WWII, and one of those was Flight Lieutenant Wilfred Fawcett, RAF. Not familiar with the usual practice of Americans to tag a nickname on their comrades, the Flight Lieutenant was somewhat dismayed when they started calling him "Leaky".

'After being addressed in this manner for a few days, and being unfamiliar with the American meaning of faucet, he went to the Group CO and said, "Colonel, somehow it has got around that I have some sort of urinary problem and it's quite embarrassing, and it's not true." Colonel Mason was just touching a glass of scotch to his lips at that moment and almost sprayed the bartender in his efforts to control his laughter.'

Of less extreme characters, it was some colourful personality that impressed, often highlighted by his laconic comments. 'Stubby' Stubblefield:

'The boys were returning from a mission and with a few other pilots who hadn't been assigned to fly I was out on the field gathered round the CO's Jeep watching the landings. The P-51s were coming in one after the other and it looked as if we had no losses. Then, as we watched, a P-51 flown by a replacement pilot appeared to have cut back too much on his speed and sure enough the plane stalled just as it approached the runway. The left wing snapped down, struck the ground and sent the plane cartwheeling. The engine smashed out and rolled away, the right wing broke off and the tail disintegrated. When the wreck finally stopped there was only the crumpled fuselage left. The crash trucks were on their way, but before they reached the wreck the pilot crawls out and walks off carrying his 'chute. We can hardly believe what we are seeing and there's a sort of stunned silence. Then Colonel Osborne, who's sitting in the Jeep, says casually, kind of matter of fact: "I thought he looked like he was too slow." '

Robert Powell also knew a similar wit:

'We had a big, affable pilot named Fremont Miller in our squadron who exhibited a laconic wit spawned from his southern heritage and western upbringing that often made us laugh. Sitting around the Pilots' Room on one occasion, one of the pilots reading the *Stars and Stripes* noted that a new highjump record of nearly six feet had just been set. Miller's comment on this achievement came with a laugh, "Well now, that fella would be plumb hard to keep corralled, wouldn't he?" '

The men of God are often remembered as characters; as indeed they were relative to the difficult task of administering to the spiritual needs of young men. This was certainly the case at Bodney, England, as Robert Powell narrates:

'The 352nd's Chaplain, George Cameron, was an unusual cleric who did all sorts of things to raise money for the Lord's work. On pay days George would get the "crap" games going by starting the "pot". Then, from the winner of each hand he would extract a pound note for the War Bond Fund. He had begun to purchase a $1,000 US War Bond for the children of any 352nd pilots who were killed in action.

'Another of his fund-raising techniques was his regular evening cornet concert of "requested tunes" over the base loudspeaker system before playing "Taps" for lights out. Special requests brought one pound sterling for the War Bond Fund or, since his tunes were not always easy on the ear, one pound sterling bought a moment of silence. George managed to have a $1 moment of silence. Eight War Bonds were presented back in the States in the name of the children, most of whom never knew their fathers.'

Perhaps the most remarkable Chaplain serving a USAAF unit in Europe was at nearby Hethel. George La Prath of the 463rd Sub Depot, was certainly impressed:

'Our Priest, Father Gerald Beck, was no ordinary priest in any sense of the word. He could serve Mass for the Catholics or hold services for any other denomination should these people not have a chaplain available. This would include the Jewish boys as well. He could do this with dignity.

'Father Beck was known among the gunners, especially, as "White Flak" because of his white hair, while often called "The Desert Rat" from his time well spent in Africa. He drove a Jeep called "Hellzapoppin" and spoke the language of his boys, those he was there to serve, and never let them down. He would be at the end of the runway to bless every aircraft that took off on a mission and be there to see them home again. He gave Communion to those aboard the planes before take-off and at times wound up going on the mission with them. He actually had an Air Medal presented to him; never wore it but carried it in his pocket. This Franciscan priest would tell you in no uncertain terms when you were wrong or when you were right. In church he would tell you to do as I say, don't do as I do.

'He lived as his men did and did many of the things they did. Most men loved this Franciscan priest, but not all of them.'

26
Return Back West

Near and after the end of hostilities USAAF airmen were involved in more peaceable activities. Aircraft that had once delivered bombs now carried food. Even in such concluding duties there were incidents that stand high in the memories of those involved, particularly for 385th Bomb Group navigator Bob Valliere:

'On May 2nd 1945 I was navigator on the "Stork Club" with a mission to drop food at Hilversum where many Dutch people were starving. A truce had been arranged with the German forces holding the area and they had agreed not to fire at our planes. As our B-17 approached the dropping zone at under a thousand feet, one of the crew shouted over the interphone that he could see some German soldiers tracking us with an AA gun. The next thing I knew was a bump. Despite the truce we had been fired at and hit. One of the gunners said we'd taken hits in the port wing and our pilot, Lt Swana, alerted us that we might have to make a forced landing or ditch in the sea because of damage to the flight controls. Luckily the damage was not as bad as it first appeared and we made it back to base safely. The incident gave us our claim to fame as the last 8th Air Force heavy bomber hit by flak in World War 2.'

Bob Valliere's unit was also, like other heavy bombers of the 8th and 15th Air Forces, engaged in the transportation of people, and this provided another memorable occasion:

'At the end of the war my Group was detailed to fly the released PoWs and forced labourers out of Germany. Our briefing took us to Linz, Austria, where we picked up Frenchmen who had been liberated by US troops. We crammed 30 of these men on board – they had no belongings to speak of – and two rode in the nose of the B-17 with me. One man insisted I take the harmonica he offered – a German make. I kept refusing it but he kept putting it in my pocket. Then it dawned on me that he wanted to be rid of anything that was connected with his imprisonment so I finally accepted. The harmonica became my permanent souvenir of that flight. Our radio-operator spoke some German and found that the PoWs could too, so he was able to converse with them. They asked him to ask the navigator – me – when the B-17 crossed the French border. When we reached it I called back to the radio room. Immediately the men there started singing the Marseillaise and it spread through the plane like a wave. Soon all thirty Frenchmen were giving voice to their national anthem.

'When we landed near Paris there was a line of trucks waiting to transport them to a reception depot. As soon as our B-17 came to a stop the French all dashed from the plane towards these trucks, until one of the older men yelled a command. Whereupon they stopped, came back and lined up in a row. The older man, wearing a worn French Army jacket and hat, went up to my pilot and saluted. Then each one of the men we'd flown out shook hands and hugged every member of our crew, said "Merci" and then ran like hell to a truck. Eager to get home I guess.'

The immediate post-war duties were not endured for long and by the end of 1945 practically all USAAF units, other than those assigned to occupational duties in Germany, had returned to the United States. In those weeks before the flight or sea journey home, there was time for relaxing and some final wild parties of the kind which were so popular with fliers. At Castellucio in Italy, the enlisted men of one squadron observed – apparently with disdain – an officers' party that did not go quite as planned. Harland Little:

'At the end of the war the officers of our squadron planned a big party. They fixed the date on Saturday, May 16 and invited nurses from the hospital in Naples and other female officers in the area. The Officers Club was all dolled up and all the hoarded whisky and beer was brought out. The officer tents were all made ready for the expected guests. Saturday finally arrived and all eyes were on the runway. Plane after plane landed with no females. At least the B-24 that was sent to Naples landed and five nurses, not the most beautiful in the world, got out. These were the only females for the big affair. The Squadron Commander and his staff escorted them to the Officers Club while the enlisted men enjoyed their embarrassment. I think every officer, except the few who didn't drink, got drunk and raised hell – the noise lasted about all night. It was assumed by us that the nurses did their duty for those willing and able. Our pilot did not drink or fool around and Sunday morning our crew was alerted to fly the nurses back to Naples. We loaded the B-24 with our hung-over, worn-out cargo and returned them to Naples. We got a great look at Mount Vesuvius!'

When, in June 1945, the liner *Queen Elizabeth* arrived in New York with several thousand USAAF men returning from Europe, a reporter asked one sergeant, who had been overseas three years, to encapsulate his experiences. The sergeant shrugged his shoulders and replied: "Just sweatin' it out man. I just been sweatin' it out with the rest of the guys." No doubt that sergeant, like the rest of the returnees, was anxious to get home. But in time there would be a lot to tell about life overseas.

Glossary

Ammo	Short for ammunition
AWOL	Absent Without Leave
Axis Sally	Female on German English propaganda broadcasts
Buncher	Radio beacon
Cajuns	Red Indians and French natives of Louisiana
Cats	Catalina flying-boats
CO	Commanding Officer
CQ	Charge of Quarters
Darky	Common frequency radio system for aircraft in distress
DDT	Chlorinated hydrocarbon used as insecticide
DF	Direction-Finding
Ditch	Forced landing on water
Dog Tags	Personal identification on metal labels worn on neck cord
DR	Dead Reckoning
EM	Enlisted Men
Faucet	Water tap
Firewalled	Quick application of maximum power – pushing the throttles fully open
Flak	Abbreviation of German word for anti-aircraft gunfire
Foxhole	Shallow trench for protection against blast
Gee	Medium-range navigational aid
GI	Government Issue
G-H	Radar blind bombing system
Goons	Slang for PoW camp staff, after comic-strip character
H2X	Airborne radar navigational and target location aid
Hardpan	Aircraft standing point off the runways
HE	High-Explosive
HQ	Headquarters
IAS	Indicated Air Speed (as per instruments)
IFF	Identification Friend or Foe system
In the hole	The centre space behind a 3-plane formation
IP	Initial Point for bomb run to target
Kriegie	PoW, culled from German Kriegsgefangener
Longhandles	Long-sleeved and legged under garment
LST	Landing Ship, Tank
MP	Military Police
OTU	Operational Training Unit
PBY	Patrol flying-boat built by Consolidated
PFF	Path-Finder Force
PoW	Prisoner of War

PPI	Pilot Position Indicator
Purple Heart Corner	Lowest and most exposed position in a bomber Formation
PX	Post Exchange – store for personal purchases
Queen liners	RMS *Queen Mary* and *Queen Elizabeth*
RAF	Royal Air Force
rpm	revolutions per minute
Rubber-necking	Inquisitive Sight-seeing
S-2	Intelligence Officer
Scrubbed	Cancelled
Shot landings	Touch-and-go landing
SOB	Abbreviated oath – son of a bitch
Socked in	Restricted by fog or low cloud
SOP	Standard Operating Procedure
SOS	Distress signal – 'save our souls'
Spam	Abbreviation for spiced ham
Togglier	Crewman detailed to release bombs on sight of leader's drop
Tokyo Tanks	Auxiliary fuel tanks in outer wing sections
USAAF	United States Army Air Forces
Very	Designer's name of signalling pistol and cartridges
WAAF	Women's Auxiliary Air Force (British)
WAC	Women's Army Corps
ZI	Zone of Interior (in USA)

List of Contributors

Connie J. Anszperger
Edward M. Anthis
Roger W. Armstrong
Robert K. Auger

Alvin G. Baker
William A. Barnett
Wesley J. Bartelt
Robert S. Bee
Robert A. Bennett
Walter Bergstrom
Don Bevan
Richard C. Boucher
F. Douglas Bowles
William E. Boyd
Robert N. Boyle
George E. Brumbaugh
Arthur J. Bryant
John W. Butler

William R. Cameron
Harold Carroll
Robert J. Cayer
C. N. 'Bud' Chamberlain
John Chopelas
Albert P. Clark
Donald R. Clark
Forrest S. Clark
Jack R. Collingwood
Robert J. Custer

V. K. 'Dave' Davidson
William A. Deane
Wayne E. DeCou
Henry A. DeKeyser
Robert E. Doherty
Roland L. Douglas

Lew Felstein

Arthur K. Fitch
Royal D. Frey
Frank D. Furiga

Frank Gaccione
William L. Garrett
T. C. Gibbs
Carl J. Gjelhaug
Francis E. Glasser
Stewart Goldsmith
John E. Greenwood

Richard Halliday
Howard Hamilton
Robert J. Hanson
Harold R. Harding
Henry Heckman
Carroll Henry
Whitmal W. Hill
Anthony P. Hmura
Fred Hollien
Edward T. Holmes
Barkev A. Hovsepian
John W. Howland
John Hutchinson

Jack Ilfrey

Robert A. Jacobs
Albert E. Jones
Donald H. Jones
Norbert S. Jost

G. Donald Kammer
Philip Kanarkowski
Ernest R. Kelly
Kenneth Kennard
John F. Kirkpatrick
George R. Klare

James R. Knaub
Walter J. Konantz
E. 'Bud' Koorndyck

Herbert Lancaster
George A. La Prath
Edward J. Laube
Saul R. Levine
Wilbur Lewis
Elinor Lilley (nee Fredricks)
Everett S. Lindley
Milton J. Lipa
Harland B. Little

Kenneth V. Maeran
James R. Martin
Edward D. McKenzie
James H. McMahon
Robert McMath
George Meshko
Harold B. Moore
Thomas B. Morrow
George L. Moscovis

Leroy W. Newby

John O'Grady
Donald W. Overdorff

Tom B. Parry
John R. Parsons
David G. Patterson
Ralph K. Patton
Irwin P. Pochter
Robert H. Powell

Edwin C. Range
Paul Reeves
Penrose W. Reagan

George F. Rich
Melvin J. Robison
Carl F. Runge
Harold Rutka

Stanley Sajdak
Cary W. Salter
Charles F. Salter
Coleman Sanders
James O. Sayre
Herbert G. Schlicker
Irving Shapiro
Everett D. Shue
Stephen Simpson
Ben Slothower
John Slothower
Harold I. Smith
Stanley K. Smith
William E. Smith
Marvin H. Speidel
Stanley Staples
Robert C. Strobell
Harley Stroven
Herman H. Stubblefield
William J. Sullivan
Arthur Swanson

David Tallichet
Ralph W. Trout
Earl Trull
Daniel Turner

Robert Valliere
Gene Venezia
James A. Verinis
Hathy Veynar
Robert E. Vickers

Hugh H. Walker
Donald R. Wassner
Ira P. Weinstein
Earl G. Williamson
John W. Wilson
Tyler C. Winton
Sheldon J. Witt
Ashley Woolridge
Louis W. Wust

John P. Zima
A. Allen Zimmerman
Harding R. Zumwalt

Index